The Theory of Mind as Pure Act

A Spiritual Philosophy of Mind

By Giovanni Gentile

Translated by H. Wildon Carr

Published by Pantianos Classics

ISBN-13: 978-1-78987-521-8

First published in 1916

This translation to English was first published in 1922

Contents

Translator's Introduction iv
Bibliography of the Writings of Giovanni Gentile ix
To Benedetto Croce x
Author's Preface xi

Chapter One - The Subjectivity of the Real 13
Chapter Two - Spiritual Reality 17
Chapter Three - The Unity of Mind and the Multiplicity of Things 21
Chapter Four - Mind as Development 31
Chapter Five - The Problem of Nature 41
Chapter Six - The Abstract Universal and the Positive 47
Chapter Seven - The Individual as Ego 57
Chapter Eight - The Positive as Self-Created 61
Chapter Nine - Space and Time 71
Chapter Ten - Immortality 82
Chapter Eleven - Causality, Mechanism and Contingency 92
Chapter Twelve - Freedom and Prevision 105
Chapter Thirteen - The Historical Antinomy and Eternal History ... 117
   Note 125
Chapter Fourteen - Art, Religion and History 127
Chapter Fifteen - Science, Life and Philosophy 133
Chapter Sixteen - Reality as Self-Concept and the Problem of Evil . 139
Chapter Seventeen - Epilogue and Corollaries 145
Chapter Eighteen - Idealism or Mysticism? 151

Translator's Introduction

THE book which I have translated is intended by its author to be the initial volume of a series of his "Philosophical Works." Giovanni Gentile was born at Casteltravano in Sicily the 29th May 1875. He was educated at Pisa and later was appointed to the Chair of Philosophy in the University of that city. In 1917 he received the appointment he now holds of Professor of the History of Philosophy in the University of Rome. He has become famous in his own country on account of his historical and philosophical writings and even more by the number and fervour of the disciples he has attracted. The present work is designed to give form to the maturity of his philosophical thinking.

The reason which has led me to present an English version is that in reading the book I have not only found a philosopher propounding a theory which seems to me to deserve the attention of our philosophers, but one who has expressed with what seems to me admirable clearness what I find myself desiring and striving to express, - the true inwardness of the fundamental philosophical problem, and the extra ordinary difficulty (of which many philosophers appear unconscious) of the effort required to possess the only concept which can provide a satisfactory solution.

The book is intended for philosophers and addressed to philosophers. This does not mean that any one may set it aside as being no concern of his. It does mean that no one may expect to understand save and in so far as he makes the problem his own. Philosophy is not understood by simply contemplating the efforts of others, each of us must make the effort his own. In saying this I am saying nothing new. Philosophy is not a pastime: it is a discipline or it is nothing. As Kant once said, there is no philosophy there is only philosophizing.

Gentile's philosophy is idealism and an idealism which is absolute. That is to say, idealism is not for him a choice between rival theories, an alternative which one may accept or reject. The problem does not present itself to him as a question which of two possible hypotheses, the naturalistic or the idealistic, is most probable. On the contrary, his idealism is based not on an assumption which may or may not be verified, but on a fundamental principle which is not in any real sense open to doubt. The difficulty in regard to it is simply a difficulty of interpretation. It arises because, when we look back and review philosophy in the history of philosophy, which is its process and development, it seems then to resolve itself into a series of attempts to systematize the principle, each attempt falling short in some essential particular, and if overcoming a defect in what has gone before, always disclosing a new defect to be overcome. In this meaning only are there idealisms and a classification of idealistic concepts. In this meaning, too, Gentile can himself distinguish and characterize his own theory. He names it "actual" idealism, and by this term he would emphasize two distinctive marks. "Actual" means that it is the idealism of to-day, not only in the sense that it is latest in time, the most recent and modern formation of the principle, but in the meaning that the history of philosophy has itself imposed this form on present thought. But "actual" means also that it is the idealistic concept of the present, the concept of an eternal present, which is not an exclusion of times past and times future, but a comprehension of all history as present act determined by past fact, eternal becoming. It is therefore in one sense the most familiar concept of our common experience, the concept of the reality of our conscious life in its immediacy. Yet to follow the concept into its consequences for theory of life and theory of knowledge is by no means easy. The philosopher who would avoid the Scylla of intellectualism (under which are included both materialistic naturalism and idealistic Platonism) on the one hand, and the Charybdis of mysticism on the other, has a very difficult course to steer.

There are two major difficulties which cling to all our efforts to attain the concept of what in modern philosophy is expressed in the terms "universal" and "concrete": two difficulties the one or other of which seems continually to intervene between us and the concept, and to intercept us whenever we feel that at last we are attaining the goal. One is the relation of otherness, which makes it seem impossible to include in one concept the reality of knowing and known. The other is the relation of finite and in finite, which makes it seem impossible that the effective presence of universal mind in the individual can be consistent with the concrete finiteness of individuality. When once the nature of these two difficulties is understood the course of the argument is clear. It may be useful to the reader, therefore, if I try to give precision to them.

The first difficulty concerns the nature of the object of knowledge, and it is this. There can be no knowing unless there is something known. This something does not come into existence when it is known and by reason thereof, for if it did knowing would not be knowing. We must, then, as the condition of knowing, presuppose an existence independent of and alien to the mind which is to know it. Let us call this the thesis. The antithesis is equally cogent. In knowing, nothing can fall outside of the subject-object relation. In the apprehension by the mind of an object, that object is both materially and formally comprehended within the mind. The concept of independent being confronting the mind is self-contradictory and absurd. Independent being is by its definition unknowable being, and unknowability cannot be the condition of knowledge. Such is the antinomy of knowledge. Can it be overcome? Yes. In one way and in one way only: it can be overcome if it can be shown that the opposition I which knowledge implies is an opposition within one reality, concrete universal mind, and immanent in its nature, and that it is not an opposition between two alien realities. If, however, such a solution is to be more than a mere verbal homage to a formal logical principle, it must put us in full possession of the concept of this concrete universal mind; a concept which must not merely continue in thought what we distinguish as separate in reality, mind and nature, but must rationalize and reconcile the opposition between them. Whether the theory of "Mind as Pure Act" achieves this success, the reader must judge.

The second difficulty is even more formidable, for if the first concerns the nature of things, this concerns the nature of persons. In theology and in religion it has taken the form of the problem: Can God be all in all and yet man be free? The task of philosophy is to show how the mind which functions in the finite individual can be infinite, although the activity of the individual is determined and restricted; and how the universal can become effective in, and only in, the finite individual. His treatment of this problem has brought Professor Gentile into friendly controversy with his colleague Benedetto Croce, and this controversy has been the occasion of an alteration of the third edition of this "General Theory" by the addition of the two final chapters. The charge of Croce is in effect that this "actual" idealism spells mysticism. The author meets this charge directly and makes it the opportunity of expounding further the distinctive character of his concept of ultimate reality.

The main argument is unfolded in the first ten chapters. It is developed continuously and reaches its full expression in the theory of space and time and immortality. The doctrine is that the unity of mind is neither a spatial nor a temporal unity; that space and time are the essential forms of the multiplicity of the real; that the unity of mind is not superposed on this multiplicity but immanent in it and expressed by it. Immortality is then seen to be the characteristic which belongs to the essence of mind in its unity and universality; that is, in its opposition to multiplicity or nature which is its spatial and temporal, or existential, expression. We may, and indeed we must and do, individualize the mind as a natural thing, an object among other objects, a person among other persons, but when we do so, then, like every other natural thing it takes its place in the spatio-temporal multiplicity of nature. Yet our power to think the mind in this way would be impossible were not the mind, with and by which we think it, itself not a thing, not *fact* but *act, pure act* which never *is,* which is never *factum* but always *fieri.* Of the mind which we individualize the author says, in a striking phrase, its immortality is its mortality. Only mind as pure act is immortal in its absolute essence. Only to the *doing* which is never *deed,* activity in its comprehension and purity, can such terms as infinity, eternity and immortality be significant. When we grasp this significance we see that these attributes are not failures to comprehend but true expressions of the essence of the real.

The later chapters of the book show the application of this principle and the criticism it enables us to bring to bear on other philosophical attempts of the past and the present.

With regard to the translation I have not aimed at transliteration but have tried to express the author's thought in our own language with as few technical innovations as possible. There are, however, two respects in which the Italian original must retain the mark of origin in the translation. The first is that the illustrations used are mainly from literature, and though literature is international the instances are drawn entirely from Italian sources. Now, however famous to us as names Dante, Ariosto, Leopardi, Manzoni and other well-known Italian writers may be, their works cannot be referred to with the kind of familiarity which Chaucer, Shakespeare, Wordsworth and Scott would have for us. I have therefore reproduced, wherever necessary, the actual passage of the Italian author which is commented on. The second is more important and requires a fuller explanation. The line of philosophical speculation in Italy has been affected by influences which have not been felt, or at least not in the same degree, in other countries. By this I do not mean merely that the individuals are different and form a national group; that Rosmini, Gioberti, De Sanctis, Spaventa are to the Italians what J. S. Mill, Herbert Spencer, T. H. Green, Caird are to English philosophers. I mean of that the line of philosophical speculation itself, whilst it is and always has been organically one with the general history of the development of thought in Europe, has had a certain bias in its tendency and direction due to conditions, political and social and religious, peculiar to Italy.

There is one deep-seated source of the difference. It goes back to the middle ages and to the Renascence. It is the historical fact that the Protestant Reformation, which produced the profound intellectual awakening in Northern Europe in the seventeenth century and stamped so deeply with its problems the philosophical development of that century, left Italy practically untouched. It hardly disturbed the even course of her intellectual life and it created no breach between the old learning and the new. And this was particularly the case with regard to the kingdom of Sicily. The Cartesian movement had almost spent its force when Vico raised his voice in the strong re-action against its pretensions to scrap history and reject authority and start science *de novo* and *ab imis*. And to-day there is a reminder of this historical origin in the lines of divergence in philosophical thought in Italy.

In recent times there have been two philosophical movements which have received in Italy the response of a vigorous recognition. One is the Positive philosophy, the leading representative of which is the veteran philosopher Roberto Ardigò of Padua (born 1828 and still living at the time of writing). In early life a priest who rose from humble origin to a high position in the church, he was distinguished by his political zeal and public spirit in pushing forward schemes of social and municipal reform, and had brilliant prospect of advancement. Suddenly, however, and dramatically, he broke with the Church and became the leader of a secularist movement, and the expounder of the principles of the philosophy of Auguste Comte. In consequence, this philosophy has had, and still has, a great following and wide influence in Italy. It is important to understand this, because it explains the constant polemic against positivism and positivistic concepts in the present work.

The other movement is Hegelian in character and idealistic in direction, and its leading exponents are Benedetto Croce and his younger colleague and friend the author of this book. The distinctive note and the starting-point of this movement is a reform of the Hegelian dialectic, but it prides itself in an origin and philosophical ancestry much older than Hegel, going back to Vico and through him linking itself up with the old Italian learning. Its characteristic doctrine is a theory of history and of the writing of history which identifies history with philosophy. It finds full expression in the present book.

In the preparation of this translation I have received great assistance from Professor J. A. Smith, Waynflete Professor of Philosophy in the University of Oxford. He has read the proofs and very carefully compared the translation with the original. But I am indebted to him for much more than is represented by his actual work on this volume. Among representative philosophers in England he has been distinguished by his sympathetic appreciation of the Italian idealistic movement in philosophy, and he felt its influence at a time when very little was known of it in this country. I would especially recommend to readers of this book his acute critical account of The Philosophy of Giovanni Gentile" in an article in the *Proceedings of the Aristotelian Society*, vol. xx.

I have appended a Bibliography of Gentile's principal writings. He is known among us mainly by his long association, which still continues, with Benedetto Croce. This began in 1903 with the initiation of *Critica,* a bi-monthly Review of Literature, History and Philosophy. The Review consists almost entirely of the writings of the two colleagues. In 1907 the two philosophers initiated the publication of a series of translations into Italian of the Classical works of Modern Philosophy. The series already amounts to thirty volumes. During this time, too, Gentile has himself initiated a series of texts and translations of Ancient and Medieval Philosophy. In 1920 he started his own Review, Giornale *critico della filosofia italiana,* really to receive the writings of the many students and scholars who owe their inspiration to him and desire to continue his work. The new series of *Studi filosofici,* now being published by Vallechi of Florence, is mainly the work of his followers. It is doubtful if there is a more influential teacher in the intellectual world to-day.

H. W. C.
LONDON, *October* 1921.

Bibliography of the Writings of Giovanni Gentile

1. "Rosmini e Gioberti." Pisa, 1898.
2. "La Filosofia di Marx." Studi critici. Pisa, 1899.
3. "L'Insegnarnento della filosofia nei Licei." Saggio pedagogico. 1900.
4. "Dal Genovesi al Galluppi." Ricerche storiche.
5. "Studi sullo Stoicismo romano." Trani, 1904.
6. "Storia della filosofia italiana" (still in course of publication). Milan, 1902.
7. "Scuola e filosofia: concetti fundamentali e saggi di pedagogia della scuola media." Palermo, 1908.
8. "Il Modernismo e i suoi rapporti fra religione e filosofia." Bari, 1909. 2nd Edition, 1921.
9. "Bernardino Telesio, con appendice bibliografica." Bari, 1911.
10. "I Problemi della Scolastica e il Pensiero italiano." Bari, 1913.
11. "La Riforma della Dialettica hegeliana." Messina, 1913.
12. "Sommario di Pedagogia come scienza filosofica." Vol. I. Pedagogia generale. Bari, 1913. 2nd Edition, 1920. Vol. II. Didattica. Bari, 1914.
13. "L'Esperienza pura e la realtà storica." Prolusione. Florence, 1915.
14. "Studi Vichiani." Messina, 1915.
15. "Teoria generale dello Spirito come Atto puro." (The work here translated.) Pisa, 1916. 3rd Edition. Bari, 1920.
16. "Sistema di Logica come teoria del conoscere." Pisa, 1917. 2nd Edition. 1918.
17. "Il Tramonto della cultura siciliana." Bologna, 1917.
18. "I Fondamenti della filosofia del diritto." Pisa, 1917.
19. "Le Origini della filosofia contemporanea in Italia." 3 Vols. Bari, 1917-1921.
20. "Il Carattere storico della filosofia italiana." Prolusione. Bari, 1918.
21. "Guerra e Fede." Frammenti politici. Naples, 1919.
22. "La Riforma dell Educazione." Bari, 1920.
23. "Il Problema scolastico del dopo guerra." 1919. 2nd Edition. 1920.
24. "Dopo la Vittoria." Nuovi frammenti politici. Rome, 1920.
25. "Discorsi di Religione." Florence, 1920.
26. "Giordano Bruno e il pensiero del Rinascimento." Florence, 1920.
27. "Frammenti di Estetica e di Letteratura." Lanciano, 1921.
28. "Saggi critici." First Series. Naples, 1921.
29. "Il Concetto moderno della scienza e il problema universitario. Inaugural Lecture at the University of Rome. Rome, 1921.

To Benedetto Croce

More than twenty years ago I dedicated to you a book which bore witness to a *concordia discors,* a friendship formed by discussions and intellectual collaboration. I have seen with joy a younger generation look up to our friendship as an example to follow.

In all these years our collaboration has become ever more inward, our friendship ever more living. But my old book is no longer alive in my soul, and this is why I feel the need to inscribe your much-loved name in this.

G.

Author's Preface

...so I print this small volume (as I hope to print others in years to come) in order not to part company with my students when their examination is over, and in order that I may be ready, if my work be not lost, to repeat in these pages my reply, or my encouragement to make them seek their own reply, when they feel the need arise and that I hope will not be seldom to meet the serious problems, so old yet ever new, which I have discussed in the class-room.

Pisa, 15th *May* 1916.

The first edition of this book had its origin in a course of lectures given at the University of Pisa, in the Academic year 1915-16. It was exhausted in a few months. The continued demand, seeming to prove that the interest in the work is not diminishing, has induced me to reprint the book as it first appeared, without waiting for the time and leisure necessary for the complete revision I wished to make. I should like to have given another form to the whole treatment and more particularly to expound several subjects hardly noticed.

I have, however, devoted as much care to the revision as the shortness of the time at my disposal made possible. I have replaced the original lecture form of the book with chapters, revising as far as possible the exposition, making it as clear as I was able to, introducing here and there notes and comments which I hope will be of use to students, and I have added at the end two chapters, originally the subject of a communication to the *Biblioteca filosofica* of Palermo in 1914. In these two chapters the doctrine is summed up, its character and direction defined and a reply given to a charge which originated in a specious but inexact interpretation of it.

The book can be no more than a sketch, fitted rather to raise difficulties and act as a spur to thought than to furnish clear solutions and proofs. Yet had I developed it in every part with minute analysis, without taking from it every spark of suggestion, it would still have needed well-disposed readers willing to find in a book no more than a book can contain. For, whatever other kinds of truths there may be, the truths I ask my readers to devote attention to here are such as no one can possibly receive complacently from others or acquire easily, pursuing as it were a smooth and easy path in pleasant company. They are only to be conquered on the lonely mountain top, and they call for heavy toil. In this task one toiler can do no more for another than awaken in his soul the taste for the enterprise, casting out the torment of doubt and anxious longing, by pointing to the light which shines on high afar off.

This *General Theory* is only designed to be a simple introduction to the full concept of the spiritual act in which, as I hold, the living nucleus of philosophy consists. And this concept, if my years and forces permit, I intend to expound in special treatises. I have this year published the first volume of my *System of Logic,* which is in fulfilment of this design. The reader of this *Theory of Mind,* who finds himself dissatisfied with it, may know then beforehand that the author is himself dissatisfied, and wants him to read the sequel, that is, if it seem to him worth while.

PISA, *October* 1917.

In this third edition the only modifications I have introduced are formal, designed to remove the obscurity which some have found in my book, due to want of clearness in expression.

As for myself, in re-reading my work after three years I have found nothing I desire to alter in the doctrine, although here and there I find in it several buds which I perceive have since opened out in my thoughts and become new branches, putting forth new leaves and new buds in which I now feel the life is pulsating. But what of this? I have never led my readers or my pupils to expect from me a fully defined thought, a dry trunk as it were encased in a rigid bark. A book is the journey not the destination; it would be alive not dead. And so long as we live we must continue to think. In the collection of my philosophical writings which my friend Laterza has proposed to publish, beginning with this *Theory of Mind* there will follow forthwith the complete *System of Logic.*

G. G.

ROME, *April* 1920.

"Par l'espace, l'univers me comprend et m'engloutit comme un point; par la pensée, je le comprends."

PASCAL.

Chapter One - The Subjectivity of the Real

Berkeley in the beginning of the eighteenth century expressed very clearly the following concept. Reality is conceivable only in so far as the reality conceived is in relation to the activity which conceives it, and in that relation it is not only a possible object of knowledge, it is a present and actual one. To conceive a reality is to conceive, at the same time and as one with it, the mind in which that reality is represented; and therefore the concept of a material reality is absurd. To Berkeley it was evident that the concept of a corporeal, external, material substance, that is, the concept of bodies existing generally outside the mind, is a self-contradictory concept, since we can only speak of things which are perceived, and in being perceived things are objects of consciousness, ideas.

Berkeley with his clear insight remarked that "there is surely nothing easier than to imagine trees in a park, or books existing in a closet, and nobody being by to perceive them; but in such case all that we do is to frame in our mind certain ideas, which we call books and *trees*, and at the same time omit to frame the idea of any one who may perceive them." [1] It is not therefore really the case that no mind perceives them, the perceiver is the mind which imagines them. The object, even when thought of as outside every mind, is always mental. This is the point on which I desire to concentrate attention. The concept of the *ideality of the real* is a very difficult one to define exactly, and it did not in fact prevent Berkeley himself from conceiving a reality effectively independent of mind.

For Berkeley, notwithstanding that happy remark, came himself to deny the ideality of the real. In declaring that reality is not properly an object of the human mind and contained therein, nor, strictly speaking, a thought of that mind, but the totality of the ideas of an objective, absolute Mind, whose existence the human mind presupposes, he contradicted the fundamental principle of his whole thought. Berkeley, indeed, even while saying *esse est percipi*, even while making reality coincide with perception, distinguished between the thought which actually thinks the world, and the absolute, eternal Thought, which transcends single minds, and makes the development of single minds possible. From the empirical point of view, at which, as a pre-Kantian idealist, Berkeley remained, it is obvious, and appears incontrovertible, that our mind does not think all the thinkable, since our mind is a human mind and therefore finite and the minds of finite beings exist only within certain limits of time and space. And then, too, we are able to think there is something which exists, even though actually it may never yet have been thought. It seems undeniable, then, that our mind has not as the present object of its thought everything which can possibly be its object. And since whatever is not an object of human thinking at one definite, historical, empirical, moment, seems as though it may be such an object at another such moment, we come to imagine another thinking outside human thinking, a thinking which is always thinking all the thinkable, a Thought which transcends human thought, and is free from all the limits within which it is or can be circumscribed. This eternal, infinite, thinking is not a thinking like ours which feels its limits at every moment. It is God's thinking. God, therefore, is the condition which makes it possible to think man's thought as itself reality, and reality as itself thought.

Now it is evident that if we conceive human thinking as conditioned by the divine thinking (even though the divine thinking does not present itself to us as an immediate reality), then we reproduce in the case of human thinking the same situation as that in which mind is confronted with matter, that is with nature, regarded as ancient philosophy regarded it, a presupposition of thought, a reality to which nothing is added by the development of thought. If we conceive reality in this way we make it impossible to conceive human thought, because a reality which is already complete and which when presented to thought, does not grow and continue to be realized, is a reality which in its very conception excludes the possibility of conceiving that presumed or apparent new reality which thought would then be.

It was so with Berkeley. He had given expression to a clear, sound, suggestive theory, strikingly analogous to modern idealistic doctrine, declaring that when we believe we are conceiving a reality outside the mind, we are actually ourselves falsifying our belief by our simple presence in the act of perceiving; and when we presume ourselves absent, even then we are intervening and powerless to abstain from intervening, in the very act by which we affirm our absence. When he had given expression to this doctrine he himself returned to the standpoint of the ancient philosophy, with the result that he failed to conceive the thinking which truly creates reality, the thought which is itself reality. This was precisely the defect of the ancient thought. For it, thinking, strictly conceived, was nothing. Modern philosophy, after full consideration, puts forward simply, with all discretion, the very modest requirement that thinking shall be something. No sooner, however, does modern philosophy acknowledge this modest requirement than it feels the necessity of going on to affirm thinking, as not simply something, as not only an element of reality or an appurtenance of reality, but as indeed the whole or the absolute reality.

From Berkeley's standpoint thinking, strictly, is not anything. Because in so far as the thinking thinks, what it thinks is already thought; for human thought is only a ray of the divine thought, and therefore not something itself new, something other than the divine thought. And even in the case of error, which is indeed ours and not God's, our thinking, as thinking, is not anything;

not only is it not objective reality, but it is not even subjective reality. Were it something new, divine thought would not be the whole.

The Kantian philosophy places us at a new stand point, though Kant himself was not fully conscious of its significance. With Kant's concept of the *Transcendental Ego* it is no longer possible to ask Berkeley's question: How is our finite thinking thinkable? Our thinking and what we think are correlative terms; for when we think and make our own thinking an object of reflexion, determining it as an object by thinking, then what we think, that is, our very thinking itself, is nothing else than our own idea. Such thinking is finite thinking; how is it possible for it to arise? It is our present actual thinking. It is, that is to say, the actualization of a power. A power which is actual must have been possible. How is it possible? Berkeley, in perceiving that this thinking is actual, feels the need of transcending it: and he is right. It is the question which sprang up in the inmost centre of the Kantian philosophy, and to answer it Kant had recourse to the concept of the noumenon. But this concept has really no ground, once we have mastered the concept of thinking as transcendental thinking, the concept of mind as self-consciousness, as original apperception, as the condition of all experience. Be cause, if we conceive our whole mind as something finite, by thinking of it as a present reality, a present with a before and an after from which its reality is absent, then what we are thinking of is not the transcendental activity of experience but what Kant called the *empirical ego,* radically different from the transcendental ego. For in every act of our thinking, and in our thinking in general, we ought to distinguish two things: on the one hand what we are thinking; on the other the we who think and who are therefore not the object but the subject in the thinking act. Berkeley indeed drew attention to the subject which always stands over against the object. But then the subject which Berkeley meant was not the subject truly conceived as subject, but rather a subject which itself was objectified and so reduced to one of the many finite objects contained in experience. It was the object which we reach empirically whenever we analyse our mental act and distinguish therein, on the one hand, the content of our consciousness, and on the other the consciousness as the form of that same content. Just as in vision we have two objects of the one experience, the scene or the term which we may call the object and the eye or the term which we may call the subject, so also in our actual living experience not only is the object of that experience an object, but even the subject by the fact that it is made a term of the experience is an object. And yet the eye cannot see itself except as it is reflected in a mirror!

If then we would know the essence of the mind's transcendental activity we must not present it as spectator and spectacle, the mind as an object of experience, the subject an outside onlooker. In so far as consciousness is an object of consciousness, it is no longer consciousness. In so far as the original apperception is an apperceived object, it is no longer apperception. Strictly speaking, it is no longer a subject, but an object; no longer an ego, but a non-ego. It was precisely here that Berkeley went wrong and failed and for this reason he could not solve the problem. His idealism was *empirical*.

The transcendental point of view is that which we attain when in the reality of thinking we see our thought not as act done, but as act in the doing. This act we can never absolutely transcend since it is our very subjectivity, that is, our own self: an act therefore which we can never in any possible manner objectify. The new point of view which we then gain is that of the *actuality* of the I, a point of view from which the I can never be conceived as its own object. Every attempt which we make we may try it at this moment to objectify the I, the actual thinking, the inner activity in which our spiritual nature consists, is bound to fail; we shall always find we have left outside the object just what we want to get in it. For in defining our thinking activity as a definite object of our thinking, we have always to remember that the definition is rendered possible by the very fact that our thinking activity remains the subject for which it is defined as an object, in whatsoever manner this concept of our thinking activity is conceived. The true thinking activity is not what is being defined but what is defining.

This concept may appear abstruse. Yet it is the concept of our ordinary life so long as we enjoy a certain feeling of life as spiritual reality. It is common observation that whenever we want to understand something which has a spiritual value, something which we can speak of as a *spiritual fact,* we have to regard it not as an object, a thing which we set before us for investigation, but as something immediately identical with our own spiritual activity. And it makes no difference that such spiritual values may be souls, with whom our own soul may not be in accord. The apprehension of spiritual value may be realized both through agreement and disagreement, for these are not two parallel possibilities either of which may be realized indifferently; they are rather two co-ordinate and successive possibilities, one of which is necessarily a step to the other. It is clear that the first step in spiritual apprehension is the assent, the approbation, for we say that before judging we must understand. When we say that we understand without exercising judgment, it does not mean that we exercise no judgment; we do not indeed judge approval or disapproval, but we do judge provisionally for apprehension. A fundamental condition, therefore, of understanding others is that our mind should penetrate their mind. The beginning of apprehension is confidence. Without it there is no spiritual penetration, no understanding of mental and moral reality.

Without the agreement and unification of our mind with the other mind with which it would enter into relation, it is impossible to have any kind of understanding, impossible even to begin to notice or perceive anything which may come into another mind. And we are driven by our thinking activity itself into this apprehension of others. Every spiritual relation, every communication between our own inner reality and another's, is essentially unity.

This deep unity we feel every time we are able to say that we understand our fellow-being. In those moments we want more than intellectual unity, we feel the need of loving. The abstract activity we call mind no longer contents us, we want the good spiritual disposition, what we call heart, - good will, charity, sympathy, open-mindedness, warmth of affection.

Now what is the meaning of this unity? What is this fellow-feeling which is the essential condition of all spiritual communication, of all knowledge of mind? It is quite different from the kind of unity which we experience when, for example, we touch a stone, altogether different in kind from the knowledge of simple nature, of what we call material nature. We find a need to be unified with the soul we would know, because the reality of that soul consists in being one with our own soul: and that other soul likewise cannot meet in our soul what is not essentially its own subjectivity. Life of our life, it lives within our soul, where distinction is not opposition. For, be it noted, within our own soul we may find ourselves in precisely the same spiritual situation as that in which we are when face to face with another soul which we fain would but do not yet understand. This means that the disproportion and incongruence which we find between our soul and other souls, when they appear to us as mute and impenetrable as the rocks and blind forces of nature, is no other than the disproportion and incongruence within our own soul between its own states, between what it is and what we would have it be, between what we can think but yet fail to realize; between what, as we shall see, is our state and what is our act.

[1] Principles of Human Knowledge, sect. 23.

Chapter Two - Spiritual Reality

To understand, much more to know, spiritual reality, is to assimilate it with ourselves who know it. We may even say that a law of the knowledge or spiritual reality is that *the object be resolved into the subject*. Nothing has for us spiritual value save in so far as it comes to be resolved into ourselves who know it.

We usually distinguish the spiritual objects of our knowledge into two classes: either they are subjects of experience, men, intelligent beings; or they are not themselves subjects of experience but the spiritual fact or mental work which such subjects presuppose. This is an empirical distinction which vanishes the moment we reflect on it; not indeed if we only bring to bear on it the reflexion proper to empiricism, but if we reflect with the reflexion proper to philosophy, that which begins with sceptical doubt of the firm beliefs of common sense. The moment we examine the nature of the spiritual facts which we distinguish from true and proper subjects of experience, we see that the distinction is inadmissible. Thus there is no science which is not particular in the sense that it is what particular, historically-determined individuals possessed in thinking it, yet we distinguish the science of men from science in itself. So, too, with language: although it is an historical product we begin by detaching it from every particular person who uses it, who is himself unique, and for whom the language he uses is, moment by moment, a unique language; we extend it to a whole people. And mentally we even detach it from all and every people, and no longer speak of a definite language, but of language in general, the means, as we say, of expressing states of mind, a form of thought. Language, so conceived and fixed by our mind, is then freed from all contingency or particular limitation, and hovers in the world of concepts, which is not only the world of the actual, but also the world of the simply possible. Language has now become an ideal fact. And lo! On the one hand there is the language sounding from a man's lips, the speech of one particular man, a language whose reality consists in the personality of the speaker, and, on the other hand, language in itself, which can be spoken, but which is what it is even though no one should speak it.

But the truth is that if we would know language in the concrete, it must present itself to us as development. Then it is the language which sounds forth from the mouths of the men who use it. We no longer detach it from the subject, and it is not a spiritual fact which we can distinguish from the mind in which it exists. The spiritual act which we call language, is precisely the mind itself in its concreteness. So when we speak of a language and believe that we mean not an historical language but a language conceived as a psychical or ideal fact apart from history, a fact as it were inherent in the very nature of mind and ideally reconstructed whenever its principle is meant; and when we believe that in this case we have completely detached it from the particular individual who from time to time speaks a particular language; what we are then really doing is forming a concept of language by reconstructing a moment of our own consciousness, a moment of our own spiritual experience. Detach from language the philosopher who reconstructs it and language as a moment of mind disappears; since language, hovering loose, transcendent and freed from time and space, is language as it is conceive, by the man, the individual, who can only effectively represent it by speaking it, and who speaks it just to the extent that he represents it. Yet do we not distinguish the *Divine Comedy* from Dante its author and from our selves its readers? We do; but then even in making the distinction we know that this Divine Comedy is with us and in us, within our mind thought of as distinct from us. It is in us despite the distinction; in us in so far as we think it. So that it, the poem, is precisely we who think it.

To detach then the facts of the mind from the real life of the mind is to miss their true inward nature by looking at them as they are when realized.

When we speak of spiritual fact we speak of mind, and to speak of mind is always to speak of concrete, historical individuality; of a subject which is not *thought* as such, but which is *actualized* as such. The spiritual reality, then, which is the object of our knowing, is not mind and spiritual fact, it is purely and simply mind as subject. As subject, it can, as we have said, be known on one condition only it can be known only in so far as its objectivity is resolved in the real activity of the subject who knows it.

In no other way is a spiritual world conceivable. Whoever conceives it, if he has truly conceived it as spiritual, cannot set it up in opposition to his own activity in conceiving it. Speaking strictly, there can be no *others* outside us, for in knowing them and speaking of them they are within us. To know is to identify, to overcome otherness as such. *Other* is a kind of stage of our mind through which we must pass in obedience to our immanent nature, but we must pass through without stopping. When we find ourselves confronted with the spiritual existence of others as with something different from ourselves, something from which we must distinguish ourselves, something which we presuppose as having been in existence before our birth and which even when we are no longer there to think will always remain the possession, or at least, the possible possession, of other men, it is a clear sign that we are not yet truly in their presence as spiritual existence, or rather that we do not see the spirituality of their existence.

This doctrine that the spiritual world is only conceivable as the reality of my own spiritual activity, would be clearly absurd were we to seek to interpret it in any other light than that of the distinction, explained in the last chapter, between the transcendental ego and the empirical ego. It is only rational when we clearly and firmly apprehend the concept of the reality of the transcendental ego as the fundamental reality, without which the reality of the empirical ego is not thinkable. Applied to the empirical ego the doctrine is meaningless. Empirically I am an individual and as such in opposition not only to all material things, but equally to all the individuals to whom I assign a spiritual value, since all objects of experience, whatever their value, are not only distinct but separate from one another in such a manner that each of them absolutely excludes from itself, by its own particularity, all the others. In the empirical domain moral problems arise entirely and precisely in this absolute opposition in which the ego empirically conceived stands distinct from other persons. The supreme moral aspiration of our being as empirical individuals is to acquire a harmony, a unity, with all the others and with all that is other. This means that moral problems arise in so far as we become aware of the unreality of our being as an empirical ego opposed to other persons and surrounding things and come to see that our own life is actualized in the things opposed to it. Though on such ground the moral problems arise, they are only solved when man comes to feel another's needs his own, and thereby finds that his own life means that he is not closed within the narrow circle of his empirical personality but ever expanding in the efficacy of a mind above all particular interests and yet immanent in the very centre of his deeper personality.

Let it not be thought that the concept of this deeper personality, the Person which has no plurality, in any way excludes and effectually annuls the concept of the empirical ego. Idealism does not mean mysticism. The particular individual is not lost in the being of the "I" which is absolute and truly real. For this absolute "I" unifies but does not destroy. It is the one which unifies in itself every particular and empirical ego. The reality of the transcendental ego even implies the reality of the empirical ego. It is only when it is cut off from its immanent relation with the transcendental ego that the empirical ego is falsely conceived.

If we would understand the nature of this subject, - the unique and unifying transcendental I, in which the whole objectivity of spiritual beings is resolved, confronted by nothing which can assert independence, a subject therefore with otherness opposed to it, - if we would understand the nature of this reality we must think of it not as a being or a state, but as a *constructive process*. Giambattista Vico in his *De antiquissima Italorum sapientia* (1710) chose as his motto: "Verum et factum convertuntur." It showed profound insight. The concept of truth coincides with the concept of fact.

The true is what is in the making. Nature is the true, according to Vico, only for the divine intellect which is creative of nature; and nature cannot be the true for man, for nature is not made by us and into its secrets it is not given to us therefore to penetrate. All we can see of these secrets is the phenomena in their extrinsic *de facto* modes of linkage (as Hume will say a little later), but we cannot know why one phenomenon must follow on another, nor in general why what is, is. When we look within nature itself all is turbid, mysterious. On the other hand, in regard to everything which we understand because it is our own doing, the criterion of truth is clearly within us. For example, what is a straight line? We know because we ourselves construct it in the inmost recess of our own thinking by means of our own imagination. The straight line is not in nature; we understand it thanks to our imagination, and not immediately but by constructing it. So later in his *Scienza nuova* (1725) Vico tells us that the human mind can know the laws of the eternal historical process, conceived as spiritual development, because the cause and first origin of all historical events is in the human mind.

The greatest effort we can make, still following Vico, to get within the processes of nature is *experiment,* in experiment it is we ourselves who dispose the causes for producing the effects. But even in the case of experiment the efficient principle remains within nature itself, whose forces we use without any means of knowing the internal mode of their working. And even in experiment our knowledge stops at the simple discovery of the *de facto* connexions, so that the inward activity of the real, which ought to be the true and proper object of knowledge, escapes us. Our experiments being operations extrinsic to nature can only yield a superficial knowledge of it. Its superficiality, or its defect as *truth,* is most clearly seen when natural science is compared with mathematics, and even more so when it is compared with the science of the human world, with what Vico called *the world of the nations*. For numbers and magnitudes, the realities studied by mathematics, are constructed by us, they are not realities in their own right but fictions, suppositions, merely postulated entities; whereas history is true and effectual reality. When we have understood history by mentally reconstructing its reality, there remains nothing outside it, no reality independent of history by which we can possibly test our reconstruction and decide whether it corresponds or not.

What then is the meaning of this doctrine of Vico? It teaches us that we can only say we know an object when there is in that object nothing *immediate,* nothing which our thought finds there already before we begin to know it, real therefore even before it is known. Immediate knowledge is *contradictio in adjecto*. Would you know what language is? There is no better answer than the remark of von Humboldt (1767-1835): true language is not ἔργον (*opus*) but ἐνέργεια (*opera*). It is not the result of the linguistic process, but is precisely that process which is developed in act. Whatever language is then, we know it, not in its definite being (which it never has), but step by step in its concrete development. And as with language so with all spiritual reality, you can only know it, so to say, by resolving it into your own spiritual activity, gradually establishing that self-sameness or unity in which knowledge consists. Destroy the degrees or steps of the development and there is no longer the development, you have destroyed the very reality whose realization and understanding is in question.

The truth is that the fact, which is convertible with the truth (*verum et factum convertuntur*) in being the same spiritual reality which realizes itself or which is known in its realizing, is not, strictly speaking, a fact or a deed but a doing. We ought then rather to say: *verum et fieri convertuntur.*

Chapter Three - The Unity of Mind and the Multiplicity of Things

The subject in this constructive process, the subject which resolves the object into itself, at least in so far as the object's spiritual reality, is neither a being nor a state of being. Nothing but the constructive process *is*. The process is constructive of the object just to the extent that it is constructive of the subject itself. And therefore instead of saying *verum et factum convertuntur,* we ought to say *verum et fieri convertuntur,* or even, *verum est factum quatenus fit.* In so far as the subject is constituted a subject by its own act it constitutes the object. This is one of the vital concepts. We must acquire firm possession of it if we would avoid the equivocal blunders of some of the ostentatious and only too easy criticisms of this idealism.

Idealism is the negation of any reality which can be opposed to thought as independent of it and as the presupposition of it. But more than this, is the negation of thought itself as an activity? if that thought is conceived as a reality existing apart from its developing process, as a substance independent of its actual manifestation. If we take words in their strict meaning we must say that idealism is the denial of being either to a mind or to mind, the denial that a mind *is*, because "being" and "mind" are mutually contradictory terms. If, speaking of spiritual reality, we say of a poet that he is, or of a poem that it is, in affirming *being* we are denying *mind*. We can say indeed that it is what the mind opposes to itself as a term of its transcendental activity. If we would say, however, what it now itself is, we can only mean, if we have a philosophical concept of it, what its development is, or more strictly, what this development is actualizing.

A stone is, because it is already all that it can be. It has realized its essence. A plant is, an animal is, in so far as all the determinations of the plant or animal are a necessary and preordained consequence of its nature. Their nature is what they can be, and what cannot be altered at will, cannot break out into new unforeseeable manifestations. All the manifestations by which their nature is expressed is already there existing implicitly. There are processes of reality which are logically exhaustible, although not yet actually realized in time. The existence of these is ideally actualized. The empirical manifestations of their being come to be conceived, therefore, as closed within limits already prescribed as impassable boundaries. This restricted nature is a consequence which follows from the fact that every thing is represented in its relation to mind, as a reality confronting it, whose being therefore is presupposed in the fact that the mind knows it. The mind itself, on the contrary, in its actuality is withdrawn from every pre-established law, and cannot be defined as a being restricted to a definite nature, in which the process of its life is exhausted and completed. So to treat it is to lose sight of its distinctive character of spiritual reality. It is to confuse it and make it merely one of the objects to which instead it ought to be opposed; one of the objects to which in so far as it is mind, it is in fact opposed. In the world of nature all is *by nature*. In the world of mind neither person nor thing is by nature, all is what it becomes through its own work. In the world of mind nothing is already done, nothing is because it is finished and complete; all is always doing. Just as all which has been understood is nothing in regard to what we want to and as yet are unable to understand, so likewise in the moral life all the merits of the noblest deeds hitherto performed do not diminish by a hair s-breadth the sum of duties there are to fulfil and in the fulfilment of which the whole value of our conduct will lie, so long as we continue to have worth as spiritual beings.

Mind according to our theory is act or process not substance. It is very different therefore from the concept of mind in the old spiritualistic and doctrine. That theory, in opposing mind to matter, materialized mind. It declared it to be substance, by which it meant that it was the subject of an activity of which it was independent, an activity therefore which it could realize or not realize without thereby losing or gaining its own being. In our view mind has no existence apart from its manifestations; for these manifestations are according to us its own inward and essential realization. We can also say of our mind that it is our experience, so long as we do not fall into the common error, due to faulty interpretation, of meaning by experience, the content of experience. By experience we must mean the act of experiencing, pure experience, that which is living and real. [1]

Let us be on our guard that we are not ensnared in the maze of language. Mechanistically analysed, not only is the noun distinguished from the verb but it is detached from it and stands for a concept separable and thinkable apart. As love is loving and hate is hating, so the soul which loves or hates is no other than the act of loving or hating. *Intellectus* is itself *intelligere,* and the grammatical duality of the judgment *intellectus intelligit* is an analysis of the real unity of mind. Unless we understand that unity there is no understanding. If the living flame in which the spiritual act consists be quenched there is no remainder; so long as the flame is not rekindled there is nothing. To imagine ourselves simple passive spectators of our soul, even after a spiritual life intensely lived, full of noble deeds and lofty creations, is to find ourselves inert spectators in the void, in the nought which is absolute. There is just so much mind, just so much spiritual wealth, as there is spiritual life in act. The memory which does not renew, and so create *ex novo,* has nothing, absolutely nothing, to remember. Even opening our eyes to look within, when it requires no effort to do so, brings work, activity, keenness, in a word, is life. To stop is to shut our eyes; not to remain an inactive soul but to cease to be a soul.

This soul, it is hardly necessary to point out, is not the object of psychology. Psychology claims to be the natural science of psychical phenomena, and accordingly adopts towards these phenomena the same attitude which every natural science adopts towards the class of objects it chooses for special study. The class of objects presented to the psychologist, like the classes of natural objects presented to the naturalist, is taken just as what it purports to be. It is not necessary therefore that the psychologist, before he can analyse the soul which is the object of his science, should have to re-live it. He can be olympically serene in its presence. What he has singled out for observation may be a tumult of emotions, but he must preserve before it the same imperturbability which the mathematician preserves before his geometrical figures. It is his business to understand, he must be perfectly impassive even before a real passion. But is the passion, when the psychologist analyses it without being himself perturbed by it, a spiritual reality? It is certainly a phenomenon which to exist must be given a place in the world of objects we can know about; and this is the ground of the science of psychology. Its particular claim to be science we will examine later. But if we are now asked: Can we think that this reality which confronts the mind and which the mind has to analyse, a reality therefore which is a presupposition of the mind whose object it is, is spiritual reality? We must answer at once: No. If the object is a spiritual reality and if our doctrine of the knowledge of spiritual reality be true, the object must be resolved into the subject; and this means that whenever we make the activity of others the object of our own thought it must become our own activity. Instead of this the psychologist, in the analysis which he undertakes from an empirical or naturalistic standpoint, presupposes his object as other than and different from the activity which analyses it. Understanding his object means that the object is not the activity of the subject for which it is object. The anthropologist who specializes on criminal anthropology does not even for one single moment feel the need to be the delinquent and so resolve the object into the subject! Just so; precisely because the reality he studies is psychology (in the naturalistic meaning) it is not spiritual reality. This means that whatever appearance of spirituality it may have, the reality in its fulness, in what it truly is, escapes the analysis of the psychologist. And every time we consider any aspect whatever of spiritual reality simply from the empirical standpoint, the standpoint of empirical psychologists, we may be sure from the start that we only see the surface of the spiritual fact, we are looking at some of its extrinsic characters, we are not entering into the spiritual fact as such, we are not reaching its inmost essence.

To find spiritual reality we must seek it. This means that it never confronts us as external; if we would find it we must work to find it. And if to find it we must needs seek it, and finding it just means seeking it, we shall never have found it and we shall always have found it. If we would know what we are we must think and reflect on what we are; finding lasts just as long as the construction of the object which is found lasts. So long as it is sought it is found. When seeking is over and we say we have found, we have found nothing, for what we were seeking no longer is. *Nolite judicare* says the Gospel. Why? Because when you judge a man you no longer regard him as man, as mind, you take a standpoint from which he is seen as so much material, as belonging to the natural world. He has ceased to be the mind which subsists in doing, which can only be understood when seen in act: not in the act accomplished, but in the act in process.

We may say of spiritual reality what the great Christian writers have said of God. Whoever seeks Him shall find Him. But to find spiritual reality one must be willing to put his whole being into the search, as though he would satisfy the deepest need of his own life. The God you can find is the God whom in seeking you make to be. Therefore faith is a virtue and supposes love. In this lies the folly of the atheist's demand that the existence of God should be proved to him without his being relieved of his atheism. Equally fatuous is the materialist's denial of spiritual reality: he would have the philosopher show him spirit, - in nature! Nature which by its very definition is the absence of mind! Wonderful are the words of the psalmist. *Dixit insipiens in corde suo non est Deus.* Only in his foolish heart could he have said it!

To have grasped the truth that mind is a reality which is in self-realization, and that it realizes itself as self-consciousness, is not enough in itself to free us from the illusion of naturalism, or Spiritual reality seems itself to be in continual rebellion against such definition, arresting and fixing itself as a reality, an object of thought. All the attributes we employ to distinguish mind tend, however we strive against it, to give it substance. *Verum est factum quatenus fit* is in effect a definition of mind as truth. What then is truth but something we contrapose to error? A particular truth is a truth and not an error, and a particular error is an error and not a truth. How then are we to define and conceive truth without shutting it within a limited and circumscribed form? How are we to conceive truth, - not Truth as the sum of all its determinations, object of a quantitatively omniscient mind, but some definite truth (such as the theory of the equality of the internal angles of a triangle to two right angles), any truth in so far as it is an object or fixed in a concrete spiritual act, how are we to conceive such a truth except by means of a fixed and self-contained concept, whose formative process is exhausted, which is therefore unreformable and incapable of development? And how can we think our whole spiritual life otherwise than as the continual positing of definite and fixed moments of our mind? Is not spiritual concreteness always spiritual being in precise, exact and circumscribed forms?

This difficulty, when we reflect on it, is not different from that which, as we saw, arises in the necessity we are under of beholding men and things in the medium of multiplicity. And it can only be eliminated in the same way, that is, by having recourse to the living experience of the spiritual life. For neither the multiplicity nor the fixedness of spiritual reality is excluded from the concept of the progressive unity of mind in its development. But, as the multiplicity is subordinated and unified in the unity, so the determinateness is subordinated in the concreteness of the system of all the determinations, which is the actual life of mind. For determinateness is essentially and fundamentally multiplicity, it is the particularity of the determinations by which each is what it is and reciprocally excludes the others. It is only by abstraction that even such a truth as that instanced, of the equality of the internal angles of a triangle to two right angles, can be said to be closed and self-contained. In reality it is articulated into the process of geometry in all the minds in which this geometry is actualized in the world.

This shows us why the concept of mind as process is a difficult concept. Against it all the fixed abstractions of common sense and of science (which by its very nature always moves in the abstract) are continually working, incessantly crowding our intellect, drawing it hither and thither, not suffering it without bitter exertion to keep its hold on the immediate intuition of the spiritual life. By that intuition alone it attains, in its vivid moments, its norm and its inspiration towards science and virtue, which the more they fill the soul the more strongly vibrate the tense cords of our internal forces.

The unity of mind, which lives in such intuition, has been more or less clearly pointed out by all philosophers, but no one yet perhaps has brought out with definite clearness its distinctive mark - *unmultipliable and infinite unity*.

The unity of mind is *unmultipliable* because, although psychology may compel us to analyse and reconstruct spiritual reality, it is impossible ever to think that mind is decomposable into parts, each conceivable by itself as a self-contained unity, irrespective of the rest. Empirical psychology, while it distinguishes the various concurrent psychical facts in a complex state of consciousness and declares different elements to be ultimate terms in its analysis, yet goes on to point out that all the elements are fused in one whole, and that all the facts have a common centre of reference, and that it is precisely in virtue of this that they assume their specific and essential psychological character. Even the old speculative psychologies (as empirical as the modern in their starting-point), when they distinguish abstractly the various faculties of the soul, always reaffirm the indivisible unity or the simplicity (as they call it) of the mind as the common basis and unique substance of the various faculties. The life, the reality, the concreteness of the spiritual activity, is in the unity; and there is no multiplicity except by neglecting the life and fixing the dead abstractions which are the result of analysis.

Modern empiricism, with its natural bias towards multiplicity, compelled to acknowledge that in any given experience consciousness is a unique centre of reference for all the psychical phenomena, and that therefore there is no multiplicity within the ambit of one consciousness, supposes that in the phenomenon of *multiple personality,* studied in abnormal psychology, multiplicity is introduced into consciousness itself. For though within the ambit of consciousness there is no multiplicity, yet when expelled from the ambit, two or more consciousnesses may exist in one and the same empirical subject. But this empirical observation itself serves only to confirm our doctrine of the non-multiplicity of mind because the duplication consists in the absolute reciprocal exclusion of the two consciousnesses, each of which is a consciousness only on condition of its not being a partial consciousness, nor part of a deeper total consciousness, but that it is itself total and therefore itself unique, not one of two.

The unity of the mind is *infinite*. For the reality of the mind cannot be limited by other realities and still keep its own reality. Its unity implies its infinity. The mind is not a multiplicity: nor is the whole, of which it is a part, multiple, the part being a unity. For if the mind belonged to a multiple whole it would be itself intrinsically multiple. The negation of intrinsic multiplicity is therefore enough to make clear the absurdity of the concept that the mind is part of a multiplicity. Atomists and monadists alike, however, have thought it possible to conceive the composite and also at the same time to conceive the simple as a constitutive element of the composite. We need not in this place discuss the strength of this thesis, we may for our present purpose even admit that it has all the value which common sense attributes to it, for, independently of every consequence of the concept of the unmultipliable or intrinsic unity of consciousness, there is a much more effective way of showing its infinity.

When we present the concept of our consciousness to ourselves we can only conceive it as a sphere whose radius is infinite. Because, whatever effort we make to think or imagine other things or other consciousnesses outside our own consciousness, these things or consciousnesses remain within it, precisely because they are posited by us, even though posited as external to us. The without is always within; it denotes, that is to say, a relation between two terms which, though external to one another, are both entirely internal to consciousness. There is for us nothing which is not something we perceive, and this means that however we define it, whether as external or internal, it is admitted within our sphere, it is an object for which we are the subject. Useless is the appeal to the ignorance in which, as we know by experience, we once were and others may now be of the realities within our subjective sphere. In so far as we are actually ignorant of them, they are not posited by consciousness and therefore do not come within its sphere. It is clear that our very ignorance is not a fact unless at the same time it is a cognition. That is to say, we are ignorant only in so far either as we ourselves perceive that we do not know or as we perceive that others perceive what we do not. So that ignorance is a fact to which experience can appeal only because it is known. And in knowing ignorance we know also the object of ignorance as being external to the ambit of a given knowing. But external or internal it is always in relation to, and so within, some consciousness. There exists no means of transcending this consciousness.

Spinoza conceived the two known attributes of substance, thought and extension, to be external to one another. He opposed *idea* and *res, mens* and *corpus,* but he was not therefore able to think that *ordo et connexio idearum idem est ac ordo et connexio rerum,* [2] because, as he tells us, res (and primarily our own body) is no other than *objectum mentis.* [3] The body is the term of our consciousness or the content of its first act. It is what Rosmini later called the basal feeling (*sentimento fundamentale*), the sense which the soul has in its feeling of what is primarily the object felt, the object beneath every sensation, the body. The *objectum mentis* of Spinoza is indeed different from the mind, but it is bound to the mind and seen by the mind itself as something different from it. In the very position then which the mind assigns to the body (and to all bodies) the mind is not really transcended. Spinoza therefore conceived mind as an *infinite* attribute of the infinite substance. Substance, from the standpoint of thought, is altogether thought.

And as we move with thought along all that is thinkable, we never come to our thought's margin, we never come up against something other than thought, the presence of which brings thought to a stop. So that the mind is not only in itself psychologically one, it is one epistemologically and it is one metaphysically; it is never able even to refer to an object which is external to it, never able therefore to be conceived as itself a real among reals, as a part only of the reality.

But this is not enough. So far we have looked at only one side of the question. A deep and invincible repugnance has in every age made the human mind shrink from affirming this unmultipliable and infinite unity of the mind in its absolute subjectivity. The mind cannot issue from itself, it can detach nothing from itself, its world is within it. And yet this concept of the self, of a centre around which every one necessarily gathers all the real and possible objects of his experience, seems to hint at something different from it, something which is its essentially correlative term. In affirming a subject we at the same time affirm an object. Even in self-consciousness the subject opposes itself as object to itself as subject. If the activity of consciousness is in the subject, then when in self-consciousness that same subject is the object, as object it is opposed to itself as the negation of consciousness, even as unconscious reality, relatively at least to the consciousness which belongs to the subject. The object is always contraposed to the subject in such wise that, however it may be conceived as dependent on the subject's activity, it is never given it to participate in the life with which the subject is animated. So that the subject is activity, search, a movement towards the object; and the object, whether it be the object of search or the object of discovery or the object of awareness, is inert, static. Consequently to the unity realized by the, subject's activity there stands opposed in the object the multiplicity which belongs to the real, hardly separated from the synthetic form which the subject imprints on it. Things, in fact, in their objectivity, presupposed as the term of the mind's theoretical activity, are many: essentially many, in such wise that a single thing is unthinkable save as resulting from a composition of many elements. A unique and infinite thing would not be knowable, because to know is to distinguish one thing from another. *Omnis determinatio est negatio.* Our whole experience moves between the unity of its centre, which is mind, and the infinite multiplicity of the points constituting the sphere of its objects.

What we have then to do here is to bring clearly into relief the character of this relation between the unity of the mind and the multiplicity of things. It escaped Kant. It refers to the exact nature of the mind's theoretical activity. Let us note first of all that if the unity of mind and the multiplicity of things were together and on the same plane, as Kant thought when he presupposed the uncompounded manifold of data coming from the noumenon to the synthesis of aesthetic intuition, then the unity of the ego would be no more than a mere name, because it could be summed up with the other factors of experience and so would participate in the totality which includes the multiplicity of the data. In such case it would be seen to be a part. To be one among many is not really to be one since it is to participate in the nature of the many. But the multiplicity of things does not stand in the same rank with the unity of the ego, for multiplicity belongs to things in so far as they are objects of the ego, or rather in so far as all together are gathered into the unity of consciousness. Things are many in so far as they are together, and therefore within the unity of the synthesis. Break up the synthesis and each is only itself without any kind of reference to the others. And therefore consciousness cannot have one of them as object without being enclosed within it and imposing on itself the absolute impossibility of passing to another. Which comes to saying that the thing no longer is one thing among many, but unique. In so far therefore as there is multiplicity there is a synthesis of multiplicity and unity.

The multiplicity of things, in order to be the multiplicity which belongs to the object of consciousness, implies the resolution of this very multiplicity, and this is its unification in the centre on which all the infinite radii of the sphere converge. The multiplicity is not indeed added to unity, it is absorbed in it. It is not $n + i$, but $n = I$. The subject of experience cannot be one among the objects of experience because the objects of experience are the subject. And when we feel the difference, and only the difference, between ourselves and things, when we feel the affinity of things among themselves, and seem ourselves to be shut up as it were within a very tiny part of the whole, to be as a grain of sand on the shore of an immense ocean, we are regarding our empirical selves, not the transcendental self which alone is the true subject of our experience and therefore the only true self.

We have not, however, eliminated every difficulty. The mind is not only bound to the multiplicity of the object or of the things. There is the multiplicity of persons. There is, it will be said, not only a *theoretical activity* by which we are in relation with things, there is also a *practical activity* by which we are in relation with persons, and thereby constrained to issue from our unity and to recognize and admit a reality transcending our own.

It is of the greatest importance to bring this difficulty clearly to light, for it has immediate consequences in regard to the moral conception of life. Let us note then that the mind is never properly the pure theoretical activity which we imagine to stand in opposition to the practical activity. There is no *theory*, no contemplation of reality, which is not at the same time action and therefore a creation of reality. Indeed there is no cognitive act which has not a value, or rather which is not judged, precisely in its character of cognitive act, according to whether it conforms with its own law, in order that it may be recognized or not as what it ought to be. Ordinarily we think that we are responsible for what we do and not for what we think. We suppose we could not think otherwise than as we think, that though indeed we may be masters of our conduct, we are not masters of our ideas. They are only what they can be, what reality makes them. This common belief, held even by many philosophers, is a most serious error. Were we not the authors of our ideas, that is, were our ideas not our pure actions, they would not be *ours*. It would be impossible to judge them, they would have no value; they would be neither true nor false. They would be, altogether and always, whatever a natural and irrational necessity had made them. The human mind, wherein they would be, altogether and always, running confusedly, would be powerless to exercise any discrimination and choice. It is absurd. For even in thinking the sceptical thesis itself we must think it, whether we will or no, as true, that is, as clothed with truth *value,* for which it *must* be thought and its opposite rejected.

Every spiritual act, then (including that which we regard as simply theoretical), is practical in as much as it has a value, practical in being or in not being what it ought to be. It is therefore *our* act and it is free. Every act is spiritual, moreover, in so far as it is governed by a law, by which an account is required from men not only of what they do but of what they say or of what they would say if they expressed what they think. This law which governs the spiritual act has nothing in common with the laws characterizing natural facts. Natural laws are no other than the facts themselves, whereas a law of the mind is, so to say, an ideal, or rather an ideal which the mind presents to itself in distinction from the fact of its own working. We are accustomed to think that the mind is one thing, the laws which govern it another. Mind is freedom; but also, and just on that account, it is law, which it distinguishes from itself as an activity higher than its own.

Yet again, the law of the mind is rational, and in that alone it is distinguished from the law of nature. The law of nature is what is, not something we are seeking behind what is. It is vain to seek the why of what is. If we ask, Why? of an earthquake or of any other *physical evil* we ask it not of nature, but of God, who can make nature intelligible as the work of mind or act of will. The spiritual law, on the contrary, in all its determinations, has a definite *why,* and speaks its own language to our soul. The poet correcting his poem obeys a law which speaks the language of his own genius. To the philosopher nothing is more familiar, more intimate, than the voice which admonishes him continually, preventing him from uttering absurdities in regard to what he discovers. Every law which others, our teachers or governors, impose on our conduct, is only imposed truly and effectively when it is rendered transparent in its motives and in its intrinsic rationality, perfectly fitted to our concrete spiritual nature.

In conclusion, if the mind be free, in so far as it is limited by laws it can only mean that these laws are not a different reality from that which it is realizing, but the reality itself. The mind cannot be conceived in freedom, with its own value, except by seeing it from the point of view of other minds, just as the "I," as subject of pure abstract knowledge, has need of the "not-I," freedom has need of another "I." And so we have man thinking of God as author of the laws imposed on him and on all other particular men. So too we have man girding himself with duties and positing around him as many minds, as many persons, as subjects are required for the rights which his duties recognize. And when we look within our own consciousness and consider the value of what we are doing and of what we are saying to ourselves, it is as though innumerable eyes were looking in upon us to judge us. The very necessity of the multiplicity of things, as we have already made clear, forces us to conceive manifold duties, many subjects with rights, many persons. Such a concept could never arise in a pure theoretical experience, for a pure theoretical experience could not be made to think of another world than that of things. But we are not a pure theoretical experience. And therefore our world is peopled with minds, with persons.

How then are we to maintain the infinite unity of mind in the face of this necessity of transcending it by a multiplicity of persons?

[1] See *L'esperienza pura e la realtà storica,* Firenza, Libreria della Voce, 1915.
[2] *Ethics,* ii. 7.
[3] *Ibid.* ii. 13. 21.

Chapter Four - Mind as Development

The difficulty instanced at the end of the last chapter concerns, as we can now clearly see, not simply the concept of mind but the concept of the real. For it is only a difficulty in the concept of mind in so far as the real in its totality comes to be conceived as mind. Since, if we take our start in the present actuality of consciousness in which mind is realized, then to posit the infinite unity of mind is to posit the unity of the real as mind.

The solution of this difficulty, which we have tried to present in all its force, is to be found in the concept already expounded that the mind is not a being or a substance but a constructive process or development. The very word development includes in its meaning both unity and multiplicity. It affirms an immanent relation between unity and multiplicity. But there is more than one way of understanding such a relation. It is necessary therefore to clear up precisely the exact mode in which in our view mind is to be conceived as development.

One mode of conceiving development is that by which we posit abstractly the unity outside the multiplicity. The unity of the development is concept then imagined as the ground or basis of development, either as its principle or as its result. The germ of a plant, for example, is represented as the undifferentiated antecedent of the vegetative process, and the growth of the plant as consisting in a progressive differentiation and multiplication of the primitive unity. In such case we may believe we are conceiving the growth of the plant but really we are making it impossible to conceive. The plant lives and grows not only in so far as there is a succession of different states, but in so far as there is the unity of all its states beginning with the germ. And when we oppose the germ to the plant, the tender seedling springing from the soil to the big tree with its wide-spreading branches, we are letting the living plant escape and setting side by side two images, two dead photographs as it were, of a living person. We have multiplicity it is true, but not the reality which comes by the multiplication into different forms of what throughout the development is and always remains one. Another example, taken not from vague fancy but from scientific and philosophical systems, is that of the old vitalist physiology and the mechanistic physiology which arose in the last century as a reaction against it. Both fell into an identical error, for extremes meet. Vitalism posited life as the necessary antecedent or principle of the various organic functions, as an organizing force, transcending all the single specifications of structure and function. Mechanism abolished this unity antecedent to the different organic processes, and these became simply physicochemical processes. It dreamed of a posthumous unity consequent on the multiple play of the physicochemical forces which positive analysis discovers in all vital processes. Life was no longer the principle but the result, and it appeared as though, instead of a metaphysical explanation starting from an idea or from a purely ideal entity, there was now substituted a strictly scientific and positive explanation, since the new point of departure is in the particular phenomena, in the object of experience. In reality for a spiritualistic and finalistic metaphysic there was substituted a materialistic and mechanistic one. The one metaphysic was worth as much as the other, because neither the unity from which the vitalists set out nor that at which the new mechanists arrived was unity. They both adopted an abstraction in order to understand the concrete. Life is not an abstract unity but the unity of an organism, in which the harmony, fusion and synthesis of various elements, exist in such wise that there is neither unity without multiplicity nor multiplicity without unity. The unity cannot yield the multiplicity, as the old physiology supposed, and the multiplicity cannot yield the unity, as the new physiology supposed, and for the following simple reason. So far as the unity and the multiplicity are not real principles but simple abstractions, there can never result from them true unity and true multiplicity, for these, far from being outside one another, are one and the same, the development of life.

There is then another mode of thinking the relation between unity and multiplicity. It can be termed *concrete* in opposition to the former which concept of clearly is abstract. This is the mode which will only let us conceive unity as multiplicity and *vice versa:* it shows in multiplicity the reality, the life of the unity. This life just because it never is but always becomes, forms itself. As we have said, it is not a substance, a fixed and definite entity, but a constructive process, a development.

From this theory that the mind is development, it follows that to conceive a mind as initially perfect, or as becoming finally perfect, is to conceive it no longer as mind. It was not in the beginning, it will not be in the end, because it never is. It becomes. Its being consists in its becoming, and becoming can have neither antecedent nor consequent without ceasing to become.

Now this reality which is neither the beginning nor the end of a process but just process, cannot be conceived as a unity which is not a multiplicity; because as such it would not be development, that is, it would not be mind. Multiplicity is necessary to the very concreteness, to the very dialectical reality of the unity. Its infinity which is the essential attribute of the unity is not denied by its multiplicity but is confirmed by it. Infinity is realized through the multiplicity, for the multiplicity is nothing but the unfolding which is the actualizing of the reality.

The dialectical concept of mind, then, not only does not exclude, it requires spiritual multiplicity as the essential mark of the concept of the infinite unity of mind. Infinite unity is therefore infinite unification of the multiple as it is infinite multiplication of the one. Let us be careful to note, however, that there are not two methods as the Platonists, with their usual abstractness, suppose: one of descent from the one, or multiplication, the other of ascent or return to the one, or unification. Such are, for example, the two famous *cycles* of Gioberti's *formula*: Being creates the existing and the existing returns to Being. [1] This is to fall back into the error already criticized, into the false mode of understanding development. Neither term (one, many) ever is, either as starting-point or end reached. The development is a multiplication which is a unification, and a unification which is a multiplication. In the growing germ there is no differentiation which splits up the unity even for one single moment. The mind therefore does not posit, or confront itself with, an other by alienating that other from itself. It does not break up its own intimate unity through the positing of an otherness which is pure multiplicity. What is other than we is not so other as not to be also our self. Ever bear in mind that the "we" which we mean when we use it as a convention in speech is not the empirical self, and is not the scholastic compound of soul and body, nor even pure mind, it is the true, the transcendental "we." It is especially important to make clear that the concept of dialectical development only belongs rightly to this transcendental "we," for only in it is it given to us to meet the spiritual reality. For there are two modes in which dialectic may be understood, and it is necessary once again to make a clear distinction. One of these modes is that of Plato. It was he who introduced the concept of dialectic into philosophy, and he meant by it sometimes the role which philosophy fulfils and sometimes the intrinsic character of the truth to which philosophy aspires. Dialectic therefore is the fundamental meaning of philosophy in Plato's system. Indeed for Plato, it is the philosopher's inquiry, his research. Dialectic is not what makes the philosopher aspire to the ideas but what makes the ideas, to the knowledge of which he aspires, form themselves into a system. They are interconnected by mutual relations in such wise that the cognition of the particular is the cognition of the universal, the part implies the whole, and philosophy is, to use his own expression, a *Synopsis*. [2] It is clear that this concept of the role of philosophy must depend on the dialectic which belongs to the ideas; it must depend, that is, on the system of relations by which all are bound together among themselves in such wise that, as Plato argues in the *Parmenides,* every idea is a unity of the one and the many. Now, it is clear that a dialectic so conceived implies the immediateness of thought, because it is the whole of thought from all eternity. It is clear therefore that such a dialectic is the negation of all development. [3]

It is not of this Platonic dialectic that we are now speaking. The radical difference between it and the modern may be seen in the fact that dialectic in the Platonic meaning, is thought in so far as it is self-identical (the thought to which Aristotle attributed, as its fundamental laws, the principles of identity and non-contra diction); whereas in our meaning thought is dialectical because it is never self-identical. For Plato every idea in the totality of its relations is what is, what it is impossible to think of as changing and being transformed. We can pass from one idea to another, and in passing we can integrate an initial idea with the cognition of relations with which formerly it had not been thought, but this movement and process in us supposes rest, fixity and immutability in the idea itself. This is the Platonic and Aristotelian standpoint, and from this standpoint the principle of non-contradiction is the indispensable condition of thought. For us on the other hand true thought is not *thought thought,* which Plato and the whole ancient philosophy regarded as self-subsistent, a presupposition of our thought which aspires to correspondence with it. For us the *thought thought* supposes *thought thinking;* its life and its truth are in its act. The act in its actualization, which is becoming or development, does indeed posit the identical as its own object, but thanks precisely to the process of its development, which is not identity, which is not, that is to say, abstract unity, but unity and multiplicity, or rather, identity and difference in one.

This concept of dialectic judged by the principle of non-contradiction, which it seems flagrantly to violate, is a paradox and a scandal. For how can we deny that the principle of non-contradiction is a vital condition of all thought? Yet when we have regard to the profound dissidence between the concept of thought thought, for which the principle of non-contradiction has a meaning, and the concept of thought thinking, the act of the transcendental ego, to which it can have no relevance, we see that the dialectic is a strictly correct concept. It is only when we descend from thought thinking, which is activity, to thought thought, which is the limit of the activity it presupposes and itself abstract, that the principle of non-contradiction applies. The world thought cannot be except as it is thought: however it is thought, it is immutable (in the thought which thinks it). But our modern aspiration to conceive mind as the transcendental activity productive of the objective world of experience, places us within a new world, a world which is not an object of experience, since it is not a world thought, but the ground and principle of experience, the thinking. The new world cannot be governed by the law which was quite right for the old world, and those who continue to point to the principle of non-contradiction as the pillars of Hercules of philosophy show that they still remain in that old world.

The distinction here emphasized between dialectic as Plato understood it, thought in its immediacy or thought thought, and our modern dialectic, thought as act or process, thought thinking, throws light on the meaning and value and inner nature or many concepts, which approximate to our concept of development. They are met with in Plato himself and before and after him, and even in our own time. They are concepts springing from the same soil in which dialectic as Plato understood it has its roots, yet they are quite distinct from the dialectic which makes spiritual reality intelligible to us, and which in its turn can only be understood in regard to spiritual reality.

The Platonic dialectic is only dialectic in appearance. If we consider it with regard to the man's mind does not possess the system of the ideas and aspires to possess it, then indeed there is a development of the unity running through the multiplicity. There is an in definite approach to the realization of dialectical unity in the ever-widening inquiry into the relations by which the ideas are inter-connected. But since the value of this inquiry presupposes that an eternal dialectic is immanent in the ideal world, or since the reality which it is sought to know by dialectic is a presupposition of the thought, the dialectic belongs to the ideas, and though it is possible to conceive a mind sharing in it, still it is not the dialectic of the mind. The ideas do not realize unity, because they are unity; and they do not realize multiplicity because they are multiplicity. Neither in the one case nor in the other have the ideas in themselves any principle of change and movement. Therefore the true dialectic is that which is no longer that of the ideas. The Platonic principle evidently depends on referring the dialectic, which is originally development and process of formation, to an antecedent which transcends it, and in which its value is thought to lie. It resolves, that is to say, the mediacy which belongs to mind in so far as it is development into the immediacy of the reality which it presupposes and which it cannot conceive therefore except as self-identical (at least in regard to the thought which thinks it), according to the laws of the Aristotelian logic.

Now, if this be the fundamental character and the intrinsic defect of the Platonic dialectic, it will cling to all the conceptions, however dynamical and dialectical we make them, which have reference to a reality opposed to the thought which thinks it and presupposed by it.

So in Plato, besides the dialectic of the ideas, we have another dialectic. Plato does not indeed speak of it under that name, but he conceives it apparently in a manner analogous to what we mean by the dialectic of development. It is the movement, the process of continual formation, the γένεσις, as he calls it, of nature. It is not, or at least he certainly does not intend it to be, immediate like the eternal world of the ideas. But Plato's Nature, if it presuppose the eternal ideas, is itself a presupposition in regard to thought, as it was for all the philosophers before him. Nature is not a presupposition in regard to thought in general, for Greek philosophy throughout its whole history cannot be said to have ever succeeded in withdrawing from the ambit of the laws of nature; on the contrary nature is for it an abstract entity, whose position, whatever it be, has no real importance for those who look only at the inner and concrete meaning of philosophical systems. Can we then say of nature so conceived, a nature which in itself, abstractly thought of, *becomes*, but in so far as it comes to be thought, *is*, and in so far as it *is*, comes to be thought, can we really say of this nature that it moves and generates and regenerates itself continually? In so far as we do not think it but only feel it, yes: but in so far as we think it (and how have we come to speak of γένεσις if we do not think it?) it does not move and can no longer be moved; it becomes rigid and petrified in the very fact that it is object of thought. And indeed Plato as the result of his criticism of sensations, and of the consequent opinions, finds no other elements intelligible except the ideas, archetypes, the images of which lying in the depths of the soul are awakened by means of the stimulus of those very sensations. So that though we *begin* by seeing confusedly the movement which is in travail with all natural things, we are not arrested by this first giddy intuition, but pass thence to the contemplation of the fixed and immutable and intelligible ideas. They are the deepest reality of nature, precisely because they are withdrawn from the restlessness of the sensible appearances, or rather because they have not, like these, a character which actually contradicts the reality which thought conceives as already realized. Yet even for Plato there is a material element which in nature is added to the pure ideal forms without disturbing their motionless perfection. But this matter is precisely what from the Platonic standpoint is never made intelligible. Plato says it is non-being. It is something for which in thought's paint-box there are no colours, since whatever is presented to thought and therefore exists for it, is idea. And what can *genesis* itself be, in its eternal truth, but idea? It would not be, were it not idea. To be, then, means that from this lower world of birth and death we are exalted into the hyperuranion of the eternal forms. And we know that when Plato had posited the transcendence of the ideas it was no longer possible for him to redescend into the world of nature.

Aristotle, although he has been called the philosopher of becoming, had no better success. He denies the Platonic transcendence. The ideal forms immanent in the matter form nature. They are subjected to the movement by which alone it is possible for the ideas to be realized in matter. There is no substance which is not a unity of form and matter. He thinks of the world therefore as mass animated by eternal movement which brings the eternal thought into act. Yet even for him thought thinks nature as its antecedent: thinks it therefore as an already realized reality which as such can be defined and idealized in a system of fixed and unchangeable concepts. Indeed there is no science for him which is not the act of the intellect. It is the human intellect corresponding, a static correspondence moreover, to the eternal intellect, which is incarnate in the material world in virtue of the purpose which rules the movement. So that nature for Aristotle, as for Plato, is not an object of science in so far as it is nature; and in so far as it is an object of science at all it is no longer nature, no longer movement, but pure form. It is a concept and a system of concepts. The Aristotelian becoming, in so far as it is not and cannot be the becoming of thought, remains a mere postulate. As thing thought of, it is not becoming; as becoming, it cannot be thought.

In saying that the whole ancient philosophy stopped at the concept of reality as presupposed by thought, we mean that this was inevitable because throughout the whole period it never failed to became possible to conceive, and in fact understand ancient philosophy never did conceive, *history, progress*. It never conceived a reality which is realized through a process, which is not a vain distraction of activity but a continual creation of reality, a continual increase of its own being. Nature, as Plato and Aristotle conceive it, supposes a perfection of being which must be realized in it, but this perfection of being lies behind its back. Man's thinking presupposes the reality of its own ideals, and can strive towards them; but only if it is alienated from them. In the beginning there shines a light, and this must be the goal of human efforts: the golden age, the φύσις (as opposed to the νόμος) of the Sophists, the Cynics and the Stoics, lies behind us, as in the Platonic idealism the ideal world precedes our corporeal life.

The idea of history, the idea of the life of the human mind, as seriously entering into the formative process and development of reality itself, was never so much as suspected throughout the whole course of the ancient philosophy nor even in the medieval so far as that continues the ancient. Even at the beginning of the modern era we find Bacon speaking of an *instauratio ab imis* which is to cancel the past of science as lost labour. We find Descartes equally denying the value of tradition, and conceiving reason abstractly as the power of the empirical individual, who must commence or recommence scientific inquiry by himself alone and start from the beginning. Yet we may hear one voice entirely new, though never understood by his contemporaries, that of Giordano Bruno. In the *Cena de le Ceneri* (1584) he championed the freedom of the new scientific thought against the authority of Aristotle. We have need indeed, he remarked, to trust the judgment of the old; but the old are not the ancients, it is we who are the old, we who come later and are therefore wiser by the experience and reflexion of the ages lived through. [4] Bruno is perhaps the first to affirm that the mind has a development which is an increase of its power, and therefore its true and proper realization. It is the first indication of the modern concept, wholly idealistic and Christian, of the importance of history.

How many are there even to-day who appreciate this concept of history as progress, gradual realization of humanity itself? The dialectical conception is possible on one condition only, and that is that in history we see not a past but the actual present. This means that the historian does not detach himself from his material and set up *res gestae* as the presupposition and already exhausted antecedent of his *historia rerum gestarum*. If he does and trusts to what is called the positive element of historical events, instead of to their organic spirituality, he comes to consider history in the same way as that in which the naturalist considers nature. It is commonly supposed that historical positivism stands on the same basis as naturalistic positivism. But it is not the same, for the naturalist, in so far as he is such, is necessarily positivist. He must set out with the presupposition that nature is and that it can be known; and its knowability depends on its being, whether its being is known or not. We mean by nature something the mind finds confronting it, something already realized when we are brought into relation with it; and positivism is nothing but the philosophy which conceives reality as fact, independent of any relation to the mind which studies it. History presents, indeed, in the positive character of its events, an analogy with nature; but its intelligibility consists in the unity of the real to which it belongs on the one side and in the mentality of the historian on the other. The history of a past is impossible if it is found unintelligible (if, for example, it is attested by undecipherable documents). Between the personages of history and ourselves there must be a common language, a common mentality, an identity of problems, of interests, of thought. This means that it must pertain to one and the same world with ourselves, to one and the same process of reality. History, therefore, is not already realized when we set out on our historical research; it is our own life in act. If then nature is nature in so far only as it precedes the thought of nature, history is history in so far only as it is the thought of the historian.

Whoever does not feel this identity of self with history, whoever does not feel that history is prolonged and concentrated in his consciousness, has not history confronting him, but only brute nature, matter deaf to the questionings of mind. A history so conceived cannot prove a progress, because it cannot be conceived dialectically as a process of formation. It cannot be so conceived for the same reason as that which prevented Plato and Aristotle perceiving the dynamical life of nature. A history which is finished, self-contained, done with, is necessarily represented as all gathered and set out on one plane, with parts which are called successive, though they have no real and substantial succession, that is, an intrinsically necessary order, in which what comes after cannot go before because it implies and therefore presupposes that which comes first. There can be no such order in the history which is simply the matter of historical representation, for the order of an historian's presentation of material is a nexus and unity which belongs to his mind. Strictly, history is not the antecedent of the historian's activity; it is his activity. This is confirmed in the fact that every organization of historical elements, although each element has its own colour and meaning as positive historical fact, bears the imprint of the historian's mentality (political, religious, artistic, philosophical). There is not a material element of history which remains point for point the same in the various representations which different historians offer, nothing which when we have despoiled a history of all the historian's subjective particularity - according to the usual empirical conception - we can fix in its skeletal objectivity.

What we have said of the concept of history, represented as existing antecedent to the mind of the historian, should suffice to clear away the absurdity of the evolutionist notion of a the concept of nature, conceived in the same way, that is, as a reality presupposed by the mind which knows it and therefore independent of the reality of that mind. Such is the nature which Darwin and his followers strive to conceive as an evolution. It is not posited as immediately and simultaneously present, but as being formed and forming itself step by step, not in virtue of a law governing the whole of nature as the process of one spiritual reality, but according to the law of natural selection, the survival of the fittest. It is called selection by a *lucus a non lucendo* since no one selects. The selection results from the inevitable succumbing of the feebler and the adaptation of the stronger to the environment. From this mechanical law, directing a reality which has been set beyond the reach of mind, self-subsistent in its brute nature, there is conceived to arise, as an effect of the mechanism itself, the highest form of animal and its soul. This soul is reason and will, a reality which puts it in opposition to all other kinds of animal and to all nature, which it understands and exercises lordship over. Now, subtract mind, suppose it not yet to have come to birth, and evolution then stands to nature, as Darwin conceived it, in the same relation as that in which dialectic stands to the world of Platonic ideas, that is, it ceases any longer to be process because it implies a system of relations all of which are already posited and consolidated. Let us imagine that there really is a moment at which one given species exists, and that at this moment there does not yet exist the superior species which, according to the evolutionist theory, must issue from it, then the least reflexion will show us that the passage of the one grade of nature into the other is unintelligible unless with the mind we pass from that moment, in which as yet the second grade does not exist, to the successive moment in which there is the first and the second grade and their relation. So that in general, in the whole chain of evolution, however long we imagine it, the first link of it is always presented as together with all the others even to the last: that is, even to man who is more than nature and therefore, by his intervention alone, destroys the possibility of conceiving nature in itself as an evolution. This amounts to saying that an indispensable condition of understanding nature, as we understand history, in its movement, is that the object be not detached from the subject and posited in itself, independent, in its unattainable transcendence. As transcendent object it can only be effectively posited as object already thought and thereby it is shown to be immanent in the thinking, but considered abstractly in a way which separates it from the thinking itself. And then it is obvious that what we find within the object is what we have put there.

To Hegel belongs the merit of having affirmed the necessity of the dialectical thinking of the real in its concreteness. He put to the proof and showed the impossibility of the dialectical thinking of the real if we begin by separating it from the act of thinking and regard it as in itself and presupposed by the act of thinking it. Hegel saw clearly that we do not conceive reality dialectically unless we conceive it as itself thought. He distinguished the *intellect* which conceives things, from the *reason* which conceives mind. Intellect abstractly represents things analytically, each for itself, self-identical, different from all the others. Reason comprehends all in the unity of mind, as each self-identical and at the same time different, and therefore both different from and identical with all the others. And yet Hegel himself, when he would define, in the moments of its rhythm, the dialectical nature of thought, the thought which understands *itself* as unity of the variety and *things* as variety of the unity, instead of presenting this dialectic as the archetypal law of thought in act, and thereby its presupposed ideal, could not avoid fixing it in abstract concepts. Thence his concepts are immobile, actually devoid of any dialectical character, and we are left unable to understand how the concepts by themselves can pass one into another and be unified in a real continuous logical movement.

The difficulties which he and many who ventured on his tracks had to meet in the deduction of those first categories of his Logic, by which the concept of becoming, the specific character of the dialectic, is constituted, are classical. Becoming is an identity of being and non-being, since the being which is not, becomes. And so Hegel has to move from the concept of being, pure being, free from every determination, which is indeed the least which can be thought, and which we cannot not think, in its absolute indeterminateness, whatever abstraction is made from the content of thought. Is it possible to pass from this concept of being, posited in this way before thought, and defined by means of its own indefiniteness, to the concept of becoming and so to prove that nothing is but all becomes? Yes, according to Hegel; because being as such is not thinkable, or rather it is only thinkable as self-identical with and at the same time different from itself. It cannot be thought, because when we attempt to think it deprived of all content, absolutely indeterminate, we think of it as nothing, or nonbeing, or being which is not; and the being which is not, becomes. But it has been said, if the absolute indeterminateness of being equates it with nothing, we are then without the unity of being and non-being in which becoming consists: there is not that *contradiction* between being and non-being of which Hegel speaks, and which is to generate the concept of becoming. For if being is on the one hand identical with, and on the other hand different from, non-being. then there is a being which is not non-being and a non-being which is not being; and there is wanting that unity of the different which gives rise to becoming. Being, as pure being, in such case would be extraneous to -non-being, as pure non-being, and there could not be that meeting together and shock of being and nothing from which Hegel thought to strike the spark of life. In the end we are left, from whichever side we approach, with two dead things which do not amalgamate in the living movement.

We might easily have brought forward other and different kinds of arguments, for this is Hegel's *crux philosophorum,* round which battle has been waged. Every one feels the necessity of giving an account of the concept of becoming, and yet no one is satisfied with Hegel's deduction of it. [5] That deduction is vitiated by the error already indicated in distinguishing the dialectic which is understood as a dialectic of thing thought, from the true dialectic which can only be conceived as a dialectic of the thinking outside which there is no thought. The being which Hegel must prove identical with non-being in the becoming, the being which alone is real, is not the being which he defines as the indeterminate absolute (how can the indeterminate absolute be other than the indeterminate absolute?), but the being of the thought which defines and, in general, thinks. As Descartes saw, thought is in so far as we think. If thought were something that *is*, it would not be what it is - act. It is in not-being, in self-positing, in becoming, that it is. [6] So that all the difficulties met with in the Hegelian dialectic are eliminated as soon as we acquire a clear consciousness of the immense difference between the reality which Plato and Aristotle conceived dialectically, the reality also which in the ordinary notion of history and the evolutionist notion of nature are conceived dialectically, and the reality which modern idealist philosophy defines as dialectic. For the one, reality is thought of, or thinkable, which is the same thing; for the other, reality is thinking.

Get rid of the ordinary and unconscious abstraction according to which reality is what you think, and which yet, if you think it, can be nowhere but in your thought. Look with steady gaze at the true and concrete reality of the thought in act. The dialectical character of the real will then appear as evident and certain as it is evident and certain to each of us that in thinking we are conscious of what thinks, just as in seeing we are conscious of what sees.

[1] "L'Ente crea l'esistente, e l'esistente ritorna all Ente."
[2] *Rep.* viii. 375 c.
[3] See Gentile, *La Riforma della Dialectica hegeliana,* Messina, Principato, 1913, pp. 3-5 and 261-3; and *Sistema di Logica,* Part I. chap. viii. s. 6.
[4] Cf. my article "Veritas filia temporis," 1912, in *Giordano Bruno e la filosofia del Rinascimento,* Florence, Vallecchi, 1920.
[5] I have given a short critical exposition of the principal attempts at interpretation in the volume already alluded to: *La Riforma della Dialettica hegeliana,* ch. i.
[6] Such is the concept I have expounded in my book just referred to, as a reform of the Hegelian principle.

Chapter Five - The Problem of Nature

Having posited a purely ideal dialectic, and a Logos, distinct from mind or thought thinking, which is the consciousness of it, the road lay open to Hegel to deduce mind from the Logos by passing through nature. For by conceiving the dialectic of thing thought as a pure thinkable, he had found a way of conceiving nature dialectically, for nature is thing thought and not a thinking. But it proves to be only a road painted on a wall. For he kept open the possibility of conceiving nature dialectically only because he had not yet discovered the true dialectic and continued to use the old, unserviceable Platonic dialectic. When we make dialectic coincide with thought we cannot, as we saw in the last chapter, even propose the problem of the dialectic of nature: it becomes an absurdity. If in place of the false conception of history which opposes history to the mind which thinks it, we have been able to indicate and put in its place the true conception of history, and if that dialectical concept eliminates the opposition and reveals the infinite unity of mind consolidated in its actuality, then the criticism we are now bringing against the dialectical concept of nature digs still deeper the abyss which yawns between mind and the concept of a reality which is resistant to all dialectical thinking. Granted the dialectical nature of mind, a limitation of its dialectic seems to carry with it a limitation of the reality of mind and so to force us to deny to it that infinity which we declared immanent in the concept of mind. Hence the problem arises: What is this nature which stands confronting the mind and is not susceptible of being presented dialectically? What is this nature which the mind finds outside itself as its own antecedent? Until we reply to this question it is clearly impossible to maintain our fundamental affirmation of the infinite unity of mind.

Before we can say what nature is we must first know whether the nature meant is thought of as general or universal, or as individual. Plato, following Socrates, who first originated the clear distinction between the general and the individual, was induced by the speculative transcendental tendency of his philosophy to think of nature as general, and so he turned the immediacy and positiveness of natural reality into the *idea* of the nature. The true horse is not for him the single, particular, individual horse but the species horse (not of course using the term in the empirical meaning of the naturalist). It is ἱππότης, horseness, and he tells us that it provoked the mirth of his opponent Antisthenes. [1] Plato could not conceive otherwise a nature which could be an object of science, or which could simply be, without an idea. But such a conception of nature fell under the criticism which Aristotle brought to bear on the Platonic transcendence. The Platonic doctrine makes the individual inconceivable, and it was the individual which, pressing upon thought with the demand that it be taken in its full actuality, had generated the problem of the Socratic universal. For Aristotle, nature, in its opposition to thought, is posited as the unity of the form or idea with matter its opposite (Plato's non-being): for Aristotle's substance is precisely the individual which is that unity. And with Aristotle nature begins to be opposed to the universality of the idea, or of the pure thought with its own individuality, which brings the incarnation of the form into the matter: an incarnation, which is the actualizing of a power, due to the realization of the form itself, of which in the matter there is nothing but the abstract and inert possibility.

The concept of the *individual* has great importance in the Aristotelian philosophy. It affirms the necessity of overcoming the abstract position of the idea, which is actual thinking as thought. But rather than a concept we should say it is a demand, or that it is the aspiration, of the Aristotelian thought to attain the immanent concept of the universal. The concept, indeed, is not attained; and it could not be attained so long as philosophy sought reality, and the reality of the individual, in thing thought instead of in thinking. It is shown indeed, that the individual we would distinguish from the idea, is distinguished as the process of realization from the reality which the idea will be. But this process of realization, as we have seen, from the Aristotelian standpoint, which coincides with the Platonic in making the reality thought of a presupposition of the thinking, is inconceivable except in so far as it has yet to begin (potency, matter), or is already exhausted (act, form). So that in analysing the individual it is necessary first to find the two elements which constitute it, and there is no possibility of understanding their relation, for it is just the process of actualization of the individual itself; and that is precisely the nature it would affirm in opposition to the transcendental reality of the pure Platonic ideas.

The thousand years' history of the problem concerning the *principium individuationis,* which had its rise in the Aristotelian concept of the individual, serves to prove how insuperable were the concerning the difficulties to which Aristotelianism was condemned, unwilling to stop at the abstract universal or Platonism, and yet completely unable to seek the immanence of the universal or rather its individuality, where alone it is possible to find it, - in the reality which is not the antecedent of thought, but thinking itself. The interpreters of Aristotle asked themselves: Of the two elements which constitute the individual, matter and form, which must be considered the principle of individualization? For if, as Plato had conceived, the form is universal, the matter likewise must itself be universal, as that from which all the forms which are displayed in the endless series of the individuals, however disparate themselves, issue; a matter which in itself has none of the determinations which are realized in it by the intervention of the forms. So that form and matter, the one as much as the other taken by itself, each excludes the very possibility of any determination or individualization. Individuality arises from their meeting. But in this meeting which of the two determines the indeterminate, making it individual?

If we start with the abstract original duality of matter and form as given, it is impossible that we should find the ground of their unity, or the true *principium individui*. Giordano Bruno in the fuller maturity of the Renascence saw this clearly, yet he could only do what Aristotle, coming after Plato, had done before: turn and affirm the need of unity. It was not given even to Bruno to perceive what he called the point of the union (*il punto dell' unione*). [2] He remained, even to the end, at the standpoint of ancient philosophy, imagining reality as a presupposition of thought: a standpoint from which it is impossible to conceive movement and development. For if we start with unity, unity remains abstract and unproductive, unable to give the ground of duality; and if we start with duality, the duality cannot but be eternal duality, because it cannot but be identical with itself and therefore incapable of being unified.

The medieval philosophers started with duality and inquired which of the two terms generates that unity which is the individual. They were divided into two opposite camps, and their conflict was interminable since they found, on the one side and on the other alike, unchallengeable reasons, the one for maintaining that the principle of the individual is in the form, and the other for maintaining that it is in the matter. They opposed and contraposed, thesis to antithesis, antithesis to thesis, without ever succeeding in extricating themselves from the antinomy. The problem is in fact insoluble because, whoever posits duality and then seeks to understand the relation of the two terms, must, since it is not an *a priori* relation (that is, a relation on the existence of which each of the two terms depends), decide in favour of one of the two. Either he thinks matter is primordial and matter only; or he thinks form is primordial and form only. To think both matter and form as together is excluded by the hypothesis of the duality, according to which each of the two terms is what it is without the other and by itself excludes the other. Now, to think matter by itself is to think a pure indeterminateness, which cannot produce determination from itself, and which cannot therefore appear individualized save by reason of its opposite, form, which will then be the individualizing principle. But this deduction is legitimate only so far as it admits the contrary. It is rendered possible in fact by the concept of the abstract matter which supposes the concept of abstract form. For to deny the concept of abstract form would involve also the denial that matter is really indeterminate, and this is the very basis on which the deduction rests. Suppose then we begin by thinking of form by itself. Lo and behold, the very term, which from one aspect appeared the origin of determinateness, now, looked at from the opposite aspect, is transfigured into the pure determinable which is absolutely indeterminate. In its pure ideality the form is the possibility of all particular individuals and not any one of the particular individuals. It must be incorporated and determined as a single existent; but this incarnation cannot be a transformation and generation from within. There must intervene something which (precisely as Plato said) is the negation of the ideal, actually universal being. And then it is evident that the individualizing principle can only be in the matter which is opposed to the form.

Hence the scales of the Scholastics, leaning now to one side, now to the other; some affirming that the *principium individui* is the form, others that it is the matter; each with equal ground in reason; each shut in by the impossibility of definitely breaking down the arguments of the opposite side. There is one doctrine, however, which though unjustifiable on the basis of scholasticism, brought into play a high speculative talent, that of Thomas Aquinas. This doctrine takes its stand not on matter abstractly conceived, *quomodolibet accepta,* but rather on matter conceived as having in itself a principle of determination, *materia signata:* matter impressed with a *signum* which implies a certain preadaptation to the form, a certain principle or beginning of it. An illogical doctrine, in so far as it framed the problem whether form or matter is the individualizing principle, it yet has the great merit that it substantially denies even the possibility of solving the problem without changing its terms. Practically it amounts to a rejection of the problem, which, like all problems admitting of two contradictory solutions or, as Kant would say, giving rise to antinomies, is wrongly stated. [3]

It must not be thought that the problem of the principle of individualization was abandoned with the disappearance of scholasticism, when the authority of Aristotle was shaken and inquiry. modern philosophy entered on a new life. We have already shown that Bruno, notwithstanding his intense aspiration towards unity, never rose above the Aristotelian conception, and, were this the place, we might trace the history of the many attempts in the modern era which have been made to solve this famous problem. It involves the essential question of philosophy. It is not merely a theme for intellectual gymnastics, such as we are accustomed to consider most of the questions over which medieval philosophers grew impassioned. The form is fundamentally the idea of the world, its ground, its plan, the Logos, God; and the matter is, in its turn, that obscure term which, irreducible to God's real essence, makes the world to be distinct from God even though it be the actualizing of his thought. All who think this world, in whatever way they think it, see in it a design, an order, something rational, which renders it intelligible in so far at least as it appears such. Galileo reduces the intelligibility of nature, which for him is the world itself in its totality, to mathematical relations, and these relations present themselves as laws conceivable in themselves, independently of their verification in natural facts, as if there were a logic presiding over the working, or rather over the realization of nature itself. Hegel constructed a complicated pure logic, by which the world is rendered intelligible to the philosopher, and this logic, in its pure element, the Logos, is posited before thought as the eternal plan, which is followed out in the world.

It is impossible ever to see reality otherwise than by the light of an idea, which, once we conceive the reality as a positive and therefore contingent fact, must ideally work loose from that fact, and posit itself as a pure idea, and so oblige us to ask: How does it become fact? The question is not substantially different from that with which the *principium individui* is concerned. This supposes, as already noticed and as it should now be clear, an original dualistic intuition. It could not be put in the monistic philosophies which denied the transcendence of the ideal to the real, of God to the world, and therefore of the form to the matter. But a philosophy must do more than merely propose to restore unity and reject transcendence, if it would gain that absolute concept of immanence for which monism strives, that in which alone it is possible to be rid of the antinomy of the principle of individualization. Hegel in this respect passes ordinarily for a more immanentist philosopher than he really is. He is responsible for pantheism being identified with immanentism and has become the prototype of the pantheists. Certainly no one before him had made such mighty efforts to free reality from every shadow of a principle which transcends it. Yet, even so, he found himself faced with the necessity of conceiving the abstract form which is not matter, and therefore the universal which is not particular and the ideal which is not real, exactly as all the other inquirers into the individualizing principle were. He too has to ask: How or whence is the individual?

The most difficult problem perhaps which we meet in the Hegelian philosophy is this: When we have posited logic, or the nexus of all the categories of reality, how or whence is nature? This nature is the particular which must intervene where there is nothing but the universal. It is the incarnating of the pure ideal in matter, beginning with its simplest determination, space. It is, in short, the Aristotelian individual. And this problem in Hegel, however his own declarations in regard to it are to be taken, remains, and must remain, unsolved. There is in fact repeated for it the difficulty of the Platonic idealism. The Logos is the thinkability, or thinking as a whole. There are therefore two alternatives, either there is nothing else than the Logos, or there is something else but it is not thinkable (intelligible). In the first case, there is no nature outside the Logos, in the second case there is nature but no philosophy of it. And if the Logos has been excogitated in order to understand nature, then the Logos is no longer Logos or rather no longer what it ought to be. So, then, the standpoint of the Logos excludes nature. And if the universality of the Logos does not satisfy us and we are athirst for actuality, for natural positiveness and particular determinateness, then there is nothing for it but to abandon the Logos, to deny the Idea, and indeed Hegel himself says so. But this negation (completely analogous to the opposition of the Platonic non-being to being), the negation which the idea itself makes of itself, can have value only if it be itself a logical act, and is therefore within the sphere of the Logos, and not an act which the Idea, remaining within that sphere and developing the whole of its logical activity, can never fulfil. It fulfils it just when it overcomes pure logicity and breaks through the enclosing bark of the universal, pushing itself forth as particular. Such a rupture is inconceivable.

Even Hegel, then, propounds the problem of the principle of individualization without solving it. He propounds it and cannot solve it, because, as we have seen, the true concept of the dialectic (its own Logos) cannot be reached as a thing thought of, or as a reality which is a presupposition of thinking, that abstract reality which had already been idealized by Plato into universals, from which, as Aristotle clearly saw, it is impossible to redescend to the individuals of nature.

By this way, then, the individual has not been and is not to be found. For a nature which with its individuals is contraposed to thought cannot be grasped.

[1] Simplicius, in Arist. *Cat.* 66 b 45 Br.
[2] *De la causa, principle e uno* (1584), in *Opere Italiane,* ed. Gentile, vol. i. p. 256.
[3] For the medieval solutions of the problem, see Gentile, *I Problemi della scolastica,* Bari, Laterza, 1913, chap. iv.

Chapter Six - The Abstract Universal and the Positive

Another famous controversy which engaged medieval philosophers and had not indeed come to an end when the modern era began, is the dispute concerning the value of universals. Even in this the concept of the individual is at stake; because, according to the way in which we interpret the value of the universal, we shall correspondingly conceive the individual. And if we fail to understand the universal in a way which enables us thereby to understand the individual, the need of conceiving the individual will necessarily remain unsatisfied.

Who has not heard of the famous dispute which divided the Scholastics of the thirteenth century? The nominalists, compromising the reality of every ideal principle which is mediated in more than one individual, and therefore even the reality of the Christian dogmas (for they affirm such principles), denied that the Aristotelian philosophy supposed universals existing as universals, in the way that Plato had conceived them. Substance, according to Aristotle, must be conceived as individual, as σύνολον, a concrete whole of form and of matter: not therefore a simple universal but a particularized universal. And it matters not that in knowing the intellect is concerned with the form only of the individual and that it has as its proper object the universal alone. The intellect knows the universal in the individuals. In the individuals the ideality of the universal is incorporated with the matter, and outside the individuals the universal is nothing but a pure name.

The realists, developing the permanent Platonic motive in Aristotelianism, objected, in their turn, that if the universal is not real, the individual cannot be real, for the individual is a determination of the universal, and only in the universal can attain the principle of its own being. The individual is real, in so far and only in so far as it participates in the universal. And precisely because we must say alike of each and every individual, that the reality of the individual is ephemeral and transient, inasmuch as it must be concurrent with the reality of all the other individuals, so we must say of the universal that in its unity it has a constant and eternal reality. So that the individual both is and is not real. The individual is not truly real if as individual it is distinguished from and opposed to the universal. The individual is real in so far as over flowing the limits of its own individuality, it coincides with the universal. For the universal is real in the absolute meaning.

Nominalism is clearly a naturalistic and materialistic theory. In confining reality to the individuals, it tends to suppress their intelligibility, for it denies the absolute value of the universals through which they are intelligible. It tends also thereby to deny that there can be value in thought by itself, for thought contrasted with what alone is real in the individuals is indistinguishable from nothing. The universal, a pure name in so far as it is present in the individuals, does not universalize them, but particularizes itself. The conceptualists who called the universal a concept are substantially one with the nominalists, for their concept is no more than a name, a universal shorn of the reality which only the individuals possess. Nominalism means, therefore, that the form of each individual, since it is not identical with the form of all other individuals, inasmuch as we can conceive the form of each independently of each of the individuals, is no longer universal but particular. It is the form given *hic et nunc,* which in its being *omnimodo determinatum* comes to be in apprehensible by thought, ineffable, non-intuitable. Reality despoiled of its form is deprived of the illumination of thought. It is no more than the pure abstract presupposition of the terms of that thought. The individual, in short, as pure individual is not even individual: it is nothing.

Realism, on the other hand, falls into the opposite fault. So true is it that *in vitium ducit culpae fuga si caret arte.* If the universal be already real and the individual can add nothing to its reality, in what then does the individuality of the individual consist? We come back to the great difficulty of Plato, who remained imprisoned within the circle of the ideas, unable to return from them to the world, although it had been in order to understand the world that he had excogitated the ideas.

The eclectic theories succeeded no better. One of these was that of Avicenna, afterwards adopted and largely developed and disseminated by Thomas Aquinas. With the nominalists, Thomas Aquinas admitted the *universalia in re,* but from these, with the conceptualists, he distinguished the *universalia post rem,* the universals man extracts from sensible experience in forming concepts; but also with the realists he maintained the value of the *universalia ante rem,* the divine thoughts which are realized in the world of natural individuals although they are real in God before they are realized in the world. As a solution it combines in one the difficulties of the opposed theses it would reconcile. Because, if the universals *post rem* are not one and the same with the universals *in re,* their difference signifies precisely, that in abstracting the universals from the individuals in which they inhere, we are withdrawing them from the reality which they have only while they adhere to the individuality. The concept, therefore, is an alteration of the object and renders more remote the real being of things which it is proposed to know by means of the concept. And it comes to this, that for Thomas Aquinas, as for every nominalist, things in their individuality are unknowable.

And the knowability of things cannot be founded on the concept of the *universale ante rem.* Because this universal also is completely different from the other two, and they therefore cannot guarantee the value of the third which is realized in the mind of man. Be sides, granting to the individual thing the reality of the universal which it actuates, but which is already realized in the mind of God, the reality of this universal makes it impossible to understand in what its ulterior actualization can consist, since it is already full reality, in all its possible determinations, not one of which can be lacking in the idea which God resolves to realize. And the conclusion is that even the *universale ante rem*, notwithstanding the company of its brethren *in re* and *post rem*, remains quite alone, imprisoned in its pure ideality, impotent to explain the being of the individual. If the idea of the world precedes the world, and the idea is real, the world is impossible. And thus we see that even in the dispute concerning universals we are confronted with an insoluble antinomy. The reality of the individual cannot be made intelligible without the reality of the universal; but the reality of the universal renders unintelligible the reality of the individual.

This antinomy is even more insistent and perplexing than that which springs from the inquiry concerning the individualizing principle: because universalizing the individual is an indispensable condition of conceiving it, it is indeed the very act of thinking it. And without the individual, *hic et nunc*, there is no nature. Every thing concrete, even the life by which we live, flies off and vanishes. But to universalize is also to idealize, and therefore to see escaping from us, in another direction, everything real, for the real is always particular, determinate and individual.

Modern philosophy began to free itself from the bondage of this antinomy when with Descartes it said: *Cogito ergo sum*. It was a beginning in so far as in the *cogito* the concreteness of the individual, the "I" who thinks, coincides with the universality of thought. But it is only a beginning, inasmuch as in Descartes the coincidence between the individual and the universal is only to the extent that the thinking is my thinking, mine who say "cogito," and I who think am; that is, in so far as the reality which is thought is the thought which thinks. So that, even in Descartes, no sooner is the thought turned away from the subject which is realized in its own thinking, to the reality which is posited before the subject in virtue of his thinking, than the co incidence disappears, and the abyss between the individual and the universal reopens, and philosophy is constrained anew to oscillate between a world which is intelligible but not real (the rational world of the metaphysicians, from Descartes to Wolf) and a world real indeed, and substantial, but not intelligible, although obscurely felt and able to shine through sensible impressions, unconnected and manifold (the "nature" of the empiricists from Bacon to Hobbes, from Locke to Hume). Either a metaphysic of empty shadows, or a prostration of reason before an unknown and unknowable Absolute!

In Kant we meet a much more vigorous effort than Descartes's to understand the immanence of the universal in the individual, and to comprehend how thereby the concept of the individual is made possible. This is the *a priori* synthesis which binds the intuition to the concept in a relation on which both the one and the other depend, and without which neither the one nor the other is. Yet Kant distinguishes the phenome non from the noumenon, and for him it is the noumenon which is the true root of the *individual* object of experience, and without experience thought would remain closed within the universal mesh of its pure forms (which are the Scholastic universals expressed in Kantian terminology). And when in Kant's successors the noumenon was dispensed with, and the individual was sought in thought itself, which is the universal, as an element or moment of it, speculation, even in affirming the impossibility of conceiving an individual other than self-consciousness, can only make self-consciousness intelligible by transcending it in nature and in pure logic. We find once again the kingdom of universals, on which, as on the empire of Charles V., the sun never sets and from which there is no going forth. The universal has indeed separated itself from the individual, by revolting against it and devouring it.

In our own time the dispute concerning universals has come again into the arena in the doctrine of the *practical character* of mathematical and naturalistic laws and concepts. This merits particular consideration, because, while it renews the old nominalism, it appears to indicate, although distantly, that doctrine of the immanence of the universal in the particular which, as we shall see more clearly in the sequel, explains the individual who is only individual, but is not nature.

Several modern epistemologists, approaching philosophy for the most part from the side of the natural and mathematical sciences, and inspired by observations which spring from the criticism of those sciences (Avenarius, Mach, Rickert, Bergson, Poincaré and others), have pointed out that the concepts of the naturalists, like the definitions of the mathematicians, derive their value purely from the definite ends which they serve. They .do not mirror the real, for the real is always diverse and therefore merely individual; and consequently, in the true and proper meaning of the term, they are not knowledge. In the case of the natural sciences they are to be considered symbols, tickets, arbitrary and mnemonic schemes, devised by man in order to guide experience, regulate with the least effort the great press of single perceptions, and communicate their own experience to others in abbreviated formulae. In the case of the mathematical sciences they are conventional constructions and their validity is willed. The validity is inconceivable as existing in itself and in that sense true; it is willed and might therefore be not willed. There is a great variety of these epistemological theories and they may all be denoted by the name *pragmatist* which some of them adopt, because, in opposing knowledge to action and truth to practical volitional ends, they deny the cognitive character and therefore the truth value of the universal concepts belonging to the natural and mathematical sciences, and they attribute to such concepts the character of actions directed to the attainment of an end.

The difference between the old nominalism and this modern form lies in this, that whilst the old maintained the necessity of the concept for the knowledge of the individual, the modern actually rejects the universal character of knowledge, and posits the individual himself in his strict individuality, confronted with his thought. The knowledge of individuality, therefore, when it is knowledge is reduced to simple immediate *intuition*. But such difference is itself more a postulate than a real deduction; since it is most difficult to prove that thought, even though it be through simple intuition, can fix itself on an object actually individual with no light whatever shed by universality. And when, more over, the object intuited is intuited as not yet an existent (and yet also not as a non-existent); when too the mind, entirely absorbed in contemplation, has not yet discriminated the object at all; it cannot invest it even with the category of the *intuited* without which there is no intuition. For this category implies the concept of being or object or however otherwise we choose to name it. So that bare individuality is not intuitable.

But what is the individual which the new nominalism opposes to the generic concept? It is not strictly pure extreme individuality stripped of every determination. An individual surely is always determinate, formed. A dog, for example, which may be here and now beside me, is not the species dog which the zoologist constructs by abstracting the differences from his ideas of single individual dogs. Without these differences there is no living dog but only an artificial type, useful for systematizing observed forms and for learning about them. Now it is clear that the individual is intuited in so far as it is determined as true to type, however artificial this type may be thought to be. We are just as vividly conscious of the arbitrariness and inexactness of our intuition of the single individual dog, which gives support to the type, as we are of the arbitrariness and inexactness of the type which is abstracted from living experience. And the more our intuition perfects itself by acquiring precision and necessity, the more perfect we see our concept become, throwing off its artificiality and becoming ever more adequate by approaching the inmost essence of the real. If at last we are persuaded, philosophically, that the inmost essence of this dog, as of this stone and of everything that is, is mind, the concept of the dog will make us intuit, and that is, strictly speaking, think, the individual dog.

But, if we insist on maintaining the presupposition that there is no objectivity except that of the individual, and that thinking must simply be adherent and cannot interpenetrate it with its constructions, and with its concepts, that is, with itself, then it is impossible to escape the consequences, disastrous for knowledge, which followed from the old nominalism and which will follow just the same from the new.

On the other hand, to the old error of expecting to attain the individual without the universal, the nominalism of the modern epistemology of the sciences adds a new one. It has its origin in the equivocation which the pragmatist conception harbours within it, an equivocation not really very new. The well-known theory expounded by Kant in the *Critique of Practical Reason,* the theory of the primacy of the pure practical reason in its union with the speculative, is pragmatistic. "If practical reason could not assume or think as given, anything further than what speculative reason of itself could offer it from its own insight, the latter would have the primacy. But supposing that it had of itself original *a priori* principles with which certain theoretical positions were inseparably connected, while these were withdrawn from any possible insight of speculative reason (which, however, they must not contradict), then the question is, which interest is the superior (not which must give way, for they are not necessarily conflicting), whether speculative reason, which knows nothing of all that the practical offers for its acceptance, should take these propositions, and (although they transcend it) try to unite them with its own concepts as a foreign possession handed over to it, or whether it is justified in obstinately following its own separate interest, and according to the canonic of Epicurus rejecting as vain subtlety everything that cannot accredit its objective reality by manifest examples to be shown in experience, even though it should be never so much interwoven with the interest of the practical (pure) use of reason, and in itself not contradictory to the theoretical, merely because it infringes on the interest of the speculative reason to this extent, that it removes the bounds which this latter had set to itself, and gives it up to every nonsense or delusion of imagination?" [1]

The speculative reason, it appears then, is nothing but philosophy from the standpoint of the *Critique of Pure Reason,* which aims at proving the possibility of mathematics and physics, and supposes no other world beyond that which these sciences propose to know, nature. The practical reason, on the other hand, is substantially philosophy from the standpoint of mind or of the moral law, which requires us to affirm freedom, immortality and God. Which of the two philosophies must prevail? Since, says Kant, the same reason which speculatively cannot transcend the limits of experience, practically can and does judge according to *a priori* principles, and enunciates propositions which, whilst they are not contrary to the speculative reason, are inseparably bound up with the practical interests of pure reason itself, that is, are such that in denying them it is impossible to conceive morality, reason in general, and therefore even speculative reason, must admit these propositions. "Admits them, it is true," he hastens to observe, "as something extraneous which has not grown on its own soil, but which is yet sufficiently attested; and it must seek to confront them and connect them with every thing it has in its power as speculative reason, *even allowing that they are not its cognitions, but extensions of its use under another aspect, that is, under its practical aspect.*" So that the conflict between the two reasons is avoided in so far as the speculative submits to the practical. It submits, according to Kant, not because reason in passing from its theoretical to its practical purpose extends its own cognitions and sees more in them than it saw before; not because the practical reason has nothing to teach the speculative; but because the practical reason rivets the chain which holds the speculative reason confined within the bounds of experience, where alone its use is legitimate according to the *Critique of Pure Reason*.

Yet, if the propositions, to which the interest of reason in its practical use is inseparably bound, are not cognitions, but simply postulates or articles of faith on which only the practical interest can confer value, they cannot be compared with the propositions of the speculative reason, and in that case there is neither the possibility of conflict, nor of suppressing them by subordinating them to the speculative reason, and the theory of their primacy is incomprehensible. For if we are to conceive a conflict and the primacy which puts an end to it, we must put the postulates of the practical reason (simple postulates, not cognitions, from the stand point of the mere speculative reason) on the same plane as the cognitions of the speculative. And this is what Kant really does when he appeals from the two reasons to the one unique reason which is always reason, as much in its theoretical as in its practical use. And then not only are the propositions of the practical reason postulates for the speculative reason, but all the propositions of the speculative reason are no more than postulates for the practical reason. The one unique reason cannot declare only the propositions of the practical reason and not those of the speculative to be mere postulates. To do so is to cheat it with words and in fact to take the side of the speculative.

In reality, the higher reason, which is philosophy, when first of all it speculates on nature, can only justify it as causality, and is compelled therefore to reject the possibility of a science of freedom. When in the second place it speculates on morality, which is spiritual reality, it discovers freedom. It does not come upon it as something already discovered in its practical use, it discovers it in its higher speculative use, which leads it to seek to give the ground of that spiritual activity whose presence has already been found in the *Critique of Pure Reason*. And when Kant confines himself to the purely practical value of the principles of the will, he equivocates between practical reason as will which concerns the object of the *Critique of Practical Reason* and practical reason according to the concept which it acquires in the *Critique* itself; between what we may call the fact, and what we may call the philosophy, of morality. From the standpoint of the practical reason as philosophy, the postulates are cognitions in the true and proper meaning, they cannot be thought of as simple postulates, not even from the standpoint of the practical reason which is truly such (for practical reason is not the object of a speculation but itself a speculation) nor even from that of the so-called speculative reason, or rather of that reason which in the Critique of Pure Reason is enclosed within the limits of experience, or as we should say to-day is simply within the limits of science. In declaring such principles postulates science discredits them and does not preserve them. And, more over, science does not submit itself to morality, but rather includes morality in itself, by naturalizing the moral act, which then comes to be considered as a simple fact conditioned by definite principles to which no necessary and absolute value is to be attributed.

Pragmatism in so far as it characterizes Kant's doctrine of the primacy of the practical reason is a kind of naturalistic scepticism. Every form of pragmatism is scepticism in so far as it depreciates an act of cognition in order to appreciate it as a practical act. There cannot be a practical act with no cognitive value, that is, an act which does not posit before the mind an objectively and universally valid reality.

So far as philosophy is concerned the Kantian moral has no (moral) value unless the postulates, to which the practical use of reason is inseparably bound, are true and proper cognitions. So likewise with regard to philosophy, the economic character of the concepts of science, according to the new pragmatists, is not really and truly economic, unless the schemes and symbols of science in order to be useful are true. We ought, therefore, rather to say that they are useful in so far as they have a truth. Pragmatic truth is different from the truth of the ideas or perceptions of the individual mind, and yet it is only by virtue of these that pragmatic truth is possible.

It is said indeed that the purpose these schemes and symbols, which are fashioned by the will, serve, is that of directing, and imposing order on, the mass of single and particular facts of experience; but is it not quite clear that they could not render this service were the cognitive character of these particular experiences cancelled? Moreover, each of these particular experiences may be thought of as useful, however superseded its usefulness may be; but it can only be useful on the condition that it is true, that it has its own proper value as experience. So in very truth is every naturalistic concept useful in so far as it effectively permeates the intuition of the particular with itself, for it is precisely in so doing that it is itself made possible as a true and proper concept.

The source of error in this matter is always in not looking at the unity of universal and particular, for it is in that unity that individuality consists. We think of the universal as the antecedent or consequent of the particular, as posited outside it and presented to thought. This in its turn is due to our thinking abstractly of the two abstract moments, which analysis discovers in the individual. They then become elements of the individuality thought (which by itself is inert and inorganic) rather than moments of the individual thinking.

Thus in philosophy to-day as in Aristotle's time there is keenly felt the need of individuality as a concreteness of the real. In the philosophies of pure experience, of intuitionism and of aestheticism there is a struggle against the abstractions of the thought which universalizes experience by including it in itself. But philosophy has never succeeded in ridding itself of the ancient alternative between the empty concept and the blind intuition. On the one hand we are offered the light, the transparency of thought to itself, the subjective elaboration of the immediate data; an elaboration which leaves the data far behind and loses all trace of them. On the other hand we are offered the datum, the immediate, the positive, the concrete, that which is *hic et nunc* but never succeeds in attaining the individual. To-day all are athirst for individuality; but what sort of thing is this individuality to which we must cling if we would escape from the fathomless ocean of thought and from its schemes devoid of any theoretical bearing? Any one who reflects will see that it is the same question which Aristotle was driven to ask when dissatisfied with the Platonic idealism. It remains to-day unanswered.

If we would reply to this question we must first direct attention to the origin of the idea of this need for the individual in the Socratic and Platonic doctrine. The consciousness of thought as reality detached from the pure immediate object of experience, for so it began to take shape for us in the Platonic speculation, made the want felt of that individual element which had wholly slipped through its meshes. What was lacking in this thought? It is clear from the Aristotelian polemic against the theory of the ideas, and from the efforts which Plato himself made in his speculation to conceive the relation of the ideas to nature, that the defect of the ideas, apparent at once, and apparent always whenever in the history of philosophy thought has been alienated from empirical reality, is this: the ideas have been conceived as ideas of the reality and not as the reality itself, just as the idea of a house which an architect is going to construct is not the house. Now the idea of an architect is a self-consistent reality in the architect's mind which may never be even translated into reality; and to understand its being we have not got to go to the constructed house. We say that so far as the idea is concerned it can arise in any one's mind who conceives it. In the house, instead of ideas and reality in general there already is the reality. We leave out the actual house when we think the ideas. We think of the idea as the beginning or cause of it. So that when ideas are in question they are actually thought of as the principle of the reality, which means that the concept of the ideas is integrated in the concept of the reality. This reality, when the ideas are posited as the thinking of it, is no other than the ideas themselves but with one difference only: *the ideas are not real; the ideas realized are the reality*. The real, which for Plato and so many after him is the characteristic of nature, is opposed to the ideal, which is the characteristic of thinking, and they are conjoined only in so far as the ideal has existence and the real is existence. When Plato says that what really exists, or, to speak precisely, *is,* is rather the idea than the thing, he means the *existing or being* in thought, not the being which Kant, and so many with him, distinguished by the fact that it has not the mark of the concept. The distinction is one which Plato himself allows when he opposes ideas to things. Neither Plato nor any one else has ever affirmed that the idea of a horse is a horse one can ride.

Now for Aristotle nature, the individual, is precisely that which *is* to be and not only ought to be. It is the *positive*. The positive is no longer *in fieri,* it is an effect or conclusion of a process. It is conceived, not as the principle only nor as the process always going on and never complete, but as the already formed result. The doing, which unfolds it, has given place to the fact; the process of its formation is exhausted. This is what we all mean by positive. The historical fact is positive when it is no longer the ideal of a man or of a race but a *de facto* reality which no one can make not be. It impresses itself, therefore, with a force which allows the mind no choice. It appears as what the mind in the purely theoretical form of its working must accept. Every fact of nature in so far as it is an observed fact is positive. It is not what will be, but what is, or to be precise, what has been. Consequently we describe a man as positive, not in so far as in his speculation and action he attains an ideal end, which might not have existed had he not brought it to pass, but in so far as he is already an effect of the past, what no one can unmake. The positive is the *terra firma* on which we can walk securely. Thought, as Plato conceived it, and as it has ever since been conceived, as the universal which is not the simple particularizing of single things, lacks, not all reality, but that reality realized which is the positive. It lacks it we already know, and it cannot generate it; since the idea while it is unreal in regard to that other reality the individual, is in itself completely realized. And the individual of which the idea goes in search is precisely the *positive*.

There are, however, two different ways in which even the positive itself may be understood. Because, if the positive be what has been posited, it may be either what is posited by the subject for whom it is positive, or posited for the subject by others. The positive of which thought as pure universal has need cannot be the positive posited by the subject. And for this reason the Platonic ideas (and the same is true of the Cartesian ideas and even of the Hegelian Logos) are themselves already positive, inasmuch as they are only thinkable in so far as they are already real (real as ideas) and have not to be realized. Yet they have not the same title to be called positive that the things which are to arise from them have, nor are they real therefore in regard to these. That is to say, the mind which thinks of ideas, and of ideas alone, thinks the ideas already real: it thinks them, therefore, as a positive reality (it imagines them, we may say, as the objects of a real positive experience in the hyperuranion). When the mind, however, thinks the ideas in relation with things it is then the things which are positive and not the ideas, in such wise that in relation to the things themselves the ideas in spite of their transcendence can no longer be thought of as already effected fact, something positive to which the subjective process of the mind which refers to them is posthumous. The ideas in so far as they serve for the knowledge of things, and fulfil therefore their peculiar function in thinking, are intrinsic to the mind and are valued for what they are worth to it. They are reproduced by ἀνάμνησις, without which their existence within the mind would be actually useless and null. In other words, the ideas so far as they are immanent in the mind are not in any sense positive, they imply and require a mental process which begins with the immanence of the ideas themselves, still implicit and obscured by the shadows of immediate sensible experience (by the darkness, as Plato imaginatively puts it, of the prison into which the soul falls). Their immanence is nothing else but the immediate presence of the truth to the mind which must acquire complete consciousness of its own content. And generally as in Plato so with all who hold the theory of *a priori* cognition or innate ideas, the universal is never positive in so far as it fulfils its function in knowledge. It is not something external to the subject and presupposed by it. It is the subject's positing and real exposition of its own activity. It is equally true of the theory of empiricism, for when empiricism opposes sensation or immediate experience to the concept, it is the subject which makes the concept its own by the very positing of it as an abstraction, a construction, or a presupposition. The positive when it is presented to the subject, already is, it only needs to be presented. This is its only title to be described as for the subject. And this is the true positive. It is posited for us, but not by us; like the individual in his particularity. Moreover, the universal either is what we make it, as the empiricist says; or else, though its reality is independent of us, it *is* only in so far as we refashion it, as the apriorist says. Thus the Italian philosopher Gioberti while he presupposes the direct intuiting of the universal (or of the necessary cognition) holds that the intuition must be revived and absorbed in the reflexion by which the consciousness of it is acquired through the gradual work of the subject. He thereby makes the activity of the subject the support of our knowledge.

The positive, then, is posited by us, but it is only in so far as we oppose it to ourselves that we can show its character of positivity. A fact is historically positive in so far as it is not our work but that of others, or if it be ours, that it is the work of a "we" which is posited in the fact and which we cannot undo. When instead of thinking of the difference between our present self and our past we think of their identity, as we do in the moral life when, for example, we are ashamed of something we have done and repent it and disown it, and so morally undo it, disowning the self which wrought the deed, then the fact loses its positivity. Morally speaking, it has no more reality than a stain which has been washed out.

The subject, we conclude then, finds himself, it seems, confronted with the positive, when he finds himself confronted with a reality realized which is not his own work. He is then in presence of the individual.

But is such a positivity really thinkable?

[1] Kant's *Dialectic of Pure Practical Reason,* Book II. ch. II. sect, iii., Abbott's Translation. Kant had previously said, "To every faculty of the mind we can attribute an *interest,* that is a principle which contains the condition on which alone the exercise of that faculty depends."

Chapter Seven - The Individual as Ego

The concept that the individual is the real positive, when we reflect on it, is seen to be absurd. It is absurd, notwithstanding that it imposes itself on thought as the only true reality which thought can find for its own support, because it is posited for the subject without being posited by the subject. This is a contradiction in terms which every one who pays attention to the meaning of the words "posited for the subject" must admit.

"Posited for the subject" simply means object. When we deny that the positive individual depends in any way on the subject, and affirm that the subject must presuppose this object in order to get its insertion into the real, we despoil or try our best to despoil the positive individual of every element in it which can bear witness to the action of the subject. We aim at purifying and strengthening its individuality when we withdraw it from every form of universality which the subject's thinking confers on it. The subject assumes it as matter which has its own independent elaboration. But there must be a limit to this subtraction and purification, beyond which the individual would cease to be the spring-board which enables the subject to leap from the pure ideas which imprison it in the sphere of subjectivity, and to communicate with the real. And this limit, it is obvious, is that within which the object is a term of consciousness, something relative to the ego and beyond which it ceases to be object for the subject. To despoil the object of this absolute relation, by which it is bound to the subject, is to destroy any value it can have as an object. So that the positive individual cannot be conceived otherwise than as relative to the subject.

To-day, and indeed ever since Kant, there has been much insistence on the value of the intuition as a necessary antecedent of thought and as the path by which thought enters into relation with reality. Aristotle was equally insistent on the necessity of sensation, - which is the same as the intuition of the moderns, - as an immediate presence of the object, not the consequence of a subjective act, and therefore not in consequence of a proportion and symmetry between itself and the object which the subject has generated. But this intuition or sensation, by eliminating from the relation between the two terms of knowing, subject and object, everything that can be thought of as secondary and derived from the action of the subject, cannot destroy the relation itself, cannot posit a pure object confronting the subject, absolutely external to the subject, fantastically conceived as originally belonging to it. The object with absolutely no relation to the subject is nonsense. The originality and the immediacy of intuition, therefore, cannot rob the individual of the truly original and immanent relativity it has to the subject.

Now what does relation mean? To say that two terms are related implies that they are different but also affirms that there is identity. Two terms different and absolutely different could only be thought of in such a way that in thinking the one we should not be thinking the other. The thought of the one would absolutely exclude the other. Such pure difference could only hold, therefore, between two terms which are unrelatable; so that if terms are in relation, however different they are, at least in thinking one we think the other. The concept of one even contains in some form the other.

In the intuition, then, the subject is indeed different from the object, but not to the extent that there is nothing whatever of the subject in the object. That is to say, the object is inconceivable apart from something which belongs to it in virtue of its being intuition, by which it is in relation to the subject. Accordingly the relation of object and subject through which the object is posited for the subject, necessarily implies the concept of the object as posited by the subject. And so the concept of the positive as that which is not posited by the subject is clearly shown to be intrinsically contradictory.

On the other hand, this does not release us from the necessity grounded in reason of integrating the universal in thought, whence the particular gets its meaning, with what is positive in the individual. We have only shown that when we oppose the individual to the universal we make the universal synonymous with the subjective. If, then, we separate from the individual everything subjective, including the positing by the subject for the subject, and suppose the positivity something outside the subject altogether, then we are also outside the intuition itself and can only get back by suppressing that "outside of subjectivity" in which we have supposed the essence of individuality to consist. And all the attempts which, under the guise of nominalism, have been made to retain this meaning of individuality have failed and will always fail.

But are we in any better case? Have we, if we cannot attain the individual which we oppose to the universal, succeeded in securing the standpoint of universal which we want to integrate? Or are we merely vexing ourselves in pursuing an empty shadow? Is the individual we require in order to endow the universal with the substantiality of effective reality an illusive appearance ever disappearing behind us?

This is the point to which we must now give careful attention, and we shall see that it is not a case of running forward or of turning back, but of stopping and embracing the true individual which is in us.

The universal is the predicate with which in the judgment the subject is invested. Every cognitive act is an *a priori* synthesis, and the universal is one of the terms of that synthesis. Even the intuition is, as we have seen, unintelligible except as a necessary relation. And this relation is an *a priori* synthesis between the ideal element whereby the subject illumines for itself the term intuited, and the subject of the judgment made explicit, which is the term intuited. So, then, the true universal, or the category, is the universal which can only work by being predicated of the subject; the individual is the subject which can only work by being the subject of predication. The category, then (as Kant proved), is a function of the subject of knowledge, of the actual subject itself; and the individual is the content of the intuition by which the subject of knowledge issues from itself. But is it possible to fix the subject of knowledge, the category, the universality? Fixing a category means defining it, thinking it. But the category thought is the category made subject of a judgment and therefore no longer predicated, no longer the subject's act. No one before Kant had ever given thought to the category, though we all use it, and many even after Kant still fail to render a clear account of it. [1] We are still accustomed to take the category in its primitive, Aristotelian meaning, as the most universal predicate which itself can never be subject. [2] It may be the category of "being" which we take as this most universal concept. Can this "being" be thought, or let us say simply can it be fixed by thinking, in the position of a universal which does not function as subject? But fixing it means saying to oneself: "Being is being." That is, we affirm "being" by duplicating it internally into a "being" which is subject and a "being" which is predicate. And then in regard to the "being" which is subject, and which alone can really be said to be fixed, it is not universal at all, but absolutely particular and definitely individual. So that if everything is "being" (meaning that "universal" comprises all things under it), "being" is not everything, since it is only itself by distinguishing itself from every other possible object of thought, as the unique being. And precisely the same applies to substance, or cause, or relation, or any similar object of thought on which we would confer the value of a category. The category, so to say, is a category only so long as we do not stare it straight in the face. If we do, it is individualized at once, punctuated, posited as a unique *quid,* and itself requires light from a predicate to which it must be referred. And then it is no longer a category.

What has been said of the category or pure universal clearly applies *a fortiori* to every universal, in so far as it functions as such, and so assumes the office of category. Each of the Platonic ideas, highest archetypes of single natural things, in order to be thought of must be individualized. For if *this* horse is horse (universal), the horse (universal) itself is horse; and if following Plato in the manner shown in the *Phaedrus* we transport ourselves on the wings of fancy to the heaven where the real horse is to be seen, that horse the sight of which will render possible here below the single mortal horse, it is clear that the real horse in heaven is only seen by affirming it, that is, by making it the subject of a judgment, precisely in the same way as in the case of any sorry nag we meet here on earth and stop to look at. So the celestial horse is unique in its incommunicable nature, and in itself, *omnimodo determinata,* it can neither be intuited nor apprehended in thought without using terms which encircle it with the light of a predicate which universalizes it. We must say, for example, "The horse is" and then "being" is the category and horse the individual.

We may conclude, then, that the universal has, even when interpreted in the most complete form by the nominalists, the need of being particularized in the individual. When, then, there is no individual and it is still to seek, the universal posits itself as individual, if by no other way, then by confronting itself with itself so making itself at one and the same time individual and universal. And the effort, therefore, to integrate the universal as pure universal which it is believed is necessary, is vain, because the universal as pure universal is never found.

We can now say that the individual and the universal in their antagonism to one another are two abstractions. Think the individual and in thinking it you universalize it. Think the universal and in thinking it you individualize it. So that the inquiry concerning the concept of the individual has always been orientated towards an abstraction, for it starts from an abstraction, namely, the concept of the universal as idea to be realized or as category to be individualized. In treating the two terms between which thought moves, the individual which has to be brought under the category, the category which has to interpenetrate the individual, no account whatever has been taken of the thought itself, in which the two terms are immanent. From the universal which can be thought of but does not think, and from the individual which can be intuited but does not intuit, we must turn to the concreteness of thought in act, which is a unity of universal and particular, of concept and intuition; and we shall find that the positive is attained at last, and clear of contradiction.

[1] Cf. my remarks on this subject in my essay, *Rosmini e Gioberti,* Pisa, Nistri, 1898.
[2] It should be remarked that the Aristotelian category, the most universal predicate, does not differ fundamentally from the Kantian category, a function of the judgment, when the predicate of the judgment, according to the Aristotelian logic, is given the full meaning which Aristotle intended. It is a universality which interpenetrates and so determines and illumines the subject that it becomes the whole matter of knowledge and the mode by which thought thinks. Whence the concept of the predicate is always, in substance, not an idea thought, but an act by which a given content is thought.

Chapter Eight - The Positive as Self-Created

The distinction between abstract and concrete thought is fundamental. The transfer of a problem from abstract to concrete thought is, we may say, the master-key of our whole doctrine. Many and various doctrines, which have thrown philosophy into a tangle of inextricable difficulties and have blocked the path of escape from empiricism, have in our view arisen entirely from looking at the abstract in unconsciousness of the concrete in which it is engrafted and by which it is conceivable. For empiricism itself is an abstract view of reality, and all its difficulties arise from the restriction of its standpoint. It can only be overcome when we succeed in rising to the speculative standpoint.

Of doctrines which spring from the soil of abstract thought we can find perhaps no more notable and significant example than that of the table of judgments, from which Kant in the *Critique of Pure Reason* deduces the categories. He distinguishes - to take one example or his method - three species or modality in the judgment, according to whether the judgment is assertorical, problematical, or apodeictical; or according to whether the relation of the predicate to the subject is thought to be actual or possible or necessary. And in classifying the judgments which are thus set in array for our thought and regarded as the content of our mind, inherent in it but detachable from it, a content communicable to others because conceivable in itself, he is right in holding that there are all these three, and no more than these three, species of modality. But when judgments are regarded in this way and found to be so diverse, the one true judgment on which, as Kant himself taught, all the others depend and from which they are in separable, the *I think,* is falsified. For example, the true judgment in its concreteness is not "Caesar conquered Gaul," but "I think that Caesar conquered Gaul." It is only the second of these judgments which is truly a judgment we can make, and in the first or abbreviated form of it the principal proposition is not absent but apparently understood and not expressed, and it is only in the full form that we find the modality of the function of judgment, and the true relation which holds between the terms which this function brings together in an *a priori* synthesis. The former of the two judgments, if taken as a distinct judgment, is clearly no more than an object of thought, abstracted from the subjective act which posits it within the organic whole of its own synthesis. It has no modality in itself since in itself it is not conceivable. And inasmuch as it is only by being presupposed as conceivable by itself that it can be posited beside other judgments different from it, so it is assertorical while the others may be problematical or apodeictic. But when, however actualized, it is not presupposed, but really thought, as alone it can be thought, as a content of the *I think,* then its differences from the other judgments (in so far as they are *judgments*) disappear. For all judgments are alike acts of the thinking I, the form of whose acts is constant. The *I think* is not assertorical, because it cannot be apodeictical nor even problematical. Or, if you call it assertorical then it is necessarily so; you must say it is apodeictically assertorical. For it is impossible to think what we cannot think we think, just as it is impossible to think that by thinking we can make it true or false that Caesar conquered Gaul. [3]

And it is not a mere question of words. Indeed it did not escape Kant himself that in all the twelve classes judgments, which he distinguished under the heads of quality, quantity, relation, and modality, we always bring judgments back to the common original form of the *I think*. We have to understand, then, that every judgment (be it assertorical, problematical, or apodeictic) is contained within a fundamental judgment which itself is outside any such classification. The serious consequence to be drawn from this criticism of the Kantian theory is that it is not judgments but dead abstractions which are classified. Judgments are spiritual acts, but judgments and all spiritual acts become natural facts when they are thought of abstractly outside their concrete actuality. In reality in Kant's assertorical judgment the real relation, which is not a necessary but a merely contingent one, is not a part of the judgment but of the natural fact, apprehended empirically, and considered in its abstract objectivity, independently of the mind which represents it. So that the distinction Kant makes is one the ground of which is in the empiricism which sees the object of thought and does not see the thought which makes it object.

This example is, as I have said, the more significant from the fact that Kant is the author of transcendental idealism. The chief characteristic of transcendental idealism is the forceful manner in which it rises above empiricism, recalling experience from the object to the subject which actualizes it. Kant himself in this as in many other cases goes about laboriously expounding artificial and untenable doctrines, because he fails to grasp firmly his own sound principle, which may be called the principle of the indwelling of the abstract in the concrete thought.

It is, then, in concrete thought that we must look for the positivity which escapes abstract thought, be it of the universal or of the individual. It is by the abstract universal that thought thinks, but the abstract universal is not thought. The abstract individual is only one of the terms of the thought which we want to intuit, to feel, to grasp as it were in a moment, to take by surprise. Neither universal nor individual is concrete thought, for taken in its natural meaning the universal is not individualized as it must be to be real; nor is the individual universalized as even it must be to be ideal, that is, to be *truly* real. When Descartes wished to assure himself of the truth of knowledge, he said: *Cogito ergo sum;* that is, he ceased to look at the *cogitatum* which is abstract thought and looked at the *cogitare* itself, the act of the ego, the centre from which all the rays of our world issue and to which they all return. And then he no longer found in thought the being which is only a simple idea, a universal to be realized, a being like that of God in the ontological argument, at least as the critics of that argument, from the eleventh-century monk Gaunilo to Kant, represented it. He found the positive being of the individual. He found in thought the individuality which can only be guaranteed by intuition, as Kant and all the nominalists, ancient, modern, and contemporary, are agreed. It is indeed only by an intuition that Descartes sees being, but by an intuition which is not immediate, such as the nominalists need, and as Kant also needs, with his theory of the *datum*, the term or matter of empirical intuition. The intuition is the result of a process: *Cogito*. I am not except as I think, and I am in so far as I think; and I am therefore only in so far as and to the extent that I think.

Here, then, is the true positivity which Plato sought, and without which it appeared to Aristotle there could be no sure basis of the ideas: the positivity which is a realization of the reality of which the idea is the principle, and which integrates the idea itself by what is intrinsic in it. For if the idea is the idea or ground of the thing, the thing must be produced by the idea. The thought which is true thought must generate the being of what it is the thought, and this precisely is the meaning of the Cartesian *Cogito*. I - this reality which is "I," the surest reality I can possess, and which if I let it go all possibility of assuring myself of any reality whatever is gone, this one and only firm point to which I can bind the world which I think - this "I am" *is* in so far as I think. I realize it in thinking, with a thought which is myself thinking. The "I," as we shall see more clearly later, only *is* in so far as it is self-consciousness. The "I" is not a consciousness which *presupposes* the self as its object, but a consciousness which *posits* a self. And every one knows that personality, definite personality, can only be thought of as self-constituted by its own inherent forces, and these are summed up in thought.

In the intellectualist theory the ideas, as Plato conceived them, confront thought, and there is no way of passing from the ideas to what is positive in the individual. The individual is the discovery which thought makes when it suddenly realizes that it has withdrawn from its original stand point, and instead of having before it the ideas which it has constructed and projected before itself, has itself confronting its own self. The individual is the realization of the process in which the ideas arise and live the moment we turn from the abstract to the concrete. In the concrete we must seek the positive basis of every reality. This, as we know, Descartes did not do. He suddenly fell back into the intellectualist position, and later philosophy has been no more successful.

The positive nature of the being which is affirmed of the "I" in the *Cogito ergo sum* consists in this. In the "I" particularity and the universality coincide and are identified by giving place to the true individual. Aristotle defined the individual as the unity of form and of matter, of the ideal element which is universal and of the immediate positive element which is particular. They are identified (and this is the point) not because they are terms which are originally diverse and therefore either of them conceivable without the other, but because they can only be thought as difference in identity. In fact, I, who am in so far as I think, cannot transcend the punctual act of the thinking without transcending myself; no greater oneness than this can be thought. But if my oneness depends on my thinking, my thinking must itself be the highest universality there can be. For the thinking by which I think myself is precisely the same thinking by which I think everything. What is more, it is the thinking by which I think myself *truly*, that is, when I feel that I am thinking what is true absolutely and therefore that I am thinking universally. The act of thinking, then, through which I am, posits me as individual universally, as, in general, it posits all thinking or, indeed, all truth, universally.

From this standpoint, whilst we are able to answer the ancient and vexed question which divided the realists and the nominalists, and at the same time to solve the problem or the principle of individualization, we are also able to see that both realists and nominalists have had more reason in their respective contentions than they ever suspected. For not only is the universal real, as the realists affirmed, but there is no other reality; and not only is the individual real, as the nominalists affirmed, but outside the individual there is not anything, not even a name, an abstract or arbitrary scheme, or the like.

The universal, not presupposed by thought, but really posited by it, is all that can be thought real. When, then, we make distinctions, as indeed we must, all distinctions fall within it. If anything could issue^ from thought it could not be thought. And universality therefore invests every principle or entity however diverse which we would oppose to thought, it being impossible in regard to concrete thought ever by any means to oppose it to thought. On the other hand, the individual (even the individual is posited not presupposed by thought) is equally everything whatever which can be thought of as real, or which is simply thinkable. Because thought in its general meaning, implying here as always that it is concrete, is all-inclusive. The *cogito* is positive, certain, individual. The world of Platonic ideas, the system of concepts in Spinoza's ethics, the world of possibles in the intellectualist system of Wolf what are all these, when we turn them from abstract thought to the concrete, but definite historical philosophies, the thought of individual philosophers, realized by them, and realizing themselves in us when we seek to realize them, in our individual minds? They deal with the cogitare which realizes itself in a definite being who is absolutely unique; who is, not one among many, but one as a whole, infinite.

The extreme nominalism, which leaves no place even for names outside the concreteness of the individual, and the no less extreme realism, which will admit nothing outside the universal, each finds its own truth in the truth of the other. Thus is ended the opposition in which in the past they were arrayed against one another. Beyond the universal which is thought there is not the individual. In being the individual the universal is itself the true individual, the fact being that outside the individual the universal is not even a name, since the individual itself, in its genuine individuality, must at least be named and clothed with a predicate, and indeed with the universality of thought.

Names, rules, laws, false universals, all the black sheep of the nominalists, are, in fact, chimaeras of abstract thought, not existences. They are real in the same kind of way as when losing patience with our fellow-men in an outburst of wrath and resentment we call them beasts, the beasts are real. In such case it is obvious that were the men we so judge really such as we judge them, we who pass judgment upon them would also be the beasts to which we liken them. It is obvious also that such angry denial to men of humanity and reason does not even abstractly mean that we deny them a share of our reason. The injustice of such denial leaps to view the moment we reflect that there are many degrees and many different forms of reason and that our own is real and imperious in so far as we realize it. A common name! - but every time a name sounds on our lips it is a new name, for it responds to an act which by its very definition, mental act, has no past. Fused in the unity of the mental act to which it belongs, it has nothing in common with all the other uttered sounds materially identical with it, used at other times to denote other objects of our experience. The rule does not include within it a multiplicity of instances, as the genus includes an indefinite series of individuals, because the rule abstracted from the instances is a rule which by definition is always inapplicable. The true rule is that which applies to instances singly turn by turn, by making them all one with it. Hence modern aesthetic knows that every work of art has its own poetry, and every word its own grammar. [4] It is the same with laws, and with all universals, whether empirical or speculative, they are never detached from the fact, from the individual. Moreover, universal and individual adhere and coalesce so long as we think of neither the one nor the other in the abstract, but in what they singly and together signify to the mind every time they are effectively thought. For then they are nothing but the logical transparency, the thinkability of facts and individuals, which otherwise would vanish beyond the outer limits of the logical horizon. They come within this logical horizon not as abstract objects of thought, but rather as moments of the life of thought, and individuals in the meaning we have indicated.

The individual we have found is positive. It is the only positive it is given us to conceive. But it is positive not, it is now clear, because, as used to be supposed, it has been run to earth along a path from which there is no escape. It is not a positive posited for the subject by some other; it is posited by the subject and is the very subject which posits it. For that subject has need to go out of itself in order to entrench itself in the positive, and the positive has not become for it fact, so long as it remains unconscious of its true being which it has projected before itself, and closed in an abstract reality. But, having acquired the consciousness of the inwardness of being in the very act by which it is sought, the mind sees it can no longer want a positivity surer and clearer than that which it already possesses in itself when it thinks and realizes itself. Common sense believes that when a man wakes up, he puts to flight his dream images, purely subjective, a world which is not *the world,* by means of sensations of material objects, the rope of salvation without which he would be unable to escape shipwreck in the ocean of the inconsistent reality of his own fantasy. The exact contrary is true. When, in fact, on awaking from sleep we look at and touch the surrounding material objects in order to recover and possess again a clear and distinct consciousness of the real, it is not in the objects themselves and in external nature that we find the touchstone of reality, but in ourselves. And the difficulty of admitting as real that external nature which is not immediately enshrined within our subjective life as it formed itself in our dream, makes us touch our body and other bodies, that is, add new sensations and develop our ideas of that external nature which at first is as it were disturbed and pushed aside and only with difficulty succeeds in affirming its reality. And if reality conquers the dream, it is because in experience, whence the dreamer draws the woof of the dream life, reality is posited through experience and not through the dream, save only in so far as it is only the reality of ourselves who have dreamed. And if we are cut off from this centre of reference of our experience as a whole, from the I, in regard to which experience is organized and systematized, we shall juxtapose reality to the things seen in fantasy and to all the life lived in the dream, without any possibility of discrimination and valuation. This comes to saying that the true and unique positive is the act of the subject which is posited as such. In positing itself, it posits in itself, as its own proper element, every reality which is positive .through its relation of immanence in the act in which the I is posited in an ever richer and more complex way. Withdraw, then, your subjectivity from the world you contemplate and the world becomes a *rêve* without positivity. Make your presence felt in the world of your dreams (as happens when one dreams and there is no clash between the general context of experience and what we are dreaming) and the very dream becomes solid reality, positive to an extent which disturbs our personality, makes us passionate, makes us vibrate with joy or tremble with fear.

To sum up: the individual and its correlative universal, as we are now able to understand them, are clearly neither two objects nor two static positions of thought. The category of being does not properly belong to them, since, strictly speaking, there *is* no individual and no universal. Nor can we even say, purely and simply, that the individual, the need of which Aristotle saw, is not nature, but thought. Because although nature *is*, it is only in so far as it is a term of the thought which presupposes it; and for the same reason Plato affirmed the *being* of the universal. But our universal is the universalizing, the making universal, or rather, since the universal is the thought itself which makes it, the *self-making of the universal*. In exactly the same way the individual is act rather than the principle or the term of an act; it consists in the individual making itself or being individualized. And the conclusion is that we can speak of universal and individual, in so far as we have in mind the subject, the I which thinks and in thinking is universalized by individualizing and individualized by universalizing.

Here the deeper meaning of the positive becomes apparent. It is not posited as the result of a process already completed and perfect, and this result does not stand confronting thought as a mystery. It is a mystery, for it is posited and we ask in vain: Who posits it? The positive is posited in so far as it actually posits itself, re-entering into that being which is in so far as it is thought. The positive rather than something posited is really the self-positing of being. Such a standpoint is secure just because it is the absolute transparence of thought as self-identical in its own act. And thought is made clear in its act because there is no surer proof of fact than being perceived; and the sureness does not depend on its being fact but on its being perceived, or rather on its being resolved into a real act of the thought which actuates and thinks itself.

When we oppose nature to mind we appear to be limiting mind. Nature is individual, and as such it particularizes and thereby determines and realizes the universal which is mind. But the specific character of nature by which we discriminate it is not in the concept of the individual. For we have shown that the individual as nature, the individual individualized, is unintelligible. The only conceivable individual is mind itself, that which individualizes.

It is true that we have not satisfied all the requirements on account of which in the history of philosophy the concept of the individual as nature arose. The individual stands for positivity as against the ideality of thought, but it also stands for multiplicity as against the unity of thought. And the positivity itself is integrated and fulfilled in the multiplicity, because the ideality arises as the intelligibility of the manifold. To over come pure ideality, therefore, it is not only necessary to grasp the real but the real which is manifold. Indeed, for Plato as for Aristotle, and also for the pre-Socratic philosophers, the positive is nature as becoming, in which all is transformed, and whereby the forms of being and the objects of experience, or the individuals, are many.

The Eleatics alone were unifiers, as Aristotle remarks in a vigorous sentence. But the objective monism of Parmenides led to the agnostic scepticism of Gorgias, and this, carrying to its logical conclusion the doctrine of Parmenides concerning the identity of thinking with being, denied the possibility of the opposition of the one to the other which is an indispensable moment in the concept of knowing, and therefore denied the possibility of knowing. To know is to distinguish, and therefore knowing implies that there are more terms than one and that we are not confined to only one. Socrates discovered the concept as the unity in which the variety of opinions concurs. The Platonic idea is the type of the manifold sensible things, and by its unity it makes their multiplicity thinkable. And what is the whole of ancient philosophy, from Thales and the first searchers for the original principle of things onwards, but one continual effort to reach unity by starting from the indefinite plurality of the existence presented in experience? This sums up the history of thought, which has always aspired to unity in order to render intelligible, without destroying, the multiplicity of individual and positive things. And this sums up logic. For if to the unity of the universal we should oppose a unique individual, the individual itself in its unity would be universal, a whole, and therefore it would in itself repeat the ideal position of the universal, and not yield the positive. Just as, were we able to think *horse* (ἱππότης) as thought of horses, then had nature produced no more than one single horse, this one horse could not be distinguished from the ideal horse, and could not therefore serve our thought as its fulcrum for the thinking of the universal. It would not be the positive of that idea. The universal is a mediation of the particulars and must therefore develop through the more positive.

We, on the other hand, have found a positivity which implies the identity of the individual with the universal. I think, and in thinking I realize, an individual which is universal, which is therefore a universal ought to be, absolutely. Other than it, outside it, there cannot be anything. But can I say, then, that I have realized something? The being which I affirm seems in its unity to reproduce the desperate position of Parmenides, for to pass from it to anything else is impossible. Is it something positive? Do I really think the "I" if I can think no other than the "I"? In making the individual conceivable, and in freeing it from the difficulties in which it was thrown by its opposition to the universal, have we not destroyed the very essence of individuality?

Against Parmenides there stands Democritus. And Aristotle's doctrine of the individual is a homage rendered to Democritus. The Democritan theory stamps the Aristotelian conception as the Eleatic theory stamps the idealistic conception of Plato. Aristotle does homage to the experience on which Plato, the great Athenian idealist, had turned his back, although continually forced to return to it. The idea is, indeed, the intelligibility of the world; but it must be the intelligibility of a world which is a multiplicity of individuals.

We also are rendering homage to the profound truth of the Democritan atomism, which is the need of difference, when we expound the concept of mind as process. The unity of mind excludes only abstract multiplicity, since the unity of mind is in itself a multiplicity, a concrete multiplicity unfolded in the unity of the spiritual process. Here, however, the need of multiplicity assumes a new aspect and this needs to be explained. It concerns the multiplicity which is imposed on mind from within, in so far as it is consciousness of things and persons. And, indeed, there is no other multiplicity than this, a multiplicity which we see arising to confront us from within our own inmost being. But to the atomist (and every one is an atomist to the extent that he feels the need of the individual as something by which he must integrate and realize thought) it appears that the multiplicity, in so far as it is positive, lies beyond this subjective multiplicity. It is not enough to conceive a world diversified and rich in particulars, because this world exists: it may be a dream. And according to the atomist it would be a dream were we unable to explain our ideas by transcending the subject and attributing the origin of ideas to the *real* multiplicity of things. It would be no use to point out, as we have pointed out, that real things and dream things do not possess in themselves the marks by which they are discriminated, they need a subject to discriminate them, without which even waking life itself would be one whole dream from which we should never awaken. It would be no use, because the atomist will always reply that the real things which the subject opposes to the dream things are not real because we have ideas of them, for ideas presuppose real things which generate ideas in us. It is rather, he will say, that we can have ideas because the things which are represented by ideas are real in themselves with a reality which is at bottom that which we attribute to them, a reality in itself, which is the true reality, the only positive reality, nature. In nature there are individuals which are real individuals, the atoms, in themselves unknowable. There we find the true positivity on which thought must lean if we are not to gasp for breath in the void, whirled among vain shadows of one's self. And there we find not the multiplicity which is only our thought (the multiplicity we cannot think without unifying), but multiplicity in itself, the familiar ground of all the individual differences and oppositions and thereby of the complex life of the reality.

So that by means of the concept of the individual, multiplicity returns to camp with the claim to pitch its tent beyond the multiplicity we have acknowledged as immanent in the process of mind, and postulating accordingly a nature in itself, the basis of the whole life of mind and a condition of an exact concept of the individual as the integrating positivity of thought.

We have got, then, to scrutinize this concept of the multiplicity. It is a multiplicity which, it is evident at once, must be obscure, for it transcends the mind. It must be chaotic, for we have withdrawn it from any unity which could hold it together as a spiritual act. Like Leopardi's *Infinite,* [5] in which even thinking itself is drowned, it is fearsome. Yet we must scrutinize it, for, in spite of its transcendence - let us recall Berkeley's warning - it seizes a place among our concepts, and even atomism is a philosophy. We cannot maintain a concept if it be inconsistent with other concepts which must coexist with it in our mind.

A pure multiplicity is not only unknowable, it is not thinkable. The many are always a totality. If each of the many were not one among multiplicity is the others, it would be one, not as a part, but as the whole. It would be an absolute unity, the unity which atomism denies. It is not such a unity. Given the multiplicity *a, b, c, d,...*, *a* must not be *b*, nor *c*, nor *d*, so likewise with *b* and *c* and *d*; but that one thing should not be the other is impossible, absolutely, unless we deny all relation between them, since relation implies some identity. Multiplicity, then, necessarily carries with it the absolute *non-relativity* of the many which go to make it. So that a not only must not be *b* but must not even be relative to *b*. And this is absurd, because the very words "not be" affirm a reciprocal exclusion, and that is a relation.

Again, multiplicity posited as pure cannot be absolute without being composed of absolutely simple elements, otherwise every composite would be an exception to the multiplicity by organizing and unifying it. But the simple (ἄτομον, ἄτομος, οὐσία) becomes in its turn a flagrant violation of the law of multiplicity, because the simple is one. The atomist, starting from the unity of experience, denies it, splits it up, divides it; this is the logic of his thought. Wherever he finds unity he must divide. He cannot stop at the atom but must divide the atom even to infinity, and then there is multiplicity no longer, for multiplicity must have its elements.

Again, even granting the atomist his multiplicity, how can he form an image of it, and what use will the image be? The atoms like the ideas are excogitated as a principle of reality. In the reality there is the unity, but there is also the multiplicity (and hence the uselessness of the ideas, as Aristotle clearly showed). In the reality there is the multiplicity, but there is also the unity, the relation, the shock of the atoms and the aggregation of matter. But if we grant the absolutely unrelated simples then the shock is impossible, because the shock is relation however extrinsic the relation be. And if we grant the shock there is an end alike of the non-relativity, of the simplicity and of the multiplicity.

The difficulty is not new. It has been more or less clearly, more or less vigorously, urged continually against atomism, and *mutatis mutandis* against every form of pluralism. But this has not prevented philosophers, however adverse they may be to pluralism, from representing the world as in space and time, and from thinking of every positive individual as determined *hic et nunc*, as existing, in so far as it exists, in space and in time. We must now consider space and time.

[1] Cf. my remarks on this subject in my essay, *Rosmini e Gioberti,* Pisa, Nistri, 1898.
[2] It should be remarked that the Aristotelian category, the most universal predicate, does not differ fundamentally from the Kantian category, a function of the judgment, when the predicate of the judgment, according to the Aristotelian logic, is given the full meaning which Aristotle intended. It is a universality which interpenetrates and so determines and illumines the subject that it becomes the whole matter of knowledge and the mode by which thought thinks. Whence the concept of the predicate is always, in substance, not an idea thought, but an act by which a given content is thought.
[3] With regard to this matter of the classification of judgments, cf. *Sistema di Logica,* vol. i. part ii. ch. 5.
[4] Cf. Gentile, "Il concetto della grammatica," 1910, in *Frammenti di Estetica e di letteratura,* Lanciano, Carabba, 1920.
[5] See the reference to this ode in Chapter X. § 3. (Trans. Note.)

Chapter Nine - Space and Time

Space and time are the two systems of the manifold. It is as such that they come to be thought of as the great depository of what is positive, effectively real, concrete, individuality. To be real, in the positive meaning, is to exist; and what exists, exists in space and in time. Nature, the realm of the existing, when contraposed to thought, is represented as just the totality of individuals co-existing in space and successive in time. Even Kant, who held that space and time are two *a priori* forms of experience, or rather two modes by which the unifying activity of mind works on the data of immediate sensibility, believed that the only way to guarantee the positive objectivity of sensible intuition was to presuppose that beneath the spatially and temporally unified manifold there was another manifold, not yet unified by the subject, but the basis of such unification. Such manifold, as any one who reflects may see, is not really deprived nor indeed can ever be deprived of all spatiality and temporality, because to affirm a manifold is at the same time to affirm space and time. So that the pure subjective intuitions of Kant, the *a priori* forms of sense, held to be insufficient in themselves, and dependent on a matter external to them, end by presupposing themselves to themselves, and so being, even before as yet there is being.

Suppose the manifold to be a positive actual manifold (not simply possible and therefore merely ideal); suppose it absolutely manifold (never mind that the absolutely manifold is an absurdity), positive and absolutely positive (not realizing or realizable but realized, which as we have clearly shown is another absurdity); and you will have the space in which we all represent things. Space in all its determinations, and apart from any question of the number of its dimensions, implies the reciprocal exclusion of all the terms of actual or possible experience.

All that we distinguish or can distinguish, and therefore all that we can posit in an actual experience, is spatial; or rather, it is resolved into elements, and in the last analysis into points, each of which is outside all the others and has all the others outside it. We may not distinguish the elements of space; and we do not, in fact, distinguish the ultimate elements, the points. But this does not prevent us regarding them as distinguishable elements in the object of an actual experience; or, what is the same thing, distinct elements in the object of a possible experience. This amounts to saying that the spatial elements are distinct with a distinction which no experience can abolish. Thence their positive objectivity, which has the appearance of being imposed on the subjective activity which generates experience.

A possible or ideal space is meaningless, although it has many times been affirmed. Thought is not spatial. The hyperuranion, of which Plato discourses, has no resemblance to the true and proper space, the χώρα of which he speaks in the *Timaeus* (50-52) as a receptacle of forms without which the ideas would remain ideas and would not have the wherewithal and the how to be realized. The ideas, however many they are, make one; they are co-ordinated and resolve dialectically all their multiplicity. The thought of space, the idea of space, has in itself no more multiplicity than any other idea. The unresolved and unresolvable multiplicity is that of the spatial elements in so far as they are given in their positivity. I can indeed represent to myself a body not given, and that body will be spatial, but it will be spatial in so far, and only in so far, as I think of it as given, that is so long as I have not the consciousness that it is merely a possibility or ideality. For when this consciousness arises, the reality is no longer the body but the idea of the body, devoid, as idea, of all spatiality.

And this, indeed, is the reason why the material world, or rather the spatially given world, is for common sense the touchstone of the existent, of what is sure and positive, and it is why, when the existence of anything is not evident, we ask, *Where* is it?

But not only do we require the *where* of what exists, we also require the *when*. Simply in space and without time experience would not be actual and the real would not be positive. For the real to be positive there must be multiplicity, and multiplicity is not absolute perfect multiplicity so long as it is only spatiality. Each point in space is a centre, to which the system of all other points is fixed, and this destroys multiplicity. The point as such is a limit of space and therefore itself devoid of spatiality. Yet just as reason compels us to divide the extended into its elements and to break up the unity of everything into multiplicity, so a point as such, limiting and thereby annulling space, is inconceivable without the concept of an ulterior multiplication which becomes a new spatialization.

We may take a point as one among the points. This is the *point of the multiplicity*, and it gives rise to the concept of space. But there is also the *point of the unity*, which cannot be fixed in its unity without making the multiplicity which depends on it fall to nothing. Thereby it spatializes itself. Let us take, for example, any element of space, any "here," what soever. In taking it in its definite elementariness, and withdrawing it from the elements together with which, and as one of which, it forms a whole, we withdraw it from spatiality. But does it then persist as something unique? No, because from its own being there arises again spatiality as a reciprocal exclusion of the elements of experience. Let us suppose it to remain always the element as defined, let us say a point, yet experience brings reciprocal exclusion in the succession of instants, it becomes without spatial change a "now" excluding other "nows."

It may be said, then, that time is the *spatialization of the unity of space.* [1] And therefore time and space can be represented schematically as two intersecting straight lines having only one point in common. It is one unique point of space which cannot be a point in space without being one of the infinite points of time. But let us beware lest our own fancy blocks our conception of this simple imaginative system of space. Let us for the moment simply keep in view the fact that there is a multiplicity of spatial points, and among these find the unity which is multiplied in time. We notice, that is to say, that we are dealing with a multiplicity which is given, or rather which is real and absolute, independently of every mental unification. And then we shall recognize that for one point of space, time is its spatialization: time as every one intuits it.

Space, then, we conclude, completes itself in time by positing itself as an absolute multiplicity, every element of which is itself a multiplicity. Not that time is the following out of the same process as the multiplication of space. Were it so there would be no point or space, nor any definite spatial unity at all. We have to arrest the spatial process by fixing an element of space, a point, in order to understand the other element, an instant, which is generated by the multiplication of the first. It also is spatialization in so far as, like the first, it is a reciprocal exclusion of distinct elements, and therefore a multiplicity, but it is only a new spatialization of the first space. And herein is the difference of time from space.

Space is a pure multiplicity immediately given. But you cannot withdraw from this multiplicity one of its units without seeing this unit in a second pure multiplicity, given in the first: and this is time. To think nature as one - as the One of Parmenides, or as the spherical whole, identical in all its parts, which Xenophon imagined and to think this one outside of time in an eternity, immobile, is to think nothing, and this it seems is what Gorgias pointed out. The object is spatially manifold; and because it is absolutely so, it is also temporally manifold. A glance - be it no more than a glance - cast on the world, holds in it a spatial multiplicity. Yet we cannot fix this multiplicity before us, neither in its whole such as it is, nor in any one of its parts. From beginning to end it is multiplied into a multitude of images of its whole or of its part and so is prolonged into the past and into the future. Either the multiplicity is spatial, or it is temporal.

In every case, then, we have a multiplicity and a multiplicity not unified. This was precisely what Kant presupposed as the antecedent of his pure subjective functions of space and time, Instead, it is the whole content of our concept or space and time. And to this concept every kind of empiricism has recourse in order to determine what by nature is positive in the richness of its individuals. So that without maintaining the concept of multiplicity in its absolute independence of every synthetic unity, it is impossible to stop short of conceiving reality as spatial and temporal. And, in fact, it is so; because the pure manifold oscillates between two extremes equally absurd without being able to rest at an intermediate point. We have already seen that either the multiplicity is thought as a whole, and then the unity of the whole comes into conflict with the multiplicity and contradicts it; or it is thought of in each of its parts, detaching a part from the whole, and then the part is itself a unity which equally comes into conflict with and contradicts the multiplicity.

It comes really then to saying that when we think of the world as spatial and temporal, and mean thereby a world in itself, what we call nature, existing before mind and independently of mind, we are thinking of nothing. The meaning of the spatiality and temporality of the real must be something different from this, and we must inquire what this meaning is, keeping hold of what is positive in space and time and rejecting the supposed transcendence of their multiplicity.

Of what we have said so far in illustration of the ordinary idea that space and time are systems of the absolute multiplicity of positive reality we may now say that while it is true it is not the whole truth. For the absurdity arises from the abstractness in which philosophical speculation has fixed an idea which is immanent in consciousness where it is integrated in the condition indispensable to its concreteness.

The inconceivability of pure multiplicity, represented by the absolute spatiality, which, as we see, is both space and time, consists in the ness of the claim to exclude the unity from that multiplicity. The unity, if admitted, would lay it under the suspicion or the intrusion of an ideal element, the suspicion that mind was present. The aim is to keep the positive element in existing reality separate from the identity with which thought is supposed to invest it, and by idealizing it, to change it from a world of things into a world of ideas. The claim comes down to us from the ancient illusion that we can place reality before thought, untouched by any subjective action, at least as a postulate of the knowledge, through which the same reality would then be presented more or less informed by the logical principles and cognitive forms of the subject. But we have repeatedly called attention to the fact that this non subjective reality itself is a reality posited by the subject, therefore itself subjective, in the absolute sense, and non-subjective only relatively to the degree or mode of subjectivity of a reality in all other respects subjective. The stimulus of a sound-sensation, as an example of a non-subjective movement, is itself something conceived by the mind, intelligible only as a function of the mental activity which reconstructs the antecedents of the sensation by means of physiology and abstract physics. When we analyse the concept of abstract reality according to this ingenuous interpretation of its non-subjectivity, or *objectivity* as we generally but inaccurately term it, we are left in no included by the doubt that its essential character is multiplicity devoid of any synthetic principle. We are left in no doubt, because the hypothesis of the object, obtained by such abstraction, is that there shall remain in what is abstracted nothing which can in any way be assigned to the subject's activity, and that every universal and synthetic principle, as an ideality which unites the multiplicity of the manifold, comes from the subject. But having made the abstraction, and having so fixed the multiplicity, we must not then go on and claim that we have shown it living by the very logic according to which it can only live in the integrity of the living organism from which we have abstracted it. It would be like cutting with a surgeon's knife a limb from the living body and sup posing we could still keep it alive, in the same physiological and biological meaning, as when it was part of the whole vital system.

Absolute multiplicity is the character of the positive in so far as it is posited, or of the object in so far as it is object. But, as we have shown, the positive is posited for the subject in so far as it is posited by it. Neither does the object transcend the subject nor can it be immanent in it save in virtue of the action of the subject itself. All the infinite elements into which the world confronting me is multiplied, and all the infinite moments into which every one of its elements, and itself as a whole, are multiplied within me, in confronting me are in me, through my work. Multiplication by which one thing is not another, is my act. And this is the great truth which Kant in his dissertation *De mundi sensibilis atque intelligibilis forma et principiis* (1770), and more clearly still, eleven years later, in the *Critique of Pure Reason,* perceived when he maintained the subjectivity of the forms of space and of time, understanding these forms as functions; a concept entirely lost sight of by the empiricist psychologists and epistemologists of the nineteenth century who sought to prove that even these forms of experience are a product of experience; and no less lost sight of by the champions of the psychology called *nativist,* who denied that Kant was right because these forms are, in fact, a *necessary antecedent of experience.* [2]

The forms of space and time are neither antecedent nor consequent. If the forms are the functions by which the object of experience is constituted, their activity and effective reality can be nowhere else but in experience.

Space and time are inconceivable as empty forms which have to be filled, as one would fill an empty vessel, with single presentations of sensible experience. Space, and time, so conceived, would be multiplicity already posited independent of the mind's activity. Instead, it is the mind's spatializing activity which generates multiplicity. It does not presuppose it. And in so far as mind has that multiplicity confronting it (or we might say in so far as there is multiplicity, since to be is always to be for mind), in so far it generates it. It is not *multiple* but *multiplication*. Multiplication is the concrete reality which gives place to multiplicity. It is only abstractly that multiplicity can be thought of as something which subsists, withdrawn from the movement which belongs to, and is, the presupposition of thought.

But if we would understand in its pure spirituality this doctrine that the reality of space is spatialization, we must abandon the Kantian standpoint of the datum of immediate sensible experience. The manifold of sense is in Kant a presupposition of empirical intuition, and this intuition is a logical antecedent of the actualization of the spatial function, and is concerned with a non-subjective multiplicity, the multiplicity obscurely imagined by Kant as outside the whole cognitive process, in the manner of the atomists and in agreement with the vague philosophical intuitions implicit in the scientific conceptions of his time. Spatiality, as we have said, is not so much order and synthesis as differentiation and multiplication. Kant insists on the unifying and order-imposing function because he presupposes (we have seen why) the manifold. He makes space the formal unity into which the mind receives the multiplicity, gathering it into a synthesis. But the multiplicity itself, if it exist, presupposes unity, for it cannot exist except as it is assembled, ordered, unified. The unity is first and spatiality consists in the multiplication of the one. So that strictly it is not the many which is synthesized, it is the one which is analysed.

Analysis, on the other hand, here as in every other moment of spiritual life, cannot be separated from synthesis. For the act which multiplies the one does not destroy it; it is in multiplying that it realizes it, and thence the multiplicity which follows from the act is a multiplicity of the one. And analysis does not disperse the individuality, rather does it enrich it, make it concrete, give it power; indeed, it strengthens it and confers on it a fuller and healthier reality. Space is, in fact, the harmonious whole of the world which we represent spatially, and what makes it one in the horizon of our consciousness. As a whole, it is unbounded in so far as our imagination enables us indefinitely to extend its limits, but it is imprisoned in us, an object of present experience, given (in so far as we make it such for our selves) and held together by the seal of time. So that every element of it, and itself as a whole, is articulated in the series of its states, connected together and forming an adamantine chain within which all that is positive in the facts is stretched out in the reality of the world. All is in us: we are all.

We, then, are not in space and in time, but space and time, whatever is unfolded spatially and has successive stages in time, are in us. But the "us" which is here intended is not empirical but the transcendental ego. It is not meant that space is located in us. It is important to make this clear. The ego is not the space in which space is, meaning space as we commonly understand it. Space is activity; and for what is spatial to be in the "I," means that it is spatial in virtue of the activity of the "I," that its spatiality is the explication, the actuality of the "I."

Kant said that space is a form of external sense, time a form of internal sense. He meant that if we represent nature, that is, what we call the external world and think or as having been in existence before our knowledge and spiritual life began in space, then we represent the multiplicity or the objects or our internal experience, or what we distinguish as diverse and manifold in the development of our spiritual life, not in space but in time. But we have insisted on the substantial identity of the scheme which is at the foundation of the idea of time and of the idea of space, and we have expounded time as the spatialization of the spatial element. Clearly then we cannot accept the Kantian distinction as a sufficient indication of the substantial diversity between nature and mind. We are not speaking of the error committed by the psychophysicists who propose to solve experimentally the problem of the measurement of psychical time, and who measure only, what alone is measurable in regard to what is psychical, the physiological phenomena held to be concomitant with the true and proper psychical act. In this case there is no more than the fallacy of double meaning. But the process of spiritual development itself, as every one allows, is subject to the form of time; chronology we know is an indispensable element of history in its more spiritual meaning; and also the !? very basis of personality lies in the memory by which the mind prolongs its present reality and is rooted in the past.

But even here we have to consider attentively what it is which is rightly temporal, and what it is which is spiritual in the reality, which in its wide meaning we crudely speak or as both spiritual and temporal. Time as Kant's form temporal of internal experience has regard to the empirical ego, that is, not the ego which is empirically (the I in so far as it is a subject of a simple experience) but the ego which is *known* empirically (the I in so far as it is an object of simple experience). And Kant distinguishes from experience the transcendental ego which by its activity makes experience possible. So that what is temporal in experience is not temporal in the absolute knowledge which understands that experience as the display of the activity of the transcendental "I," the true "I" and the act which is properly spiritual. This "I" does not come within the horizon of empiricism, for empiricism must be true to itself; but it is revealed and attracts attention when we become conscious of empiricism. This *consciousness of empiricism* is not itself empirical but absolute knowledge, for it has to give an account of empiricism. What is temporal as an abstract object of the real "I" is not an "I," is not something which has freedom or any spiritual value, because it is what is done, not what is doing. It is the positive in so far as it is posited.

An historical fact as regards time is a past fact but our judgment concerning it can only have meaning if we take as its valuation, not the accomplished fact, but the historian's consciousness and personality, of which indeed the idea of the historical fact is an inherent part. Only spiritual acts have value, we do not judge pure facts such as fair or foul weather, deformity or fine stature. Now it is true that each of us is his past, just as civilization and learning are what is retained and remembered, but what we retain is in fact what we now understand, and it is obvious that the intellect with which we now understand is no longer identical with that with which we formerly understood, were it for no other reason than that our intellect having once understood is thereby made more intelligent. When we bring to mind in a present act the past fact of our spiritual life, a past coloured in our soul, now with a sad regret, now with a sweet and tender yearning, now with joy and now with sorrow, we are not really comparing two realities, one present one past, but two empirical representations both equally present as the actuality of the "I" which compares and judges: equally present because, although variously assorted in the time series, all our past states are compresent in the temporalizing act of the mind.

We are now able to see what is in the true meaning spiritual in regard to time. The temporal as mere positive fact is not spiritual, but the act by which the temporal is temporal, the act through which the temporal fact acquires its positive character; this act is spiritual. It is natural in living our experience to multiply our states and see ourself as a many. But the "know thyself" of philosophy ought to open our eyes, revealing to us the act of experiencing and multiplying, which is the root of temporal multiplicity.

The *coexistence* of the elements of space has its exact counterpart in the *compresence* of the elements of time. The compresence of the time existence and elements gives us the exact significance and compresence. enables us to understand the coexistence of the spatial elements. Compresence is the convergence of all the moments of time (past, present and future in their infinite distinctions and consequent multiplications) in a *present* which is no longer a present situated between a past and a future, but a negation of all temporal multiplicity and of all succession. It is not *duration,* as time deprived of spatiality has been some what fancifully defined (in so far as it is time it cannot be deprived of spatiality, since time is already space), but eternity, which is the principle and therefore a negation of time. The eternal present on which all the rays of time converge and from which all irradiate, is the intelligibility of time. Time is unintelligible only so long as we are anxious to set it above us as pure time, without eternity: pure nature without mind, multiplicity without unity.

Coexistence is convergence of all the points of space in a *point* which is outside all the points and so a negation of their multiplicity: a point which is the "I" itself, a spatializing activity from which all points irradiate and on which all are centred. This merely ideal, or as we should say transcendental point, by its spatializing activity posits all the points of space and all the moments of time, thus generating the positive character of the real in space and time.

It is clear that without coexistence and cornpresence there cannot be space and time. And both are unintelligible if we seek to understand them as the actual multiplicity which each is, except on one condition, namely, that space is the spatiality of the point and the point is non-spatial, and time is the temporality of the instant and the instant is non-temporal. Both therefore are contained in one reality, by which they attain their being, and this is eternal in regard to time, in so far as it is absolutely instantaneous; and it is one in regard to space, which is the fundamental process of its multiplication. Nature, in short, even in this aspect, is only intelligible as the life of mind, which however it is multiplied remains one.

This doctrine of space and time as absolute spatialization, which is only multiplicity in so far as multiplicity is absorbed in the unity of mind, does not mean that the multiplicity of the coexistent things in space and of the compresent series of the events in time is reduced to a simple illusion. If we say, as we certainly can and ought to say, that reality is neither spatial nor temporal, because reality is mind and mind is neither in space nor in time, this need not imply that no form of reality can be represented rightly as space and time. We only mean and we cannot insist too strongly on its importance that space and time are not adequately conceived when they are assumed to exist in their pure and abstract manifoldness, immobile and irreducible. They have a real multiplicity, however, but only in so far as it is posited, in the mobility, in the life, in the dialectic of the actual position which mind makes for them by realizing in them its own unity.

We may say, indeed, that what we ordinarily think of space and time, as we effectively conceive them before we attain the view-point of the pure act, is quite true, but not the whole truth. It is as it were no more than the half-truth, which for its completion must find the other half. It does not indicate a real division, but only the half-truth of immature philosophical reflexion, incapable of apprehending in its integrity the spiritual act which is posited as space and time. This other half is that which reconciles the abstractness of positive reality in the naturalistic meaning, in a positive reality which renders possible the first by actualizing it.

In logical language, spatiality is the antithesis of which mind is the thesis. Mind, however, in so far as it is simple thesis opposed to its antithesis is no less abstract than spatiality. The concreteness of each consists in its synthesis. The synthesis is not a *tertium quid* supravening on mind or unity and nature or spatiality, and reconciling their opposition by unifying their terms.

The synthesis is original, and this means there is neither thesis without antithesis nor antithesis without thesis. Just as there is no opposition without opponents, though it be of the one to itself as different and identical. And this duality of the terms is thrown into relief and made to appear an absolute duality which is not unity when we bring an abstract analysis to bear on the unique living spiritual process, in which the thesis is the antithesis, and the antithesis is the thesis.

Our conclusion is, then, that not only is the naturalism which thinks that space and time are presuppositions of the mind, false, or, what is the same thing, half true, but also that an idealism which should deny space would be false. Because just as it is false to think the antithesis without the thesis which is the ground of it, so it is false to think the thesis without the antithesis which is the structure raised upon it.

All philosophies which have failed to attain the concept of mind as pure act, the concept which alone makes it possible to understand spatiality as mind, have been naturalistic, even those which hold that there is no way of conceiving nature without a mind which creates it and explains it. Because a mind which is supposed to stand outside nature and be antecedent to nature as the idea is antecedent to the creation, must be conceived as outside of, and antecedent to, the mind which knows this nature. Such a mind is both pre-mental and pre-natural, the ground both of nature and of the mind whose idea nature is. Now this mind can only be posited by and for the present mind, the mind which it is urgently necessary to understand, the mind which in no other way but that of understanding can guarantee the truth of what it thinks. And this extra-mind is posited for present mind just as nature is posited for it. It is posited as a reality, which is all reality, already realized, while the mind which now is has yet to arise and be.

When mind is assigned this place in regard to the transcendent reality, space can only be the abstract multiplicity, absolutely inconsistent with any unity, which has been shown to be unintelligible and absurd; and this notwithstanding any effort philosophy may make to conceive it as subjective and as unity. On the other hand, it cannot be said that there has ever been an idealism really opposed to such naturalism. We may see in Spinoza a true and distinctive negation of the multiplicity which is spatiality. It is the basis of his system, as it was generally of the neo-Platonic pantheism with which Spinoza's speculation is akin, as seen in his reconstitution of Stoicism and Eleaticism. But that negation does not annul the multiplicity of nature in the unity of mind, but rather in an immediate natural unity. It may be regarded as an anomaly of naturalism, and it becomes in fact a kind of mysticism, which is the negation of nature as such, and a retracting of the mind within itself, by cancelling all the determinations of its object and so blocking the way of knowing it as a positive object, or as a true and proper *natural* object.

No abstract idealism has ever been absolute, nor is such an idealism possible, because from the absolute standpoint it would be aware of its own abstractness. Yet we are not without a relative abstract idealism, relative because we find it in the end, as I shall show, turning into a pure naturalism. This is the philosophy of Leibniz, who held that mind cannot be conceived except as a pure unity cut off from all multiplicity. The *monad,* as Leibniz called it, is absolutely simple, a substance which exists in so far as it is separate from all relation with the manifold. The monadism of Leibniz is the most significant and conspicuous instance of the abstract idealism which I have called relative. It is a real compromise between the reasoning of the mind and the plain and ingenuous naturalistic intuition of reality. Leibniz is idealist and monist in his conception of the quality of substance, because for him there is no other substance but mind, but he is pluralist in his mode of conceiving the being of substance according to the most rigidly naturalistic conception, that of the atomists. Atomist or mechanist he is not, inasmuch as he denies that the phenomena spring out of inter-atomic actions, or, in his own language, out of actions exercised by one monad on the others. All that happens resolves itself for him into the internal life of each monad which is appetition and perception, or rather mind and nothing other than mind. But this mind is both self-sufficient and insufficient. It is self-sufficient since the monad has no windows and receives nothing from without; but it is insufficient in so far as the monad originally mirrors the universe in itself, and therefore all the other monads as others, are originally and substantially others. They are not the monad yet they condition it, through the monad of monads, God, who presides over all and is himself the condition of each. So that each monad is, in so far as all the others are, which others it cannot make exist. And therefore the monad is not self-sufficient. Moreover, as free, it is nothing, because appetition is its essential being and it develops in so far as it acquires ever clearer and distincter perception, not of itself, but of all the others, the consciousness of which can never be self-consciousness in it, and therefore true and proper realization of the monad in its autonomy, because the others are outside it. The monad therefore, I repeat, is self-sufficient and in sufficient. In so far as it is self-sufficient it is mind, in so far as it is insufficient it is no longer mind but changed into the plurality of its objects, naturalistically. The monad, in fact, as true monad, as the unity which to be mind it must be, cannot be a monad among the monads. Together with the others the monad ends by being multiplicity (a multiplicity which in its turn postulates a unity, which it interprets by making it one sole multiplicity) and the multiplicity will be the true unity. The Leibnizian monad is only a monad relatively to a subjective point of view. And even this, according to Leibniz, there is power to transcend, by rising to the absolute or divine point of view which recognizes the infinite multiplicity of the monads, more absolutely unrelated than any atomist had ever had the courage to conceive his material elements. Its absolute irrelativity makes the monadology, in this respect, a more naturalistic conception even than that of materialistic atomism.

There is an equal abstractness in the idealism of the dualists, an idealism also relative and leading fatally towards naturalism. The dualism of soul and body, or of spirit (a divine transcendent personality) and nature (man being included in nature, through what he is *naturally*), is idealistic so long as it is a question of conceiving mind in itself, without putting it in relation with its opposite; but no sooner does it seek to integrate the concept in the whole than the rights of mind are suppressed and nature alone becomes compact, uniform and infinite. The soul, which is not body, simply is, and by its pure being excludes from itself all spatial multiplicity, and therefore is free. Yet the soul which is not body is with the body; and with the body it makes two. But as the body is a great multitude of parts, the soul, situated in the heart or in the brain or in a particular point of the brain such as the pineal gland (to which even so great a philosopher as Descartes assigned it), is added to the number of all the parts, together composing the multiplicity which is explicitly or implicitly spatial. So there may be as many souls as there are bodies; and they may form companies as souls, although by means of bodies. They will constitute a spatial manifold because they must be distributed on the face of the earth with intervals between them, and having relations with the various natural and local conditions which will be mirrored in the diverse natures of the souls themselves. So in a thousand ways naturalism invades the spirituality of the soul conceived in this dualistic way.

Analogous considerations can be set forth in regard to the dualism of God and nature, the conjoining of which is impossible without assimilating one term to the other. In every case the error is not in the duality but always in the abstractness of the duality. In the concrete the duality rules only on the basis of the unity.

[1] This unity, being always a unity, may be like the unity of the point, that is of a spatial element, or like the unity of space in its totality, for space itself is always a relative totality.

[2] The only one who saw clearly the common error in the genetic and nativist theories in psychology in regard to Kant was Spaventa in his article *Kant e l'empirismo* (1881). By taking space to signify spatiality he indicated the only way in which the doctrine of Kant can be interpreted and verified. We have followed the same plan in this chapter. See Spaventa, *Scritti filosofici*, ed. Gentile, Napoli, Morano, 1900, p. 85 ff. In that article it seems to me we are given a glimpse of the concept of space as act.

Chapter Ten - Immortality

If mind is the principle of space and has that principle in itself, there is not a space which contains the mind and therefore it is impossible to attribute to mind any of those limits by which every spatial reality is circumscribed. And in this we may see both the ground of the finiteness of space and the profound meaning of the infinity of mind.

Space is indefinite, not infinite. It has no assign able limits, yet it is not the negation of every limit, for it cannot be conceived otherwise than limited. Space as an object of the mind is a datum: it represents that positive multiplicity which the mind itself posits. It is not an undefined or indefinite object because to be an object of the mind really means that it is some thing the mind has defined. Space is antithesis as such, as we have already said, and the antithesis stands confronted by the thesis, not as something which may be, but as a definite position. This positive and effectual determinateness of space (and of every thing which is posited before us as spatial) implies the limit of space, implies that it is precisely a certain space. But, on the other hand, as it is posited by the mind, and only subsists as the mind posits it, it has no independent being of its own but a being which depends on a continuous and inexhaustible spiritual activity. Spiritual activity, therefore, posits space not by positing it finally once for all but by continuing in the actuality of positing it. Or rather in the very act which posits space, space is never posited, but always is to be posited. And the limits of space, like its own being, are not something fixed but a boundary which is mobile, always living and present.

The conclusion is that space exists only in so far as there is and at the same time as there is not a spatial limit. Or, we might even say, space exists in so far as the limit which determines spatiality is displaceable to infinity. The limit can never be lacking and yet it can never be fixed; because, it does not belong to an object which exists for itself and is originally independent like an absolute substance. It is the attribute of an object produced by the immanent act of a subject, whose reality consists in the production and therefore in the limitation of its own object.

Space accordingly is finite without being a fixed finite thing. This negativity of every definite limit, with the consequent impossibility of assigning to it an absolute limit, constitutes its indefiniteness. This indefiniteness of space is a consequence of the infinity of the mind. For the negativity of the spatial limit is the intrinsic character of the limit, not in so far as it is posited by an act which completes it, but in so far as it comes to be posited by the act *in fieri;* by the act, that is, which is always act, a pure act, and which here is the act of limitation. If we could free the limit from the spiritual act, it would rest fixed, but it is not fixed, and is displaced because limit means limitation and is conceivable only through its immanence in the mind's act. This act does not fix the limit once for all, and then cease to act. The unfailing absoluteness of the act implies the immanence of the limitation, and thence the negativity of the limit, the ever positing and at the same time the never being posited of the limit.

It follows that space how vast soever it be is always within the mind, the mind, that is, is superior to it, can look beyond its limits towards remoter limits; and only in so far as every space is contained within a greater space, is the contained space determinate, that is, a representable space. Now infinity is precisely this immanent negation of every spatial limit, which whilst subjecting every spatial reality to limits, overrules or transcends these limits by spiritual activity. Not that there is a space without limit, but that there is no limit which is not negated. It is the mind which always negates and never recognizes the limit, which, in positing it, removes it and thus manifests its own absolute infinity. This absolute infinity, on the other hand, does not imply abstention from all limitation (because limitation, which is its own multiplication in spatiality, is its very life), but only the transcending of every limit and therefore the impossibility of being stopped at any assignable limit however remote. The infinite, in short, is the exclusion of every limit; an exclusion which coincides with the immanent assigning of the limit to the object, in its immediate positivity. Leopardi in his ode *L'Infinito* has very finely expressed that dizziness which comes over the mind when it is withdrawn from all limits not only of the infinite but even of the indefinite. It leads, he shows us, not to the exaltation but to the annihilation of the mind.

> Mirando interminati
> Spazi di là da quella, e sovrumani
> Silenzi, e profondissima quiete
> Io nel pensier mi fingo; ove per poco
> Il cor non si spaura.
> Così tra questa
> Immensità s' annega il pensier mio;
> E il naufragar m' è dolce in questo mare.

(Contemplating the boundless spaces beyond, and superhuman silences and profoundest rest, there in thought I bring myself where the heart has so little to fear. So midst this immensity my thought itself is drowned and even shipwreck is sweet to me in this sea.)

"Thought is drowned," because the one retires from the many (which is never immeasurable but always bounded) and is thereby withdrawn from the essential condition of its own being which is to be actualized as the one in the many.

Infinite in regard to space, the mind is also infinite in regard to time. How can it be otherwise if time is a kind of spatiality? But as spatial infinity is the infinity of what is opposed to space, so temporal infinity is the infinity of what being opposed to temporal reality is withdrawn from time. The want of an exact doctrine of time has rendered impossible in the past a rational doctrine of the infinity of mind in regard to time.

The problem of the immortality of the soul is not an invention of philosophers; and the question of the origin in time of the belief in immortality is a meaningless question if we are thinking, not of the empiricized forms of the mind, but of its essential nature and functions, for these are eternal.

The affirmation of the immortality of the soul is immanent in the affirmation of the soul. For this affirmation is the "I" affirming itself, and it is the simplest, most elementary, and therefore the indispensable act of thinking. The extreme difficulty of describing the essence of this most primitive and truly fundamental reality, and consequently the inadequate conceptions with which for so long the human mind has been in travail, have led to the formulation of many different ways, all inadequate, of understanding the relation which binds the "I" to the object, and the soul to the body and through the body to all which is spatial and which being spatial must also be temporal. These have given rise to various, totally unsatisfactory, modes of conceiving, and even modes of denying, immortality. Yet even negation by the soul of immortality is an affirmation of its own power and value which in a way affirms the immortality it denies.

What is the meaning of immortality? The soul posits itself as "I," and to affirm its being as "I" requires no support of psychological and metaphysical doctrines, for every such doctrine, and indeed every breath of our spiritual life, presupposes such affirmation. But the soul, the "I" which posits itself, in opposing itself to every reality, posits itself as different from all other reality. When, then, it is the natural world with which the soul finds itself confronted, world and soul are not the same thing. As the world is manifold, the soul is joined with its multiplicity. Since this multiplicity is *Nature,* - spatial and temporal, where nothing is its other, in which everything at first is not, then is, and after it has been is not, where everything is born and dies, so the soul comes to be conceived like all the other elements of the manifold as born and destined to die, as sharing in the vicissitudes of all transient things, to whose company it belongs. But the "I" is not only a multiplication, the positing of its other and the opposing of itself to this other, it is also, and primarily, a unity, through which all the co-existents in space are embraced in one single survey in the subject, and all the events in time are compresent in a present which is the negation of time. The "I" dominates space and time. It is opposed to nature, unifying it in itself, passing from one of its terms to another, in space and in time, breaking through and thrusting beyond every limit. The mind cannot marshal its forces amidst the manifold without some glimmering of the fact that it subdues, dominates and triumphs, by withdrawing itself from its laws. It gets a glimpse of this (a glimpse which is essential to it and original) as soon as ever it perceives the *value* of its positing the object and contraposing itself to it, or rather when it perceives that the value of every real affirmation is in its discrimination between the true and the false, without which the mere affirmation as such is unintelligible. If we think at all we must think that what we think of is as it is thought of and not otherwise; that is, we cannot think of anything except as being true in distinction from its contrary of being false. And the true is not relative, as it were an element of a multiplicity in which there are many elements. The true is one, absolute; absolute even in its relativity, for it cannot be except what it is. The element of the manifold has the other elements surrounding itself, but the true, if it is true, is alone. Truth, therefore, cannot be subject to the spatiality and temporality of natural things; it transcends them even in being what must be thought about them. It posits itself as eternal. The eternity of truth implies the eternity of the thought in which truth is revealed. Speculation in pursuing truth may detach from it this eternity, but only in so far as it finds it. So that even when in making a speculative induction the conclusion seems to transcend the eternal nature of truth, it yet presupposes a certain presence of the eternal in mind, and a certain identity of the two terms, thinking and eternal. And this is why, having made truth transcendent we must make mind transcendent, endowing it with the ultramundane, if not premundane, life of the soul. Feeling truth in one's self can only be feeling the eternal in one's self, or feeling that we participate in the eternal, or however otherwise we like to express it.

In its origin and in substance the immortality of the soul has no other meaning. All the grounds upon which faith in immortality has rested, it we set aside reasons prompted by desire to prove its rationality, so often attached to inadequate philosophical concepts, resolve themselves into the affirmation of *the absoluteness of the value of all the affirmations of mind*.

Philosophy of religion and natural religion have placed the immortality of the soul among the constitutive principles of religion itself. But the contrary rather is the truth. If it be true, as Kant thought, that religion *within the limits of reason* leads necessarily to the concept of immortality, it is no less true that there have been religions which have had no explicit doctrine of immortality. Moreover religion within the limits of reason is not religion, but philosophy. Religion, as we shall see later, is the position in which the absolute is taken in its abstractly objective aspect, and this involves the negation of the subject, and leads to mysticism, which is the subject's self-negation of its individuality, and its immediate self-identification with its object. Immortality, on the contrary, is the subject's self-affirmation of its own absolute value. From this it follows that there are certain forms of naturalistic atheism which deny immortality because they deny transcendence in any form, which yet become substantially more positive than some mystical tendencies with regard to the affirmation of the immanent value of the soul, than they would be if they affirmed the concept of immortality. But we shall see further on that religion in its extreme and ideal position is unrealizable; because the very mysticism which is the denial of the value of the subject is the activity of that subject, and therefore the implicit affirmation of its value. Absolute transcendence cannot be affirmed of mind without denying it. God can only be God in so far as he is very man. And so the development of the awareness of this immanent relation of the object with the subject development due to the work of the thought in which philosophical reflexion consists leads on the one hand to the contamination of the purity of religion with the rationality of the subject, and on the other to the commingling and integrating of the eternity of God with the eternity of mind. Thus it is not the concept of God which posits the immortal soul, but the concept of God in so far as it is our concept and therefore a manifestation of the power of our mind. Or we might even say it is the concept of our soul, which in turning to God finds its own concept unknowable except as eternal. It implies immortality. It is therefore the concept of our own immortality, or of the absolute value of our own affirmation, which generates that concept of God with which is bound up the concept of an immortal soul, or rather, the concept of a true and real God who is eternal being.

Whatever we value - our children, our parents, the God in whom we trust, the property we have acquired as the result of our labour, the art and philosophy which is the work of our mind - possesses value to the extent that it triumphs over the limits of our natural life, passes beyond death into immortality. The man who aspires to be united with God, and to rejoin his dead in another world than this world of experience, is united even in this world to those whom he leaves behind, to his heirs to whom he bequeaths the fruit of his labour, and to his successors to whom he commends and trusts the creations of his mind, because his whole personality becomes eternal in what he values as the reality of his own life.

Whatever the particular form which faith in immortality may take, that faith is immanent, because substantially, immortality is the mentality of mind, the spirituality of spirit. It is just that absolute value which is the essential character or every form and of every moment of spiritual activity. All the troublesome puzzles which surround immortality are derived from the mind's projection of its own value into the object, which is the realm of the manifold, the world of space and time. These puzzles, consequently, are mirrored in the embarrassments of those who in every age have travailed with this concept of the absoluteness of value, in giving birth to the scepticism inherent in all the naturalistic and relativistic conceptions of knowing and of acting and of whatever is conceived as spiritual act.

All these puzzles disappear when the problem of immortality is set forth in its own terms. Immortality belongs to mind, and mind is not nature, and precisely for that reason and only for that reason it is not included within the limits of any natural thing, nor of nature generally, which is never a whole. Nature is not infinite either in space or in time. The same reason which, as we saw, proved that it is indefinite in space applies equally to time. It is identical with that in which Kant found his solution of the first of the antinomies. [1] Nature is not temporally infinite but temporally finite; its limits are displaceable; and their essential displaceability implies that time for nature is indefinite. But the indefiniteness of time is the temporal infinity of mind in its unity which remains one even in being multiplied, since multiplicity always supposes unity. To inquire what was at the beginning of nature and what there will be at the end is to propound a meaningless problem, because nature is only conceivable as a given nature, *this nature,* enclosed within certain limits of time, only assignable in so far as they are not absolute and as the mind passes beyond them in the very act of supposing them. But this indefiniteness of nature, in its turn, would not be intelligible were it not an effect of the infinity of mind, which supposes all the limits of time, by passing beyond them and therefore by gathering in itself and reconciling in its own immanent unity all temporal multiplicity.

The conclusion is that if we think of ourselves empirically as in time, we naturalize ourselves and imprison ourselves within definite limits, birth and death, outside of which our personality cannot but seem annihilated. But this personality through which we enter into the world of the manifold and of natural individuals, in the Aristotelian meaning, is rooted in a higher personality, in which alone it is real. This higher personality contains the lower and all other empirical personalities, and as this higher personality is not unfolded in space and time we cannot say that it is before the birth and after the death of the lower, because "before" and "after" applied to it would cause it to fall from the one to the many, and by destroying it as the one we should thereby also destroy the manifold. But this personality is outside every "before and after." Its being is in the eternal, opposed to time, which it makes to be. This eternity, however, does not transcend time in the meaning that it stands outside time as one reality is outside another. Is it not clear, then, that the eternity of mind is the mortality of nature, because what is indefinite from the standpoint of the many is infinite from the stand point of the one? Life, the mind's reality, is in experience (in nature, the experience of which is consciousness). But it lives within nature without being absorbed in it, and without ever itself becoming it; moreover, it always keeps its own infinity or unity, without which even nature with its multiplicity, that is, with space and time, would be dissolved.

The only immortality, then, of which we can think, the only immortality of which we have ever actually thought, when the immortality of mind has been affirmed, is the immortality of the transcendental "I"; not the immortality of the empirical individual "I," in which the mythical philosophical interpretation of this immanent affirmation of mind has been imaginatively entangled. In this way it has come to project multiplicity, and consequently the spatiality and temporality of nature, into the realm of immortality.

Nor does it leave unsatisfied the heart's desire. Only those who fail to place themselves at the standpoint of our idealism will think it does. That standpoint requires that we shall in every case pass from abstract to concrete thought, and so keep ever before us the reality whose indispensable condition it is to be inherent in thought, in thought as present reality, not in thought when we only mean it as an abstract possibility, something distinct from its present activity. But whoever attains this standpoint must take heed. He must, as it were, keep his attention fixed and not divided, one eye on concrete thought in which the multiplicity is the multiplicity of the one and nature therefore is mind, and the other on abstract thought in which the multiplicity is nothing but multiplicity and nature is outside and beyond mind. This is the case of those who protest and assure us that they understand and know the transcendental "I," that unity to which we must refer the world of experience, and who then turn and seek in that world of experience itself the reply to the problems which arise in the depth of their soul, problems, that is to say, which arise precisely in the activity of the transcendental "I."

The heart - for by that name we are accustomed to express the inmost and concrete concerns of our spiritual individuality - does, it is true, demand immortality for the empirical "I," rather than for the transcendental "I." It wants the immortality of our individual being, in its concrete form of a system of particular relations, depending on the positive concreteness of natural individuals. My immortality is the immortality of all which for me has absolute value. My immortality therefore includes, for example, that of my children and my parents, for they with me form a complex multiplicity of individuals. It comes to saying generally that my immortality is only a real concrete thing in the immortality of the manifold.

But, in the first place, we must remember that in so far as I attribute to the manifold, or recognize in it, the value which makes me feel the need of affirming its immortality, I am not myself one of the elements of the manifold, I am the One, the activity which in itself is unmultipliable because it is the principle of the multiplicity. And in the second place, we must remember that the multiplicity which I prize, and in prizing cannot but affirm its immortality, is the multiplicity which has value, the multiplicity which is not abstracted from the activity which posits it, and is not abstractly multiple. It is not a multiplicity, for example, in the sense that I and my child are numerically two and I and my parents are numerically three, for it is a multiplicity actually realized in the present unity of the mind. It is as though the multiplicity, fixed as it is, as we analytically make it, issued forth from the eternal to be flung into the abstract and self-contradictory time, which is chaotic multiplicity: but mind, in so far as it does not fix the multiplicity but lives in it, that is to say, from the immanent standpoint, never abandons the empirical reality to itself. It holds it, reconciles it eternally in itself, eternizes it in its own eternity. We have an example of this immanent eternity whenever, without plunging into idealistic speculation, we have the intuition and affirmation which is the recognition of a work of art, for a work of art is immortal. But how is it immortal? As one among other works of art, chronologically fixed in a series? As a fact? No, clearly not. Its immortality is in the mind which withdraws it from the multiplicity. And the mind withdraws it in understanding and enjoying it, that is, in re-creating it in itself by a creative act. In this way, and in this way alone, the work of art is present reality, reality with neither antecedents nor consequents, unique with the unity which rules time and triumphs over it by the judgment regarding the value of the work itself, a judgment immanent in the creative act. But how if it be not read, if it be not re-created? The supposition itself removes the problem; for we are asking what is meant by the immortality of art, that is, of art as it *is*, and art *is* only in so far as it is known or is *for us*.

Will it not be said, however, that immortality is only of the immortals, and even of these it is not their whole individuality which lives in memory, but only those moments of supreme universal value, which highly privileged souls have known how to live, and deeds such as they have only once in their lives performed? The case of art which we have instanced is no more than an example, but since what is material in it is an intuition of speculative truth to be found in ordinary thought, it may aid us to rise at once to the truth itself in its lull universality. The immortals - the poets, the philosophers, all humanity's heroes - are of the same stuff as all men, and indeed of the same stuff as things. Nothing is remembered and all is remembered. Nothing is immortal if we recognize immortality only by its mark on empirical memory; everything is immortal if memory, by which the real is perpetuated and triumphs over time, means what strictly it only can mean. We have already shown that memory, as the preservation of a past which the mind has mummified and withdrawn from the very series itself of the elements of time, is a myth. In this meaning nothing is remembered, nothing abides or is repeated after having been, and the whole of reality is inexorably clothed, by definition, with the "innumerabilis annorum series et fuga temporum," of which Horace speaks in the well-known ode: [2]

> Exegi monimentum aere perennius
> regalique situ pyramidum altius,
> quod non imber edax, non Aquilo impotens
> possit diruere aut innumerabilis
> annorum series et fuga temporum.
> non omnis moriar multaque pars mei
> vitabit Libitinam: usque ego postera
> crescam laude recens, dum Capitolium
> scandet cum tacita virgine pontifex.
> dicar, qua violens obstrepit Aufidus
> et qua pauper aquae Daunus agrestium
> regnavit populorum, ex humili potens
> princeps Aeolium carmen ad Italos
> deduxisse modos. sume superbiam
> quaesitam meritis et mihi Delphica
> lauro cinge volens, Melpomene, comam.

What escapes the grasp of the goddess Libitina and abides, - a monument more lasting than bronze, - is the song in the poet's imagination, with its eternal value by which it will always rise and live again in the human imagination, not because it is always the same written poem, but because every poem is always a new poem, real in the act of its restoration, in a way which will always be new because always unique. Horace's ode, which we can localize at a particular point in the series of years, is swept away by the "fuga temporum." Horace as the man who was born and died is indeed dead, and his monument rises up in us, in an "us" who, in so far as we are subject and immanent act, are not different from Horace himself. For Horace, besides being an object among the other manifold objects compresent in history as we know it when we read it, is presented to us, not as something different from us, but as our brother and father, even as our very self in its inner transparence, in its self-identity. What is real, then, in memory does not come to us from the past but is created in the eternity of our present, behind which there is no past and in front of which there is no future.

The poet's true eternity, then, is not the poet in so far as he belongs to the manifold, but the poet in so far as he is one with the unity of the transcendental "I," with the immanent principle of every particular experience, in so far, that is to say, as the poet and we ourselves are one. But if this be the meaning of eternity, who or what is not eternal, dissolved in the One that abides? What word is there, though it sound for an instant only in the secrecy of our soul; what grain of sand is there, buried it may be in the ocean depths; what star is there, imagined to exist beyond every possible limit, beyond all astronomical observation; which does not concur with, and which is not concentred in, that One in relation to which all is thinkable? What would our body be, our body as we represent it empirically, could we not think of it as a point around which the whole of a nature which is indefinite gravitates? And what would it be if we detached it in its spatial and temporal multiplicity from the I, from that transcendental energy which posits it and is posited by it? And how could a word sound in our inner being without being a determination of our own soul, and therefore a reality gradually propagating itself, or concentrically resounding in and across our life, in the universal reality, which even empirically represented cannot be thought except as forming one whole system? And who is there who in such an hour has not been or is not a poet and cannot say with Horace, "Exegi monimentum acre perennius"? Nothing which happens can be represented empirically except as flowing, as compresent with the future in the actuality of the present. Understood in the speculative mode of philosophy it means that there is no present poised between the two opposed terms past and future. The present is the eternal, a negation of all time.

The part of us and of those dear to us which dies is a materiality which has never lived. For real materiality is not the simple abstraction from the spiritual act which appears as materiality. When, as in ordinary thought, we have this abstract materiality in mind, we are unconscious of the spirit which gives it life and makes it be. Abstract materiality is not immortal, for the simple reason that it does not exist. The materiality which is a multiplicity of the mind is in the mind; it is in it, and has value just so far as it is its realization. *Its immortality consists in its mortality.* Because the unity of mind is the intelligibility of the multiplicity of nature. And this multiplicity, when not taken in the abstract, is the nature of mind (the manifoldness of the one). It participates, therefore, in its immortality. But it cannot participate in mind's immortality by destroying mind, but by itself being destroyed as nature. It is just this which happens, in virtue, let us clearly understand, not of nature itself which is the externality of the spiritual act, but of the spiritual act which, as we have shown, does not posit the manifold without unifying it in the very act which posits it, and therefore does not give life which is not also death. Were the life of the object posited by the mind not also its death, it would imply the abandonment of the object by the mind itself. Life would be a petrified life, which is absolute death. True life, on the other hand, is made one by death, and therefore the immortality of the manifold (things and men, for men in so far as they are a many are things) is in their eternal mortality.

Is the individual, then, mortal or immortal? The Aristotelian individual, who is the individual in the ordinary meaning, is mortal; that is, its immortality is its mortality, because its reality is within the mind which is immortal. But the individual as spiritual act, the individual individualizing, is immortal. The mind's act as *pure act,* outside which there is nothing which is not an abstraction, is the realm of immortality.

If a man were not this act and did not feel, however obscurely, in his very being that he is immortal, he could not live, because he could not escape that absolute practical scepticism which is not simply an attempt not to think (which the theoretical or abstract scepticism, that so often has made inroads on the human soul, has always been), but the effective arrest of thought, of the thought by which alone we can perceive truth in the world of the eternal. Can we be and not think, if being is essentially thinking or rather thinking itself? The energy which sustains life is precisely the consciousness of the divine and eternal, so that we always look down on the death and vanishing of everything perishable from the height of the immortal life.

[1] The first antinomy said in the thesis, "The world in time has a beginning and as regards space is enclosed within certain limits"; and in the antithesis, "The world has neither beginning in time, nor limits in space, but is infinite in regard to time as in regard to space."
[2] Horace, *Odes,* iii. 30.

Chapter Eleven - Causality, Mechanism and Contingency

Our doctrine of time and space has brought us back to the concept with which we started of the infinite and unmultipliable unity of mind. As positive the individual is posited in a spatial multiplicity which is also temporal, but without ever destroying the mind's unity, or ever being able to transcend it. From the womb of space we have seen infinite mind reborn, and from the womb of time immortal mind.

And now some one may object. You tell us that the past of time and the spatial form of nature are annulled in the unity of the spiritual act; and yet you say that the past is confluent in the present. The present, then, is conditioned by the past, without which accordingly it cannot be conceived. And you say also that the multiplicity of coexistents is made one and reconciled in the unity of the spiritual act. Even the act, then, is conditioned by the multiplicity of the co existents. And even if both these multiplicities be a production of the mind it is no less true that their ultimate unification, and in this the development of mind consists, is conditioned by the antecedents. These antecedents cannot be thought to be immediately identical with the consequent unity."

Here too we might very easily dispose of the objection by referring to what we had said on the inconsistency of the manifold in its abstract opposition to unity, and simply call attention to the principle that the condition is not to be conceived abstractly as separated from the conditionate and standing by itself, limiting as it were the conditionate itself. Our rejoinder would in truth miss its effect if we did not in this case also submit to a strict examination the concept of *condition* on which not only empiricism but also transcendentalism rely as their second plank of safety. These two modes of philosophizing are, as we know, much more akin than is commonly supposed.

"Condition" may have two quite different meanings. It may mean what is simply *necessary* or it may mean what is *necessary* and *sufficient*. The necessary condition of a real thing (real in the metaphysical and in the empirical sense) is another real thing, the realization of which makes the realization of the first possible. The sufficient condition of a real thing is another real thing, realization of which makes its realization necessary and infallible. In the first case the conditionate cannot be thought without at the same time thinking its condition, but the condition can be thought without thinking the conditionate. In the second case an absolute relation holds between condition and conditionate, and neither can be thought without the other.

The absolute character of the relation between the two terms, and the necessity that the conditionate follow the condition, are the constitutive elements of the *metaphysical* concept of cause. We can in fact define cause as the real thing whose realization renders necessary the realization of another real thing. This causality has been called metaphysical from the necessity of the relation which it posits between condition and conditionate, cause and effect. It is a necessity which cannot be learnt by experience, for if experience bears witness to relations at all, it is only to contingent relations of facts. It is an *a priori* necessity, only knowable *a priori* by analysis of concepts. For this reason in the metaphysics of Descartes and Spinoza it is reduced to mere logical deduction based on the principle of identity.

But the strictly metaphysical character of such a causality lies deeper. It lies in a principle of which the necessity of the relation between cause and effect is a consequence. It needs a very clear exposition because the prevalence of empiricism as a result of the writings of Locke and Hume, and the insinuation of it into meta physics in the works of Geulincx, Malebranche, and even of Leibniz, led in modern philosophy to the supersession of the concept of metaphysical causality. Metaphysics is a conception of the unity underlying the multiplicity of experience (meaning by experience, , what may be thought). The "water" of Thales is a metaphysical reality, in so far as it has in itself the possibility of all the forms displayed by nature to sensible observation and is the principle of them. The "being" of Parmenides is metaphysical, for it is the unity to which thought reduces all things by willing to think them. Plato's "idea" is metaphysical in so far as it unites in itself the dispersed and flowing being in the many and transient objects of space and time. Empiricism is the intuition of the real which sets its face towards the multiplicity; metaphysics is the intuition of the real which sets its face towards the unity. Causality, the necessary relation between two terms of thought, must, from the metaphysical stand point, be conceived in the light of the unity, or rather by means of a unity, which lies at the base of the duality. How can the reciprocal necessity of conceiving the one term together with the other, by which the realization of the effect is presented as the necessary realization of the cause, be itself conceived, unless the duality of the two terms is reconciled in a fundamental unity? Now so long as the condition is necessary to the conditionate but not the conditionate to the condition, there is lacking that absolute relation which we have already had occasion to expound as having its roots in the unity. But when the concept of the condition is such that we cannot conceive the condition without conceiving the conditionate, or rather such that the essence of the condition implies the essence of the conditionate, then the two concepts are no longer two, they are merged in one single concept. The pantheistic concept of the world, for example, is the concept of God and the concept of the world bound together or fused into one single concept, so that to conceive God is the same as to conceive the world.

Necessity is the identity of the necessary term with the term for which it is necessary. In the case of the necessary and sufficient condition, the cause is necessary for the effect, the effect is necessary for the cause, and therefore the effect is identical with the cause and *vice versa*. On the other hand, in the case of the necessary and non-sufficient condition the conditionate is not identical with the condition because it is not necessary for it, but the condition is identical with the conditionate because the conditionate is impossible without the condition. In so far as there is necessity there is identity, and only when the relation of necessity is not reciprocal is the identity not whole and perfect. In the conditionate, therefore, besides the identity with the condition there is required the difference. Thus the theistic theory of creation makes the concept of God independent of the concept of the world, but not the concept of the world independent of that of God. God, in this theory, is the necessary but not the sufficient condition of the world, because though there were no world there could be God. But, on the other hand, in so far as there could be no world without God, God is in the world. Therefore, God is identical with the world without the world being identical with God. Besides the being of God the world must, in fact, contain the nonbeing of God, that which is excluded from the divine essence. Were the world being, and nothing else but being, it would be identical with God and therefore indistinguishable from him. Such at least is the out come of theistic dualism, which makes God necessary and the world contingent. In the same way psycho-physical dualism, when it would explain sensation, assumes movement to be the necessary but not the sufficient condition of sensation. This clearly implies a difference between movement and sensation; but also it implies an identity, not indeed of the soul with the body, but of the body with the soul, because had the soul no body it could not even be a term of physical movement. [1]

The passage from the necessary and sufficient condition to the simply necessary condition introduces an empirical element into the metaphysical intuition, and this empirical element always characterizes the case of the intuition of necessary and non-sufficient condition. The empirical element is statement of fact and affirmation of simple contingency, of a positive datum of experience. Necessity, in fact, has to disappear in order that the empiricist conception, which admits no identity in the real but only an absolute multiplicity, may set itself up in all the force of its logic. In the absolute manifoldness of the real, the unity of identity, according to the empirical principle, can only be an intrusion of the subject, extraneous to the immediate reality. For the concept of *metaphysical causality* there is substituted, therefore, the concept of *empirical causality*. It received precise form in Hume, but it existed before, however obscurely, in Vico's sceptical doctrine of the knowledge of nature, expounded in the *De antiquissima Italorum sapientia*. [2] Ordinarily, the empirical concept of cause is distinguished from the metaphysical concept by this difference, that the metaphysical is the concept of efficient cause, the empirical the concept of simple succession. [3] But the efficiency of the cause is an obscure idea, which when cleared up is shown to be the unity or identity of the cause with the effect; because the efficient cause is that which is conceived as necessary and sufficient, that is, as a reality whose realization is a realization of the reality of which it is the condition. This reality of the conditionate issuing from the essential reality of its condition (which is nothing else but the impossibility of conceiving the process of the condition otherwise than as expanding into the conditionate) is the efficiency of the causality. This is too obvious to be missed in the intellectualistic and abstractly rationalistic position of a metaphysic such as Spinoza's, which claims to construct the real world - an object of the mind, though how or why we know not - on the basis of the substance, *causa sui,* whose essence implies its existence. It must therefore say axiomatically, *ex data causa determinata necessario sequitur effectus,* since everything is reduced finally to a conceptual relation and *effectus cognitio a cognitione causae dependet et eandem involvit.* [4] The efficiency is a logical deduction which implies and supposes identity and adds nothing to the identity. And empiricism rending the network of concepts which the metaphysical intellect weaves around itself, and bent on breaking through to the immediate reality, can meet nothing but absolute multiplicity. When for the logical relation of necessity it substitutes the chronological relation of the succession of antecedent and consequent, it can do so only because it has no consciousness of the unity, which is all the while present in the simple relation of time, which implies a subjective elaboration of the presupposed sensible material. Should it become conscious of the subjective unity in the true relation, the causal chain in the pure multiplicity would be broken and empiricism would lose every criterion and every means of making the real intelligible. But empiricism remains, in its unconsciousness of the subjectivity of time, the extreme limit to which it is possible to push the empirical conception of the relation of condition and conditionate, and the last support on which the negation of unity can lean.

Between efficient or metaphysical causality and empirical causality there stands, then, the concept of a necessary and non-sufficient condition, a hybrid scheme of the intelligibility, or sufficient rather of the unification, of the real, half metaphysical, half empirical. A two-faced Janus which from without, from the effect to the cause, looks metaphysically at the unity and at the necessity, and from within, from the cause to the effect, looks empirically at the difference and at the fact. It is a self-contradictory concept. On its metaphysical side it affirms empiricism, and on its empirical side, metaphysical rationality. For when working back from effect to cause it sees the necessity of the cause, that necessity implies not only an identity of the cause with the effect but also of the effect with the cause: or rather, it is that absolute identity for which the cause is not only the necessary but also the sufficient condition. *Vice versa,* when working from the cause to the effect it sees the contingency of the effect, the contingency means diversity, and there cannot be diversity of the effect from the cause without there also being diversity of the cause from the effect. And it is impossible to get rid of the dilemma by refusing to choose either of the two ways, from the effect to the cause or from the cause to the effect, because if we should affirm the unity and identity of the two, and, in short, consider that there is no difference between the relation of cause to effect and that of effect to cause, then clearly we restore entirely the meta physical character of the condition as not only necessary but sufficient.

There is another compromise between metaphysics and empiricism one which has played an important part in the history of philosophy from the promise of beginning of the modern era, the concept of occasional causes, which we owe mainly to Geulincx (1627-69) and to Malebranche (1638-1715). These philosophers sought by it to cut the Gordian knot of psychophysical causality, in the Cartesian doctrine of the two substances, soul and body. Occasionalism denied that physical movement can be the efficient cause of ideas, or ideas the efficient cause of physical movement. The parallelism between them was explained as an agreement between soul and body depending on God. It was analogous to that which we may see between two clocks constructed by the same artificer, an agreement brought about, not through the action of one on another, but through their common dependence on the clockmaker's skill. [5] The occasional cause, when we reflect on it, is not a cause at all, except in so far as we transcend it and pass from it to God, in whom is the real principle of its causality, through the relation which it always implies between movement and sensation. And when Leibniz extended occasionalism, giving it a profounder meaning and making its anthropomorphic bond between the physical and psychical substances the type of the universal relations of all substances or monads, it became in the system of the pre-established harmony the concept of the reciprocal unrelatedness of the monads in their common dependence on God. But through God the occasional cause necessarily conditions its correlative term, although, on the other hand, such condition may be non-sufficient, and for this reason occasionalism can retain a certain metaphysical value, and need not end once and for all in empiricism. That is, the occasion and the occasionate in themselves, the one in opposition to the other, are a mere contingent concomitance, actually like the succession to which the empiricist reduces causality. But the occasion is an occasion in so far as we do not think of it only in itself and in respect of the occasionate, but in relation to God who makes one term the occasion, the other the occasionate. And when this system of "occasion = God = occasionate" is constituted, then the reciprocal relation of the two extreme terms participates in the necessity of the relation between God and the occasion, no less than between God and the occasionate. The relation is that of a necessary but non-sufficient condition. Whence the occasion becomes a necessary and non-sufficient condition of the occasionate, and inversely this of that, even obliging us to think of each of the two terms, the one either as the occasion of the other or as occasioned by the other.

So that the characteristic of occasionalism is to unfold the relation of necessary and non-sufficient condition by duplicating it, in so far as between the occasion or the occasionate the conditioning is reciprocal. Through this duplication the relative contingency of the effect in regard to the cause, in its character of necessary and non-sufficient condition, can be turned into the relative contingency of the cause in regard to the effect. And therefore the empiricism of the occasionalists is more accentuated than that to which we have called attention in the system of the simply necessary and nonsufficient condition, since with the double contingency the multiplicity appears actually loosened from every chain of metaphysical unity.

I say appears, because the so-called duplication, if on the one hand it duplicates and confirms the contingency, on the other it duplicates and strengthens the necessity of the cause in regard to the effect. The body necessarily supposes God who creates the soul, and the soul necessarily supposes God who creates the body. And in the system of the monadology every monad supposes God, the creator of all the monads, and therefore supposes all the other monads. In such reciprocity of conditioning between occasion and occasionate, the relative necessity of the cause in regard to the effect becomes reciprocal relative necessity, or rather it becomes necessity which excludes all contingence and therefore all empirical multiplicity.

Between the unity, then, of metaphysics and the multiplicity of empiricism all attempts to fix a relation of condition and conditionate, as a relation which mediates between unity and multiplicity, are destined to fail.

Setting aside the possibility of stopping at an inter mediate point between the metaphysics of efficient causality and the empiricism of causality intended as simple contingent concomitance, is it perhaps possible to stop at the concept of metaphysical causality or at its extreme opposite, that of empirical causality?

It is obvious that the concept of metaphysical causality as necessary and sufficient condition is absurd. The concept of condition implies the duality of condition and conditionate, it implies therefore the possibility of conceiving each of the two terms without the other, yet this possibility is negated by the concept of metaphysical causality, which is an *a priori* relation, and implies the unity and identity of the two terms. To use the word causality, therefore, in the metaphysical meaning, if we would give an exact account of what we have in mind, is to mean what has no meaning.

We are left with empirical causality. Let us not insist now that, whilst all causality implies a relation, empiricism excludes every relation by postulating a multiple reality of things unrelated. Let us even admit the hypothesis that there may be such a manifold and that causality may take place in it. Let us simply inquire whether on the basis of pure atomism it may nevertheless be possible to maintain the concept of causality as plain empirical causality. Atomism is always finding itself at the cross roads. It has either to maintain rigidly the original and absolute multiplicity of the unrelated, and in that case it must give up the attempt to explain the phenomenon which it has resolved into the unrelated atoms; or it has to explain the phenomenon by making it fulfil effectively for the atoms the purpose for which they are destined, by the principle of the reality given in experience. Now to do this it must endow the atoms with a property which renders possible a change in their primitive state, that is, in their state of unrelatedness and absolute multiplicity, in order to bring about their meeting and clash. Movement (the effect of weight) as a property of the atoms is already a negation of their absolute unrelatedness, because we can only speak of movement in terms of the relation of one thing to another, and movement itself, as Epicurus remarked, must be different in the different atoms (through the differences which the new relations and correlation imply) if by means of movement the atoms are to be aggregated and so generate the phenomenal things. For if all the atoms move in the same manner, and in the same direction, and with the same velocity, it is clear that their meeting is for ever impossible, and the atomic hypothesis is useless.

Atomism, therefore, has always of necessity been mechanism, one of the most coherent logical forms of the conception of reality, conceived as a presupposition of mind. Mechanism in resolving all reality into matter and force (atoms and movement) starts with the postulate that nothing of this reality can be lost and nothing can be added to it. Qualitatively and quantitatively, therefore, being is immutable, and all change is no more than an alteration of the disposition in the distribution of the elements of the whole. The intelligibility of the new is a perfect mathematical equation of the new with its antecedents. The sum of matter and force at the moment n is equal to the sum of matter and force at the moment $n - 1$, and also to that at the moment $n + 1$.

Whether it resolves force into matter with the old materialism, which saw in movement the external manifestation of the intrinsic property of epistemology matter; or whether with the chemists and physicists to-day, who think they have got away from materialism because they no longer speak about matter, it resolves matter into force or energy; mechanism, apart from any imaginative representation of the atom and of movement, consists in the conception of absolutely manifold being, the result of elementary units. These units can be variously added up, but always give the same result, so that the possibility of a novelty which is not merely apparent, and of a creation which is really new existence, is absolutely excluded. In its particular application it is clear that in mechanism a relation of condition to conditionate is only thinkable as empirical causality. If a ball struck by another ball moves, mere empiricism must be limited to the discovery that the ball after having been struck had moved, without supposing any other relation between the antecedent stroke and the movement which followed it. And this, indeed, is the assumption of empiricism when it insists on what it would have us understand is the true character of causality. But empiricism, when from the particular it passes to the universal and has to make its own metaphysics of reality, in order to enable it to explain the particular itself according to its own scheme of intelligibility, and thereby make credible the mechanism according to which there cannot be a movement which had not a previous movement to account for it, cannot observe the temporal contiguity of the movement of the ball with the stroke received by it without thinking that the movement of the struck ball is one and the same with the movement of the striking ball, the one communicating to the other just as much as it loses itself. And lo and behold, the duality of the facts of experience is resolved into a unique fact, whereby in a whole the new is equalized with the old. And when empirical causality wants to affirm concomitance between phenomena, and, in general, multiplicity without unity, what it comes to is that by empiricizing the causality it attains to mechanism, or rather to the crudest form of metaphysical monism it is possible to conceive.

Against the mechanism necessarily prevalent in modern science since Descartes, Galileo and Bacon, there has arisen in the latter part of the last century in France a philosophy, the leading concept of which has been termed *con-

tingency, famous for its vigorous vindication of freedom. Modern science, following Bacon, has pronounced itself empirical, and even if, following Galileo and Descartes, it has been mathematical, it has always been conceived with the logic of empiricism. Reality for it is a presupposition of thought, and self-identical in its already perfect realization. The new philosophy of contingency, conscious of the freedom of the mind in its various manifestations, has opposed to the concept of a reality always self-identical that of a reality always diverse from itself. [7] Contingency is, in fact, an attempt to conceive freedom by denying the unity or identity in which mechanistic empiricism ends, without, on the other hand, abandoning the concept of conditioned reality, that is, of that multiple reality which is empirically given.

In order to understand the starting-point of the philosophy of contingency, let us begin by quoting the first page of Boutroux's thesis on *The Contingency of the Laws of Nature.*

"By what sign do we recognize that a thing is necessary? What is the criterion of necessity? If we try to define the concept of an absolute necessity we are led to eliminate from it every relation which subordinates the existence of one thing to that of another as to its condition. Accordingly, absolute necessity excludes all synthetic multiplicity, all possibility of things or of laws. There is no place, then, in which we could look for it if it reigns in the given world, for that is essentially a multiplicity of things depending more or less one on another. The problem we have to deal with is really this: By what sign do we recognize relative necessity, that is to say, the existence of a necessary relation between two things? The most perfect type of necessary connexion is the syllogism, in which a particular proposition is proved as the consequence of a general proposition, because it is contained in it, and so was implicitly affirmed at the moment the general proposition itself was affirmed. The syllogism, in fact, is only the demonstration of an analytical relation existing between the genus and the species, the whole and the part. So that where there is an analytical relation, there is a necessary connexion. But this connexion, in itself, is purely formal. If the general proposition is contingent, the particular proposition which is deduced from it is, at least as such, equally and necessarily contingent. We cannot reach, by the syllogism, the demonstration of a real necessity unless all the conclusions are attached to a major premise necessary in itself. Is this operation compatible with the conditions of analysis? From the analytical standpoint the only proposition which is entirely necessary in itself is that which has for its formula $A = A$. Every proposition in which the attribute differs from the subject, and this is the case even when one of the terms results from the decomposition of the other, leaves a synthetic relation subsisting as the obverse of the analytic relation. Can the syllogism reduce synthetically analytic propositions to purely analytic propositions?" [7]

Starting from this principle it is not difficult to argue that the necessity arising from absolute identity is not to be found in any proposition and tingencyor is not in the syllogism. So that if necessity. mechanics is mathematically conceivable, physics is no longer simple mechanics, and biology is not physics, and neither is biology psychology, nor psychology sociology; and in short, whenever science with its mechanical interpretations is forced to bring a new order of phenomena into line with another, it lets the difference between the one order and the other escape. Therefore, while remaining within the limits of simple experience, the world cannot but appear a hierarchy of different worlds each of which has something irreducible to what is found in the antecedent. The world, then, is not necessary if necessity mean necessary relation, and if necessary relation mean identity.

To begin with *being*. In its greatest universality and abstractness, can we say that it is necessary? Can we deduce the existence of *being* analytically from its possibility, just as from the premises of a syllogism we deduce the conclusions? "In one sense no doubt there is no more in being than in the possible, since whatever is was possible before it existed. The possible is the matter whose being is fact. But being when thus reduced to the possible remains purely ideal, and to obtain real being we must admit a new element. In themselves, indeed, all the possibles make an equal claim to being, and in this meaning there is no reason why one possible should be realized rather than another. No fact is possible without its contrary being equally possible. If then the possible is given over to itself, everything will be eternally floating between being and non-being, nothing will pass from potentiality to actuality. So far, then, from the possible containing being, it is being which contains the possible and something besides: the realization of one contrary in preference to the other, actuality properly so called. Being is the synthesis of these two terms, and the synthesis is irreducible." [8] And this is the contingency of being. If being is contingent, everything is radically contingent, inasmuch as it is being. And if from the abstractness of being we rise gradually to the greater concreteness of the reality presented in experience, we see the range of necessity becoming ever more restricted, that of contingency growing ever larger, and thereby making ever wider way for that freedom, which in the mechanical and mathematical conception of the world is absurd.

It is evident then that the philosophy of contingency is an empiricism incomparably more empirical than the naturalistic and positive mechanism of the ordinary empiricism. Should it mechanism of succeed in making freedom, or a possibility of freedom, spring up within nature, which for empiricism alone is real, we should be able to say that it had conquered empiricism with its own weapons. Contingency, in fact, does no more than affirm the reality of the differences or rather of the multiplicity of the real. In it *a, b, c, d,* do indeed constitute a system, but *a* is not *b*, nor *c*, nor *d*. To make each term the conditionate of the preceding term and the condition of the following term is not to make the preceding term originate the following term because between the one and the other there is no equivalence such as there is between a and a.

Suppose there were such equivalence and that $b = a$, as mechanism requires, the relation between b and a would then be necessary, as necessary as the relation of a with a, and representable in a purely analytical judgment. But if we suppose only a given, by making abstraction from the multiplicity and from every external relation, then it is only a in itself which is absolutely necessary. So if b is not identical with a, it is different; and in so far as it is different and irreducible the juxtaposition of a and b can never give rise to an analytical relation. (Strictly, it could not give rise to any relation whatever, because, as we know, relation is already identity.) It cannot give place to it because $a = a$ and $b = b$. No term is contingent in regard to another (that is, relatively not necessarily) except on condition that it is absolutely necessary in regard to itself. And all the terms one by one are only contingent relatively to points of view external to their definite and particular essence, whereas, considered absolutely, they are completely necessary. But the necessity which clothes them is only that which mechanism affirms, except that, instead of being monochrome, it is many-coloured like a harlequin's dress.

"Being" is not deducible from "possible." The proposition is self-evident, - but why? Because being is being, and the possible is possible, shorn of the realization of itself which is purely the exclusion of its contrary. But if behind the realized being which is not the possible, we know not how to think any other than this possible, *toto caelo* different, it is clear that being is thinkable only in so far as it is thought as immediate; not as realizing itself but as a reality already established. As such it is self-identical, immutable, in such wise that self-identical must not even mean identical with itself, since even identity is a relation of self with self. And with one term only which can have no other confronting it, even though that other be only itself unfolded and contraposed to itself (and this is precisely the spiritual relation, the basis of every other relation), there is no possibility of relation. [9] And even when we come to the perfection of being in man and mind, and recognize that "the human person has an existence of its own, is to itself its own world; that more than other beings it can act without being forced to make its acts enter into a system which transcends it; and that the general law of the conservation of psychical energy breaks up into a multitude of distinct laws each of which belongs to each individual"; that moreover, "for one and the same individual the law is subdivided again and turned into detailed laws belonging to each different phase of psychical life, and the law tends to approximate to the fact...and the individual having, from being alone, become the whole kind to which the law applies, is master of it"; [10] it still remains true that the individual in his concrete individuality is what he is, just what "being" is in regard to "possible," what life is in regard to physical and chemical forces, what psychological fact is in regard to physiological fact; in short, what every reality is in regard to that with which experience compares it: not contingent except relatively, in itself absolutely necessary. Nothing behind the individual in his positive concreteness can be considered as his principle, since, whatever can be thought as distinct from him is another with which he has no necessary relation. And, consequently, he is thinkable just in so far as he is and not as that self which is not and is to be, which makes itself what it ought to be rather than what it ought not to be, in which freedom really consists.

The philosophy of contingency, in short, by accepting the purely naturalistic standpoint of empiricism, may seem to make freedom possible by insisting on the differences which mechanism cancels. In reality it does no more than smash the compact nature of the mechanist, keeping the inert materiality and the qualitative, abstractly conceived, identity which is the fundamental law of the unity of nature to which mechanism has regard. And if this be true, the philosophy of contingency falls back into the mechanical intuition of the reality which is the characteristic of empiricism. Its contingency has no value which is different from that of the concept of empirical cause, and it lands it in the same absurdity as that which we have exposed in that concept.

Neither metaphysical causality nor empirical causality, neither occasionalism nor contingency, are successful, then, in overcoming the unsurmountable difficulties which arise from the concepts of condition and conditionate.

[1] The other identity, that of soul with body, is required, when this psychophysical psychology, in its theory of volitional process, comes to expound the will as a principle of external movement, for it makes the will a necessary but not a sufficient condition of the movement.
[2] See Gentile, *Studi vichiani,* Messina, 1915, pp. 101 ff.
[3] It is sometimes thought necessary to say *invariable* succession. But the invariability is either assumed as fact (the not varying) and the adjective is then a simple pleonasm, or it is assumed as a law of the succession, and then there is an end of the empirical character of empirical causality, which moreover can be nothing more than simple succession.
[4] *Eth*. i. axioms 3 and 4.
[5] "Imagine two clocks or watches which agree perfectly. Now, this may take place in *three ways*. The *first* consists in a mutual influence; the *second* is to have a skilful workman attached to them who regulates them and keeps them always in accord; the *third* is to construct these two clocks with so much art and accuracy as to assure their future harmony. Put now the soul and body in place of these two clocks; their accordance may be brought about by one of these three ways. The way of influence is that of common philosophy, but as we can not conceive of material particles which may pass from one of these substances into the other this view must be abandoned. The way of the continual assistance of the creator is that of the system of occasional causes; but I hold that this is to make a *deus ex machina* intervene in a natural and ordinary matter, in which, according to reason, he ought not to co operate except in the way in which he does in all other natural things. Thus there remains only my hypothesis: that is, the way of harmony. From the beginning God had made each of these two substances of such a nature that merely by following its own peculiar laws, received with its being it, nevertheless accords with the other, just as if there were a mutual influence or as if God always put his hand thereto in addition to his general cooperation" (Philo-

sophical Works of Leibniz, G. M. Duncan's translation, chap. xv.). (Compare also the *Troisième Éclaircissement* and the *Système nouveau*, Erdmann, p. 127.) We may remark that the comparison of the two clocks is not Leibniz's own invention, for we find it being commonly cited by the Cartesians as a scholastic illustration (v. Descartes, *Passions de l'âme*, i, 5, 6, and L. Stein in *Archiv für Geschichte der Philosophie*, i. 59). We may remark, too, that Leibniz's distinction between occasionalism and his system of the pre-established harmony has no great speculative importance 5 for it is easy to see that to dispense with the work of God from the different moments of the process of reality after it has been set going does not eliminate the speculative difficulty of the miraculous character of God's extrinsic inter vention. Without this intervention causality remains just as unintelligible as the harmony, which is already affirmed in occasionalism, and which Leibniz cannot help extending to his pluralism.

Geulincx, also (*Ethica*, i. sect. ii. § 2), explains the agreement of the two substances, soul and body, as that of two clocks: "Idque absque ulla causalitate qua alterum hoc in altero causat, sed propter meram dependentiam, qua utrumque ab eadem arte et simili industria constitutum est." The body therefore does not think nor make think ("haec nostra corpora non cogitant, licet nobis occasionem praebeant cogitandi"). But bodies not only do not think, they do not act, they do not move of themselves, for the only mover is God. This most important doctrine was taught by Geulincx in his *Metaphysica* (published in 1691): "Sunt quidam modi cogitandi in me, qui a me non dependent, quos ego ipse in me non excito; excitantur igitur in me ab aliquo alio (impossibile enim est ut a nihilo mihi obveniant). At alius, quicumque sit, conscius esse debet hujus negotii; facit enim, et impossibile est, ut is faciat, qui nescit quomodo fiat. Est hoc principium evidentissimum per se, sed per accidens et propter praejudicia mea et ante coeptas opiniones redditum est nonnihil obscurius; jamdudum enim persuasum habeo, res aliquas, quas brutas esse et omni cogitatione destitutas agnoscebam, aliquid operari et agere. Existimavi v. gr. ignem, quod ad ejus praesentiam sensum in me caloris produceretur, calefacere; et hoc calefacere sic interpretabar, ac si esset calorem facere. Similiter solem illuminare, juxta similem interpretationem, lumen efficere, lapides cadere, ut interpretabar, se ipsos praecipites dare, et motum ilium efficere, quo deorsum ruant; ignem tamen, solem, lapidesque brutos esse, sine sensu, sine cognitione haec omnia operari existimabam. Sed cum intellectual intendo in evidentiam hujus principii: *Quod nescis quomodo fiat, id non facis,* non possum non videre, me falsum fuisse, et mirari mihi subit, cum satis clare agnoscam, me id non facere, quod nescio quomodo fiat, cur de aliis aliquibus rebus aliam persuasionem habeam. Et qui mihi dico, me calorem non facere, me lumen et motum in praeceps non efficere, quia nescio quomodo fiant, cur non similiter, igni, soli, lapidi idem illud improperem, cum persuasum habeam ea nescire quo modo effectus fiant, et omni cognitione destitui?" (*Opera philosophica*, edition Land, ii. 150). It is remarkable that in this passage the negation of efficient causality (*operari et agere*) is connected with the empiricist opposition between subject and object affirmed in the principle indicated by Geulincx and so nearly resembling the principle of Vico: *Verum et factum convertuntur.* This in its turn is closely connected with a sceptical theory of the knowledge of nature, analogous, as I have already pointed out, to that of Hume.

That occasionalism and the pre-established harmony both arise from the need of maintaining the unity of the manifold is evident in the proposition which is one of the earliest accounts Leibniz has given of the doctrine (in 1677, in a note to a letter of Eckhard): "Harmonia est unitas in multitudine ut si vibrationes duorum pendulorum inter se ad quintum quemlibet ictum consentiant" (*Philosophische Schriften,* edition Gerhardt, i. 232). For the genesis and the ancient and medieval precursors of occasionalism consult Zeller, *Kleine Schriften,* i. p. 316 n., and two writings of Stein, *loc. cit.* i. 53 and ii. 193.

[6] There are several indications of this doctrine in Lachelier, but it was first definitely formulated by Emile Boutroux in *De La contingence des lots de la nature,* published in 1874, republished in 1895, and in many subsequent editions.
[7] *Op. cit.* pp. 7-8.
[8] Op. cit. pp. 15-16.
[9] Compare my *Sistema di Logica,* i. pp. 152-5, 175 *et seq.*
[10] Boutroux, *op. cit.* p. 130.

Chapter Twelve - Freedom and Prevision

The philosophy of contingency does not rise above the position which Hume reached when he denied the objective value of causality by emphasizing the difference between cause and contingency effect, condition and conditionate, thus bringing into relief the uniqueness of every fact as such. Hume's position, the position to which natural science has now been brought and cannot get past, is that of strict empiricism. As we have already shown, empiricism regards reality as the antecedent of immediate experience, and sup poses that this reality is in itself manifold, and only unified phenomenally in the ideal connexions which the subject in one way or another forms of it in elaborating experience.

The real, the antecedent of immediate experience itself, is the *fact,* and empiricism is confident it does not transcend it. This fact, in its bed-rock position, is the absolute necessity which the theory of contingency considers is at once got rid of when we leave the scientific point of view; yet there it stands as fact, the fundamental postulate, we may say, of contingency. Whether nature, this world of experience, be taken in its complexity, or whether it be taken in each of its elements, it is fact: fact which being already accomplished is bound by the iron law of the past, and *infectum fieri nequit;* fact of which the Greek tragedian said:

μόνον γὰρ αὐτοῦ καὶ θεὸς στερίσκεται,
ἀγένητα ποιεῖν ἄσσ' ἂν ᾖ πεπραγμένα. [1]

(Of this alone even God is deprived, to make what has been done not to have been.)

Fact precisely is that absolute identity of being with itself which excludes from being even the possibility of reflecting on itself and affirming its own identity. It is natural, unmediated, identity.

The necessity which characterizes fact, which is the extreme opposite of freedom, is a concept common to empiricism and to contingency, if we keep to the real meaning of the so-called natural laws with which empiricism, apparently in contradiction of its own principle, invests the natural event and appears so far to differentiate itself from contingency. Contingency conceives reality to be a continual creation, or rather to be something new continually taking place which is different from its antecedents, whereas scientific empiricism, which mechanizes nature, in formulating laws by which nature becomes knowable, denies the differences and conceives the future as a repetition of the past, and says therefore, with Auguste Comte, that knowing is foreseeing. It is true that in recent criticism of the epistemology of the sciences, the objective value of natural laws, as concepts of classes of phenomena, has been denied, and thereby the foundation on which the concept of the foreseeability of the future rests has been shaken. But it is also true that this criticism does not in the least prevent the empirical sciences from formulating laws and foreseeing, so far as it is foreseeable, the future. Nor, as we have seen, can we accept the merely economical interpretation of such logical processes, on which, without exception, science would insist.

The problem which such criticism has sought to solve, is wrongly formulated. The law cannot be thought, nor do we in fact think it, natural in separation from the fact of which it is the law, and which would include the fact by imposing on it a necessity extrinsic to its own being. Empiricism has never acquired a clear consciousness of its own logic. It has been said that its logic depends on the postulate of the uniformity of nature. Galileo, one of the most sagacious inquirers into the logical foundation of the sciences, used to say that nature is "inexorable and immutable and caring nothing whether its recondite reasons and modes of working are or are not open to human capacity; because it never transgresses the limits of the laws imposed upon it": [2] a sure confidence which yet did not prevent him disputing the supposed immutability of the celestial substance, which the Aristotelians held to be free from the continuous vicissitude of the generation and corruption which belong to natural things, the objects of our experience on earth. With clear insight he remarked that the life both of the body and of the soul consists in change, without which we should be as though we had "met a Medusa's head which had turned us into marble or adamant." [3] Immutability, then, is continual change, the one does not contradict the other. Natural law is not the negation of change (as Plato thought, and Aristotle after him, with the consequent immutability of their heavens, from the forms of which [ideas, laws] the norm of terrestrial nature must come) but the negation of the mutability of the change. Change is fact, and if it is fact, it is immutable. It is fact, since we propose to know it; and there it is ready for us, and nothing caring, as Galileo said, that the reasons and modes for and by which it has come to pass should be open to our capacity. That is to say, it confronts us, not posited by us, and therefore is independent of us.

Now the distinction between the two moments, past and future, by which we are able to speak of "foreseeing," does not imply that foreseeing is a different act from simple knowing and added to it. We foresee in so far as we know, because in the very past of the fact which stands before us as accomplished fact the future is present. A fact is immutable when it is such that thought cannot think it as not yet accomplished but in course of accomplishment (for then it would not be *factum* but *fieri*). The future, indeed, is foreseen, but only in so far as it is present in the object as we empirically conceive it; it exists not as what is not yet and will be, but as what is already (the past). Marvellous in their insight, therefore, are Manzoni's words:

> E degli anni ancor non nati
> Daniel si ricordò. [4]
> (And Daniel remembered the years not yet born.)

In astronomy we have the typical case of prevision. There it is nothing but the result of a mathematical calculation on facts which have already taken place. Calculation, for the astronomer, is actual objective knowledge of already given positions, distances, masses, velocities, so that what appears as prevision is nothing but projection into the future of what is really antecedent to the act of foreseeing: a projection of which the logical meaning is simply the concept of the immutability of the fact as such, a concept which annuls the future in the very act in which it posits it. The movement of the comet which at a certain moment will arrive at a certain point of the sky, is continual change; but the fact of its changing is unchangeable; and it is in so far as it is unchangeable that the movement is defined and the prevision takes place. The prevision (this foreseeing of the past in the future) would be impossible if in the movement itself we could admit a variation which did not form part of the picture we have formed of its properties, by means of which the movement is thought of as determined. For in that case the movement would not be determined, as by the hypothesis it is, from the standpoint of the empiricist who apprehends it as a *fact*.

"Judge no man till he is dead" says the proverb. Because man makes himself what he is and is not made. Yet we need not wait till a man is dead to speak of him as having been born, for being born of particular parents is a fact. The movement of a comet is a fact like the birth of a man; it is not an act like a man's moral or intellectual life. And when we suppose the course of a man's moral life can be determined *a priori,* like that of a celestial body, we are denying the freedom or power of creation belonging to him as spirit, debasing him to the level of natural things which are what they are, and supposing his destiny to be already formed in a character which can never produce any thing unforeseeable, since all that it will produce is already fatalistically determined in its law.

The law of the empiricist, therefore, is the fact in so far as it is immutable (even if the fact consists in a change). Fact, in so far as the mind affirms it in presupposing it as its own antecedent, is immutable, necessary, and excludes freedom. To reject and destroy this attribute of fact, it is no use appealing to the *novelty* of facts, as the theory of contingency does, we must criticize the category of fact itself, we must show its abstractness and how it implies an even more fundamental category, the spiritual act which posits fact.

This character of the past which belongs, as it were, to the future in so far as it is foreseen, and the consequent impossibility of conceiving a foreseeable future to be free, have been marked in history by the constant but always vain attempts of theodicies to freedom. reconcile the two terms of divine foreknowledge and human freedom. The terms are *a priori* unreconcilable when we recognize the identity of the concept of the freedom of the mind with the concept of its infinity. But when we conceive God as outside the activity in which the human spirit is actualized, we are denying this infinity. The problem tormented Boethius, in prison, seeking consolation for his misfortunes in a philosophical faith. From Boethius the Italian humanist Valla took the problem as his theme in the dialogue *De libero arbitrio*. He stated it with such clearness that Leibniz, in the *Theodicy,* [5] took up the problem at the point to which Valla had brought it, and desiring to reach a full justification of God from the moral evil which must be imputed to Him were mankind, by Him created, not free, could find no better means than that of continuing the lively dialogue of the sharp-witted humanist. It is hardly worth while even to indicate his solution, for, as Leibniz says, it rather cuts the knot than unties it.

It is instructive and entirely to the point, however, to read what Valla says concerning the necessity of the foreseen future, and his comparison of it with the necessity which is attributed to the past known as past. The reader may enjoy it the more if I reproduce a little of it in his witty Latin. One of the interlocutors, who is attempting the reconciliation, taking up an argument of Boethius says: "Non video cur tibi ex praescientia Dei voluntatibus atque actionibus nostris necessitas defluere videatur. Si enim praescire aliquid fore, facit ut illud futurum sit, profecto et scire aliquid esse, facit ut idem sit. Atqui, si novi ingenium tuum, non diceres ideo aliquid esse, quod scias illud esse. Veluti, scis nunc diem esse; nunquid, quia hoc scis, ideo et dies est? An contra quia dies est, ideo scis diem esse? ...Eadem ratio est de praeterito. Novi, iam octo horis, noctem fuisse; sed mea cognitio non facit illud fuisse; potiusque ego novi noctem fuisse, quia nox fuit. Atque, ut propius veniam, praescius sum, post octo horas noctem fore; ideone et erit? Minime; sed quia erit, ideo praescisco: quod si praescientia hominis non est causa ut aliquid futurum sit, utique nee praescientia Dei" (I cannot see why the necessity of our volitions and actions should seem to you to follow from God's foreknowledge. For if foreknowing that something would be makes it that it will be, then to know that something is makes that something to be! But, if I rightly judge your intelligence, you would never say that something is but that you know it to be. For example, you know it is now day; is it day because you know it? Is it not, on the contrary, because it is day that you know it? The same reasoning applies to what is past. I knew eight hours ago that it was night; but my knowledge did not make it night; rather, I knew it was night because it was night. But, I will come to the point, I foreknow that in eight hours it will be night; will that make it so? Not in the least; but because it will be, I foreknow it. If, then, human foreknowledge is not the cause of something future existing, neither is God's foreknowledge.) To this the other speaker, who in the dialogue presents the difficulties which are raised by the solution of Boethius, objects with admirable clearness: "Decipit nos, mihi crede, ista comparatio: aliud est scire, praescientia hac, praeterita, aliud futura. Nam cum aliquid scio esse, id *variabile esse non potest:* ut dies qui nunc est, nequit fieri ut non sit. Praeteritum quoque nihil differens habet a presenti: id namque non turn cum factum est cognovimus, sed cum fieret et praesens erat, ut noctem fuisse non tune cum transit didici, sed cum erat. Itaque in his temporibus concede non ideo aliquid fuisse aut esse, quia ita esse scio, sed ideo me ascire, quia hoc est aut fuit. Sed alia ratio est de futuro, quod variabile est; nee pro certo sciri potest quod incertum est. Ideoque, ne Deum fraudem praescientia, fateamur certum esse quod futurum est, et ob id necessarium." (Your comparison, it seems to me, is deceptive. It is one thing to know the past with this foreknowledge, another thing to know the future. For when I know something is, *that something cannot be variable:* for instance, the day which now is cannot become that it is not. The past, indeed, is not different from the present: [6] we knew it when it was making and present, not when it was over, just as night was not then when you discoursed of it but when it was. And so with these times I grant that nothing was or is because I know it, but what it is or was, it is or was, though I am ignorant. But concerning what is in the future another account must be given for it is variable; it cannot be certainly known because it is itself uncertain. Hence, if we are not to deny foreknowledge to God, we must admit that the future is certain and therefore necessary.) The former speaker having replied that the future, although future, can yet be foreseen (for example, that in a certain number of hours it will be night, that summer is followed by autumn, autumn by winter, then spring, then summer again), the critic rejoins: "Naturalia sunt ista, et *eundem cursum semper currentia:* ego autem loquor de voluntariis." (The instances you cite are natural things ever flowing in an even course: but I am speaking of events dependent on will.) And the volitional thing, he remarks, is quite different from the fortuitous thing (what in the philosophy of contingency would be called the contingent). "Ilia namque fortuita suam quandam naturam sequuntur; ideoque et medici et nautae et agricolae solent multa providere, cum ex antecedentibus colligant sequentes; quod in voluntariis fieri non potest. Vaticinare tu utrum ego pedem priorem moveam; utrumlibet dixeris, mentiturus, cum alterum moturus sim." (For fortuitous things follow their own nature; and therefore physicians and sailors and farmers are used to foreseeing many things, when they are the sort of things which follow from their antecedents, but this can never be the case with voluntary things. You may foretell which foot I shall move next when you have done so you will be found to have lied because I shall move the other.) This may be so when it is man who foretells but when God foresees the future, since it is impossible He should be deceived, it is equally impossible that it should be granted to man to escape his fate. Imagine, for example, that Sextus Tarquinius has come to Delphi to consult the oracle of Apollo and has received the response: *Exul inopsque cades, irata pulsus ab urbe.* (You will die an exile and wretched, driven in wrath from the city.) To his distress and complaint, Apollo can reply that though he knows the future he does not make it. But suppose from Apollo, Sextus has recourse to Jupiter, how will Jupiter justify to him the hard lot the poor wretch has to expect? By the haughty pride of Tarquinius and the future misdeeds it entails? Apollo, perhaps, will say to him: "Jupiter, ut lupum rapacem creavit, leporem timidum, leonem animosum, onagrum stolidum, canem rabidum, ovem mitem, ita hominum alii finxit dura praecordia, alii mollia, alium ad scelera, alium ad virtutem propensiorem genuit. Praeterea alteri corrigibile ingenium dedit, tibi vero malignam animam nee aliena ope emendabilem tribuit." [7] (Jupiter, as he created the wolf ravenous, the hare timid, the lion bold, the ass stubborn, the dog savage, the sheep gentle, so he formed some men hard-hearted and some soft-hearted, some with a propensity to crime, others to virtue. Whilst to others he has given a mind which is open to correction, he has endowed thee with an evil soul which can by no outside help be made good.) This is clearly to take all responsibility and all value from Sextus, and to attribute his conduct to Jupiter. It makes man a natural being and his future actions nothing but facts in so far as they are foreseeable. It makes him, in regard to Apollo who can foretell and generally in regard to a foreknowing God, a reality already realized, that is, a past.

Leibniz, not content with Valla's mystical and agnostic solution, which has recourse finally to the inscrutable divine wisdom, continues the fiction and supposes that Sextus has come to Dodona to the presence of Jupiter to inquire what will give him a change of lot and a change of heart. And Jupiter replies to him: "If thou art willing to renounce Rome the Fates will spin thee other destinies, thou mayst become wise and be happy." Then Sextus asks, "Why must I renounce the hope of a crown? Can I not be a good king?" "No, Sextus," the God replies, "I know better than thou canst what befits thee. If them goest to Rome thou art lost." Sextus, unable to reconcile himself to so great a sacrifice, leaves the temple and abandons him self to his appointed destiny. But when he is gone, Theodorus, the priest, would know why Jupiter can not give Sextus a will different from that which has been assigned to him as king of Rome. Jupiter refers him to Pallas, in whose temple at Athens he falls asleep and dreams he is in an unknown country, where he sees a huge palace. It is the palace of the Fates, which the Goddess makes him visit. And therein is portrayed not only all that happens, but all that is possible, and he is able to see every particular which would have to be realized together with and in the system of all the other particulars in its own quite special possible world.;< Thou art aware," says Pallas to Theodorus, "that when the conditions of a point which is in question are not sufficiently determined and there is an infinity of them, they all fall into what geometricians call a locus, and at least this locus (which is often a line) is determined. So it is possible to represent a regulated series of worlds all of which will contain the case in point and will vary its circumstances and consequences." And all these worlds existing in idea were exactly pictured in the palace of the Fates. In each apartment a world is revealed to the eyes of Theodore; in each of these worlds he always finds Sextus: always the same Sextus, and yet different in relation to the world to which he belongs. In all the worlds, therefore, is a Sextus in an infinity of states. From world to world, that is from room to room, Theodore rises ever towards the apex of a great pyramid. The worlds become ever more beautiful. "At last he reaches the highest world, at the top of the pyramid, the most beautiful of all; for the pyramid had an apex but no base in sight; it went on growing to infinity," because, as the Goddess explained, "among an infinity of possible worlds there is the best of all, otherwise God would not have determined to create any, but there is none which has not less perfect ones beneath it; that is why the pyramid descends to infinity." They enter, Theodore overcome with ecstasy, into the highest apartment, which is that of the real world. And Pallas says, "Behold Sextus such as he is and as he will in fact be. Look how he goes forth from the temple consumed with rage, how he despises the counsel of the Gods. See him going to Rome, putting all in disorder, ravishing his friend's wife. See him then driven out with his father, broken, wretched. If Jupiter had put here a Sextus happy at Corinth, or a King in Thrace, it would no longer be this world. And yet he could not but choose this world which surpasses in perfection all the others and is the apex of the pyramid; otherwise Jove would have renounced his own wisdom, he would have banished me who am his child. You see, then, that it is not my father who has made Sextus wicked; he was wicked from all eternity and he was always freely so. He has done nothing but grant to him the existence which his wisdom could not deny to the world in which he is comprised. He has made it pass from the realm of the possible to that of actual being." [8]

The conclusion is obvious. The proposal to renounce Rome which Jupiter makes to Sextus at Dodona is a cheat, because from eternity there has been assigned to Sextus his own destiny in this possible world to which Jupiter has given existence. And the conclusion, so far as it concerns our argument, is, that the knowledge of the empirically real supposed to pre-exist the mind (whether really or ideally pre-existing is the same thing) is knowledge only of facts; and when we attain to foreknowledge we know nothing except fates which are facts: systems of reality wholly realized in their knowability. The future of the prophets, and of Apollo who can inspire them, is exactly like the future of the astronomer, an apparent future which in the concrete thought in which it is represented is a true and proper past.

One other remark we may make in confirmation of what we have said. It is that when Jupiter chooses the best of the possible worlds, that which stands at the apex of the pyramid, he not only cannot leave Sextus free to choose his own lot, but neither is he free himself to choose it for him. The world which he realizes is in reality already realized, and precisely because it is realized he can know it, and choose it. That world is in itself before Jupiter wills it; and it is the best of all possible worlds. The willing it adds nothing to its goodness. It is in its very absoluteness incapable of development and growth. It is like the Platonic ideas, which are in them selves, and bound dialectically by a law which is their very being, when they can be known or, it may be, willed.

In short, the divine foreknowledge not only renders impossible the freedom of the human mind, but even the freedom of the divine mind; just as every naturalistic presupposition not only binds the object of the mind in the iron chain of nature, but also the subject, the mind itself. The mind can no longer conceive itself except as bound up with its object, and therefore naturalistically. The concept, then, of the divine foreknowledge is a mark of the naturalistic conception of God.

Reality, we can now say, cannot be distinguished into condition and conditionate except on the clear understanding;: that the two realities are conceived as in every way one reality only; a reality which, in its turn, being the negation of the freedom of the mind, is unintelligible save in relation to it.

Reality is not duplicated but is maintained in its unity even when distinguished into condition and conditionate; because neither metaphysics nor empiricism can present the condition in its immanent relation with the conditionate, nor the conditionate in its immanent relation with the condition, except as a unity of the two terms.

Metaphysics with its efficient causality, empiricism with its empirical causality, one as much as the other, both tend to the identification rather than to the distinction which is essential to the concept of condition ally. So that, taken strictly, the concept of meta physical causality aims at considering the cause, from which the effect is not really differentiated, as alone absolutely real; while, on the contrary, empiricism represents the absolute as the simple effect (fact) into which the cause itself is resolved. And the philosophy of contingency is a manifestation of the empirical tendency to free the effect from its relation to the cause without making it thereby acquire any other right to freedom. But neither can metaphysics stop at the cause without an effect, nor empiricism at the effect without a cause; not only because the cause is not a cause unless it is cause of an effect, and an effect without a cause is a mystery which the mind cannot admit, but for a deeper reason, which we have already indicated more than once. It is that undifferentiated reality is inconceivable, even as self-identical, for identity implies a relation of self with self and therefore a moment of opposition and duality, which the pure undifferentiated excludes.

The abstract unity, with which metaphysics as well as empiricism ends, in absorbing the conditionate in the condition, or the condition in the conditionate, is what is called the *unconditioned,* not in the meaning of *freedom* but in that of *necessity:* the necessity which the doctrine of contingency dreads, and into which it falls headlong. Now this unconditioned cannot be affirmed without being denied, in accordance with our usual appeal from the abstract to the concrete thought. Because in so far as we think it, the unconditioned comes to be thought, not as the purely thinkable, but precisely as the thing thought, or rather as that which we posit in thought. Unconditioned it is, then, but, so far as it is such, thought, or in thought, which is therefore the condition of it. In other words, it is unconditioned for the thought which abstracts from itself, and thinks its object without thinking itself, in which its object inheres. It is conditioned in so far as the object thus unconditioned is thought in its immanence in the subject, and as this subject is conscious of positive activity which belongs to that unconditioned. In short, the object is conditioned by the subject even when the object, as pure abstract object, is unconditioned.

The relation, then, of the subject with the object is that of conditionality. It can only be effectively conceived by bringing together the unity and the duality, and therefore by requiring thought neither to shut itself within unity, which is absurd, nor yet to end in abstract duality, which is equally absurd, because it reproduces in each of the elements the same position of unity. Evidently it is the relation of the *a priori* synthesis belonging to the act of thinking, which is realized in the opposition of subject and object, of self and other than self.

The ignorance of such a relation is the explanation of the origin of all the difficulties of metaphysics and of empiricism with which we have been dealing. The conditionate of metaphysics must in fact, when accurately thought out, be merged in its condition, since the condition is not a true and proper condition, it being itself the conditionate. Aristotle, in the well-known argument based on the absurdity of the process to infinity, believed indeed he could make God an immobile mover, an unconditioned condition or first cause; but his God cannot explain the world as other than Himself; and from Aristotle, therefore, we must necessarily pass to Plotinus. God as the mover is no other than the movement which it is required to explain. He is the very form, whose reality philosophy studies in nature and so finds already realized before nature. He is indeed nature itself, thought and hypostasized beyond immediate nature; that is, the opposite of thought. This opposite is always pure fact in so far as it is never apprehended in the making through the process of thought. In empiricism, on the contrary, the condition must be resolved into the conditionate, because a condition which is not thought itself but the presupposition of thought (and this is what it must be for the empiricist) is nothing else but an object of thought, a conditionate of the activity of thought.

The condition of metaphysics cannot explain its own efficiency and productivity, since it is not productive, being rather itself a simple product of thinking: a thought which supposes the activity of the thinking which realizes it. And the empiricist Hume was right in his opposition to metaphysics because he saw the full consequence of the metaphysical point of view. Metaphysics contraposes the cause (the only true cause is God, alike for the Scholastics and the Cartesians) and the thought which thinks it as cause; and, granted the opposition, it is impossible that thought should penetrate into the working of the cause, as it must in order to understand it, and perceive thereby the necessity of the relation by which the cause is connected with the effect. To that extent it is true that the empiricist criticism of the principle of causality is the profound consciousness of the implicit scepticism in the transcendent metaphysical intuition. As we have already pointed out, we find the consciousness of this, even before Hume, in Vico, a metaphysicist who denied the certainty of knowledge concerning the working of the natural cause, precisely because that cause is an object of thought and not thought itself.

The empiricist, on the other hand, if he would endow his empirical causality with a minimum of logical value, must maintain some connexion between condition and conditionate. Having no other way he thinks it permissible even for empiricism to maintain the chronological chain of succession, which indicates a kind of synthesis, and therefore a principle of unification, chargeable to the work of the subject. Even then he does not realize his concept of pure *de facto* conditionality; and it is impossible for him to do so because, just as the metaphysicist posits the condition, so he posits the conditionate as confronting the thinking. Therefore for the empiricist the unity of the manifold is inconceivable, it presents itself to him as mere temporal connexion, as to the meta physicist it presents itself as efficiency.

The *a priori* synthesis of condition and conditionate is dialectic, and it is obvious from our standpoint that a dialectic outside thought is inconceivable. When, instead, we look at the condition and dialectic in thought, then the thinking or metaphysical causality, as or every other form of the concept of conditionality, is relieved of all the difficulties we have enumerated. For the fundamental difficulty of metaphysics is to understand in what way the one can generate another than itself, in what way the identical can generate the different. But when by the "one" metaphysics means the "I," this "I" is precisely found to be the self-engendering principle of the other, of difference from self. So, when empiricism acquires the consciousness of the immanent relation of the other, precisely as other, in its condition, which is the "I," it will still continue to see the other and the manifold, but with the unity and in the unity.

So, then, just as metaphysical reality and empirical reality are each (in the unconsciousness of abstract thought) posited as conditioned, that is as necessity without freedom, so the reality of concrete thought posits itself as condition of that unconditioned which is then shown to be conditioned. And thereby it posits itself in the absoluteness of its position, as the Unconditioned which in being necessary is free. The first unconditioned we may call *Being,* the second unconditioned, *Mind.* The one is the unconditioned of abstract (and therefore false) thought, the other is the unconditioned of concrete (and therefore real) thought. Being (God, nature, idea, fact, the contingent) is necessary without freedom, because already posited by thought. It is the result of the process: the result which *is,* precisely because the process has ceased. That is, we conceive it as having ceased by fixing and abstracting a moment of it as a result. The necessity of the future, object of the divine foreknowledge, comes by conceiving the future itself as "being," or as something which confronts thought. (So that we know what "can be" only by reason of thought which when it posits it confronting itself, in so far as it does so, posits itself confronting itself.) This necessity is the necessity of natural fact, of fate, of death, necessity thought of naturalistically. It excludes the miracle of the resurrection which mind alone can work, and does work when nature obeys it, and that is when nature is no longer simply nature but itself also mind.

The necessity of being, however, coincides with the freedom of mind, because being, in the act of thinking, is the act itself. This act is the positing (and thereby it is free), presupposing nothing (and thereby it is truly unconditioned). Freedom is absoluteness (infinity of the unconditioned), but in so far as the absolute is *causa sui.* [9] *Sui,* we must notice, supposes the *self,* the subject, the self-consciousness, whence the being caused is not an effect, but an end, a value, the term to which it strives and which it gains. Such freedom is not a negation of the necessity, if we do not mean a necessity which competes with the abstract objectivity of being, but a necessity which coincides with the necessity of being, which in the concrete is the mind's dialectic.

Such a dialectic, in resolving all multiplicity and thereby every condition into its own unity, in positing itself as the principle of every synthesis of condition and conditionate, eliminates even the category of conditionality from the concept of mind, once more re-establishing the infinite unity of it. Moreover, as the criticism of individuality enabled us to discover the concept of individualization, and the criticism of space and time gave us the concept of the infinity of the mind in opposition to the indefiniteness of nature, and gave us also the concept of the eternity and true immortality of mind, so now, through the criticism of the category of condition, we have gained the real concept of freedom.

Metaphysicians and empiricists will not be completely satisfied with this concept of freedom which we have now given. Restricted to their false view, and the concept which follows from it, of a reality presupposed by the subject, they will maintain that by the a-priori synthesis of the condition and conditionate in the dialectic of mind, which is posited as subject of an object and so as unity of condition and conditionate, all that we have succeeded in finding is an epistemological relation. Beyond this, they will say there always remains the metaphysical or real relation, at which the metaphysicist aims with his causality, and which even the empiricist has in view when he conceives mind conditioned by a nature in itself. It may even be, they will say, that the subject's cognitive activity posits its own object in positing itself, in knowing, as the unconditioned condition of the phenomenon. This cannot mean that it is unconditioned *realiter;* that it is *realiter* is a condition of every thinkable object. Mind is dialectic on the basis of the condition to which it is really bound.

That the basis of mind cannot possibly be nature is clear from what we said in proof of the purely epistemological value of the reality which we call nature. Nature as space and time, for example, is no more than an abstract category of thought. Mind abstracts from its own infinity which is a root of space, and from its own eternity which is a root of time. As a basis of mind, to take another example, nature cannot be race, another naturalistic concept, which so many historians and philosophers of history suppose it necessary to assume as a principle of the historical explanation of human facts. This is evident to every one who recognizes that the individuality of a race is realized and characterized in its history. The history of a race is not the spiritual activity conditioned by the race, but the very meaning of the concept of race when withdrawn from the abstractness of the naturalistic position in which it is an empty concept, and carried into the realm of spiritual reality where alone it can have meaning: a realm in which it is no longer the race, but the history, the mind. What is it in general you wish to prove? Is it that you can think something which is a condition of your mind, your mind which is actualized in you in thinking its condition? The condition must be, if you succeed in thinking it, a reality unthought (not entering into the synthesis of your thought). That is, it must be thought to be unthought. Berkeley will laugh at you. We will be content to point out to you that it is an abstraction which can only live in the synthesis of thought.

To escape the tangle we must keep before our mind that the transcendental "I" is posited as empirical, and as such it is conditioned. And if by reality we are not meaning only what is in the object of experience (pure experience), then undoubtedly our synthesis, in which the "I" is an unconditioned absolute, free, and therefore a condition of every thing, is a purely epistemological and not a real synthesis. But in meaning by reality the object alone cut off from the subject, we must by this time be convinced that we are meaning something which is meaningless. The only remedy is to look deeper, to go to the root of the reality wherein the object is the life of the subject, whose synthesis is therefore absolutely real.

We see here at last how the oscillating of thought between the concept of mind as pure act and the concept of mind as fact, as object of experience, generates the historical antinomy of mind which only in the exact concept of the pure act can find its adequate solution.

[1] Agathon, quoted by Aristotle, *Eth. Nic.* vi. 2, p. 1139 b 19.
[2] "Inesorabile e immutabile e nulla curante che le sue recondite ragioni e modi d operare sieno o non sieno esposti alia capacita degli uomini; per lo che ella non trasgredisce mai i termini delle leggi imposteli." Letter to B. Castelli, Dec. 21, 1613.
[3] "Caro l'incontro d'una testa di Medusa, che ci convertisse in un marmo o in diamante." *Opera*, ed. Naz., v. 234-5, 260.
[4] In his poem *La Resurrezione*. The stanza is -
Quando Aggeo, quando Isaia
Mallevaro al mondo intero
Che il Bramato un di verria;
Quando assorto in suo pensiero
Lesse i giorni numerati,
E degli anni ancor non nati
Daniel si ricordo.
[5] Leibniz, *Theodicy*, 405 *et seq*.
[6] Because in reality the present as an object of cognition is past and not present.
[7] *Opera*, ed. Basilea, pp. 1002-3, 1006.
[8] Leibniz, following an original concept of Augustine, according to which evil is justified as an instrument of good, makes Pallas conclude, "The crime of Sextus subserves great things. Of it will be born a mighty empire which will produce splendid examples, but this is nothing in regard to the value of the complexity of this world" (*Theod.* sec. 416).
[9] The expression is Spinoza's; but Spinoza retains the meaning which Plato's αὐτὸ κινοῦν (*Phaedrus*, 245 c) and Plotinus's ἑαυτοῦ ἐνέργημα (*Enn.* vi. 8, 1 6) must have. Compare my edition of the *Ethica*, Bari, Laterza, 1915, pp. 295-296. Spinoza's substance, like Plato's idea and Plotinus's God, is the abstract unconditioned, which cannot be *causa sui*, because it is not mind but its opposite. The *sui* therefore is a word deprived of its proper meaning.

Chapter Thirteen - The Historical Antinomy and Eternal History

What we call the *historical antinomy* is the antinomy which arises from the concept of mind as pure act when we consider it in its essential relations with the concept of history. We can formulate it in the thesis: "Mind is history, because it is dialectic development," to which is opposed the antithesis: "Mind is not history, because it is eternal act." It is the antinomy in which at every moment we find ourselves entangled in studying and understanding man, who presents always two aspects, each of which appears to be the negation of the other. For we cannot understand man apart from his history in which he realizes his essence; yet in history he can show nothing of himself which has that spiritual value entirely on account of which his essence comes to be conceived as realizing itself in history.

In what way and why is man history? Man is history because the essence in virtue of which he is contraposed to the necessity of nature is freedom. Nature *is*, mind *becomes*. Mind becomes, in so far as it is free. This means that it realizes its end. Its life is value, it is what ought to be. It is knowing truth, creating images of beauty, doing good, worshipping God. The man who is man for us is one who knows truth and to whom we can therefore communicate our truth (which we cannot do to the brute). When he errs we believe he can be turned from his error in as much as he can correct himself, that is, knows the truth, not completely realized at a moment (that, strictly speaking, would not be a realizing but an already realized *being*) but in realizing it. This is the man into whose society we enter and who in history is our neighbour, since our society is not limited to those few men of our time who come within the sphere of direct personal relationship.

The language we speak, the institutions which govern our civil life, the city in which we live, the monuments of art which we admire, the books, the records of our civilization, and the religious and moral traditions which, even if we have no special historical interest, constitute our culture, bind us by a thousand chains to minds not belonging to our own time, but whose reality is present in us and intelligible only as free spiritual reality. Our historical consciousness is peopled with names of nations and of men, the actors in this reality of civilization, its prophets, artists, men of science, statesmen, generals. With the energy of their minds they have created the spiritual world which is the atmosphere in which our soul breathes. To take an example, let us suppose it is Ariosto's *Orlando Furioso* we are reading and enjoying, finding in it food for our imagination and re-living it. History can tell us the origin of this poem. It can tell us that there was a man, Ariosto, who was the author, whose mind, which created this work of art, we can only know in the poem itself. Ariosto, then, is a man for whom we can only find a place in the world when we think it in the form of time and in the form of space. In the series of years he was living from 1474 to 1533 of our era, and his life was spent in the part of the spatial universe we name Italy, and in various different localities of that peninsula. But the Ariosto who wrote the *Orlando Furioso* does not fill the fifty-nine years which elapsed between the poet's birth and his death; that Ariosto belongs only to those years during which the composition and correction of the poem occurred. And no more than we can say that Ariosto is his own father can we call the Ariosto of the years in which his poem was written the Ariosto of his earlier years. The Ariosto of the years before the poem, in the life he then lived, in his reading and in the first essays of his art, is indeed the antecedent which renders historically intelligible the author of the poem, or rather, the reality of his divine poetry. We see, then, that in knowing Ariosto we know two quite different men: one is a mind, the unconditioned, a condition of every conditionate, an act which posits time and all temporal things; the other is a reality like any which is conditioned by its antecedents. The one Ariosto is eternal, the other historical. One an object of aesthetic criticism when we see in Ariosto solely the eternal beauty of his art; the other an object of historical criticism, when we see in Ariosto solely fact, conditioned in time and in space, and intelligible, like every other fact, in relation to its conditions.

If instead of a poet we take a philosopher, he will in exactly the same way duplicate himself before us into two personalities. One will be the personality of the philosopher in reading whose works (if we understand them) we make his thought our thought. Thereby we know it as mind, appreciate and judge it; it is his true personality in the strict meaning of the word. The other personality is that by which he is fixed in the particular age in which he lived, and his thought is determined by the conditions of the culture of that age, or rather, by the historical antecedents of his speculation. This being given he could not think but as he did think, just as the animal born a cat does not bark but mews.

In general, when the mind is historicized it is changed into a natural entity; when its spiritual s History value only is kept in view, it is withdrawn and spiritual from history and stands before us in its values. eternal ideality. This presents no difficulty so long as the eternal reality of mind comes to be conceived as a hypostasis of the content of mind, in the way that Plato conceived the idea, which, in its transcendence, is, by definition, withdrawn from contact with the historical flux. But when the transcendence is demolished, and we conceive spiritual reality in its eternity no longer as something fixed but as process in act, then we no longer have history outside the eternal, nor the eternal outside history. The difficulty then consists precisely in the concept of reality which is both eternal and historical. It consists in the concept, by which, in the example of the *Orlando Furioso,* the poem itself, even while we distinguish it in knowledge from its antecedents, yet in itself is a process which develops by degrees, each degree presupposing those which have gone before and being what it is by reason of them, and in that way conditioned by them. And the philosophy of a philosopher, when we regard it in its maturest and most perfect expression, can only be understood as a system of ideas developed stage by stage just as the poem is.

It was this difficulty of conceiving the eternity in the history and the history in the eternity, which led Plato to deny value to history and to imprison all being in a transcendent reality. And it leads the empiricists of all times (from Protagoras onwards) to deny any absolute value, any value raised above the plane of particular and contingent conditions. And the antinomy arises from the impossibility of confining ourselves either with Plato to a transcendent value which is not mind (a negation of history), or with Protagoras to the purely historical fact of mind (a negation of its value). It arises of necessity, for Plato and for Protagoras alike, in their contradiction.

How is the antinomy solved? It is solved, as all antinomies are solved, by bringing the spiritual reality, value and history, from abstract thought to the concrete. The spiritual reality actually known is not something which is different from and other than the subject who knows it. The Ariosto whom we know, the only Ariosto there is to know, author of *Orlando Furioso,* is not one thing and his poem another. And the poem which we know is known when it is read, understood, enjoyed; and we can only understand by reason of our education, and that is by reason of our concrete individuality. So true is this, that there is a history not only of Ariosto, but of criticism of Ariosto, criticism which concerns not only the reality which the poem was in the poet's own spiritual life, but what it continues to be after his death, through the succeeding ages, in the minds of his readers, true continuators of his poetry. The reality of Ariosto for me then, what I affirm and what I can refer to, is just what I realize of it. So then, to realize that reality to the best of my ability, I must at least read the poem. But what does reading mean? Can I read the poem unless I know the language in which it is written? And what is the language? Can I learn it from the dictionary for all the writers of the same literature? And can I know the language of any writer as his language, unless I take into account what there is individually real in the process of a spiritual history, which no longer belongs only to the empirically determined individual but lies deep in the spiritual world in which the mind of the writer lived? And so we must say that reading Ariosto means in some way reading what Ariosto had read and re-living in some way the life which he lived, not just when he began to write

> Le donne, i cavalieri, l'arme e gli amori;

but before, long before, so long as we can trace back the whole course of his life of which *Orlando* was the flower. And this in substance is not two things, the poem and its preparation taken together; it is one concrete thing, the poem in its process of spiritual actuality. It will exist for us, always, in so far and just so far as it is realized as the life of our own "we."

If we want to have the conditioned Ariosto we must abstract him from this reality. When we have made the abstraction we may then proceed, or try to proceed, to introduce him mechanically into the process to which he belongs. The reality is in the process. But can this process, - in its actuality in which the reality of the poem and its valuation lie, - posit itself at every moment as conditioned by its preceding moments? Evidently not, for the very reason that such conditioning supposes the pulverization of a process which is real in its unity. It does indeed posit itself as multiplicity, but as a multiplicity which is resolved into unity in the very act in which it is posited, and which cannot, except abstractly, be thought as a pure multiplicity. So in like manner I can always distinguish empirically my present from my past, and posit in my past the condition of my present, but, in so doing, I abstract from that true *me*, for whom past and present are compresent in the duality by which the relation of condition and conditionate is made intelligible; whereas the true *me* immanent in each temporally distinct *me*, the past *me* and the present *me*, is the root of this as of every other conditionality.

There are, then, two modes of conceiving history. One is that of those who see nothing but the historical fact in its multiplicity. It gives a history which cannot treat mind without degrading it from a spiritual to a natural reality. The other mode is ours, rendered possible by the concept expounded above, of the spatialization of the One, which posits the fact as act, and thereby, being posited in time, leaves nothing at all effectively behind itself. The chronicler's history is history hypostatized and deprived of its dialectic; for dialecticity consists precisely in the actuality of the multiplicity as unity, and as unity alone, which is transcended only in transcending actuality.

When, then, we say "historical process," we must not represent the stages of this process as a spatial and temporal series in the usual way in which, abstractly, we represent space and time as a line, which, in the succession of its points, stands before us as we intuit it. It is in the intuition of the line, an intuition which constructs the line, by always being and never being itself, that is, never being the complete intuition it would be, that we ought rather to say progress consists. The process is of the subject; because an object in itself cannot be other than static. Process can only be correctly attributed to the object in so far as in being actualized it is resolved into the life of the subject. On the other hand, the subject is not developed by realizing a stage of itself and moving therefrom to the realization of a further stage, since a stage from which the subject can detach itself, a stage which is no longer actuality or act of mind *in fieri*, falls outside mind: a kind of Lucifer, a fallen angel. Such a stage is an abstraction. It is a past which the mind detaches from itself by making abstraction from itself, and all the while the very abstraction is an act affirmative of itself, and so an embrace by which the mind clasps to itself this fallen Lucifer.

The antinomy, therefore, is solved in the concept of the process of the unity, which in being multiplied remains one. It is the concept of a history which is ideal and eternal, not to be confused with Vico's concept, for that leaves outside itself a history which develops in time, whereas our eternal is time itself considered in the actuality of mind.

The clearest confirmation we can give of the doctrine of the identity of the ideal and eternal history with the history which is developed in time, is that which in recent years has been formulated in Italy in the theory that philosophy and history of philosophy are a circle. Empirically we distinguish philosophy from its history; not in the sense in which Plato, or, according to tradition, Pythagoras, distinguished divine philosophy (σοφία), which is the true science of being, and human philosophy (φιλοσοφία), which is only an aspiration towards that science: the one eternal in its transcendent position, the other subject to the becoming which infects all natural things. We may say indeed that for Plato a history of science, in the strict meaning, is impossible, because for him either science has a history and is not science, or is science and has no history. The empirical distinction was made when the history of philosophy first began to be a distinct concept (a concept which did not arise before Hegel and the general movement of Romanticism in the beginning of the nineteenth century). It contraposes the history of philosophy to philosophy, as the process of formation can be contraposed to its result. Hegel, who has been charged with having confused the history of philosophy with his own philosophy, and also with having done violence to the positivity of history by the rationalistic logic of his system, did not fail to distinguish his own philosophy from the whole historical process. He conceived his own philosophy as a result, a recapitulation, or epilogue, an organization and system of all the concepts which had been brought stage by stage to the light, in the time of all the precedent systems. For his method the history of philosophy is the condition of philosophy, just as no scientific research is conceivable which is not connected with what has gone before and which is not its continuation.

When we have made this distinction, and thereby raised history of philosophy into a condition of philosophy, it is obvious that the relation which makes philosophy a conditionate must be reversible. And so we find in Hegel himself, and also in all historians of philosophy who are conscious of the essentially philosophical as distinct from the philological value of their discipline, the vital need of conceiving philosophy as the necessary presupposition of its history. If philosophy *in re* require as preparation for it and development of it, the history of philosophy which appears its antecedent, this history cannot but be valued also *post rem,* in the mind, as cognition of the history of philosophy, since this cognition has the value that it is the actual preparation for and condition of an actual philosophy. Now were this history of philosophy not what we have learnt and therefore know, what could it be but the empty name of a history which had no subject-matter? And if it be abstracted from present cognition, must it not be after it has been learnt and, indeed, after it has been reconstructed? Or again, if it be reconstructible in itself, must it not be reconstructed with precisely those determinations which will fit it when it is, if it is, reconstructed in act? History, however, is rationally reconstructible history. How is it reconstructible? For Hegel the history of philosophy is reconstructible, because, indeed, the philosophy is his own: so, too, with every other philosopher, the philosophy whose history he reconstructs is his own. Well, then, what will each include in his own history as matter which belongs to the history of philosophy? A choice of material is inevitable; and a choice requires a criterion. And the criterion in this case can only be a notion of the philosophy. Again, every history disposes its own materials in an order and in a certain perspective, and each disposes its materials so that what is more important stands out in relief in the foreground and what is less important and more remote is pushed into the back ground, and all this implies a choice among various possible orders and dispositions. And this choice of order and disposition of the already chosen material itself also requires its criterion, and therefore the intervention of a mode of understanding and judging matter which here can only be a philosophy. So we reach the conclusion that the history of philosophy which must precede philosophy presupposes philosophy. And we have the circle.

For a long while it was suspected that it was a vicious circle. Were it so, it would be necessary to choose between a history of philosophy which presupposed no philosophy but was itself presupposed by it, and a history of philosophy not presupposed by philosophy nor a basis of it. But more accurate reflexion has shown that the circle is not logically vicious, it is rather one of those which Rosmini in his *Logica* calls solid circles (*circoli solidi*), that is, circles which are unbreakable, or regresses (*regressi*), as they were termed by Jacopo Zabarella, the Italian sixteenth century philosopher. [1] And it has been shown that no philosophy is conceivable which is not based on the history of philosophy, and no history of philosophy which does not lean on philosophy, since p*hilosophy and its history are together one as process of mind*. In the process of mind it is possible to distinguish empirically an historical from a systematic treatment of philosophy and to think of either of the two terms as presupposing the other, since speculatively the one is itself the other, although in a different form, as the various stages of the spiritual process considered abstractly are always different. [2]

There is a difficulty, and it will meet us continually, the difficulty of seeing clearly the identity of the process in which philosophy and history of philosophy are identical and at the same time, and while always maintaining their identity, also different. It comes from the habitual error we commit when, instead of conceiving the two terms in the actuality of the thought which thinks them, we presuppose them abstractly. It is because both are conceived as external to the thinking in which alone their reality consists that the necessity arises of conceiving philosophy as external to the history of philosophy and this as external to philosophy. Instead, the history of philosophy, which we must keep in view if we are to see it as identical with philosophy, is the history which is history of philosophy for us in the *act of philosophizing*. If from that standpoint we should maintain the difference to be pure difference, it is evident we should not be able to think the history of philosophy at all, for it would be different from his thinking who is the philosopher philosophizing. Moreover, it cannot be denied that the whole history of philosophy consists in what has been philosophized, it is only history of philosophy through philosophizing. So, on the other hand, in making the history of philosophy we imperil a system of concepts which is the historian's philosophy. If I compare Kant's *Critique of Pure Reason* with F. A. Lange's *History of Materialism* (to instance the history of a Kantian philosopher), Kant's philosophy is not Lange's history. And yet the Kantian philosophy is the whole of Lange's history, the whole history, that is, which is seen from within the horizon of that definite thought which is realized in the *Critique*. And, on the other hand, Lange's *History* is Lange's system of thought, that is, the whole philosophy which is such for him within the ambit of the problems he propounds. Neither in the one philosophy is there the whole of history nor in the one history the whole of the philosophy, but there is no specific difference which distinguishes history of philosophy from philosophy. There are, indeed, differences common to all parts, as we say, or rather to all the determinations and individualizations of philosophy. We may distinguish them, for example, as aesthetical, or ethical, or logical; not one of them is the whole of philosophy, yet each of them is a philosophy always and whenever in the thinking of a universal aspect of reality it really succeeds in thinking systematically, however superficially, the inner reality in its unity. For the totality of philosophy does not consist in the scholastically encyclopaedic completeness of its parts so much as in the logically systematic character of the concepts in which it is realized. A system embracing organically universal reality may be contained in a most specialized essay and altogether wanting in a voluminous encyclopaedia. The identity of philosophy with its history is the typical form and culminating point of the resolution of temporal into eternal history, or indeed of the facts or mind into the concept or spiritual act. It is the culminating point, because philosophy is the highest and at the same time the concretest form of spiritual activity, the form which judges all the others and can itself be judged by none. To judge philosophy, in fact, is to philosophize. He who looks at the history of philosophy with a philologist's eyes sees nothing in it but facts which once were and no longer are thought; or regarding which the one thing that matters is that they were, not that they are, thought with the value of thought in the historian's eyes. [3] But this philological conception is absurd because it postulates an objectivity in historical fact, or rather it postulates the object of historical knowledge, completely outside the subject, a postulate there is no need for us now to criticize. As actual fact there is no historian who does not take a side in his history, bringing into it his own categories of thought. These categories are indispensable not merely for such judgment as he may bring to bear on the facts after they have been presented in their strictly objective configuration, but for the very intuition and presentation of the so-called facts. The historian who shows himself no partisan in indicating any particular speculative direction is the sceptic who believes no philosophy. But in the end, even the sceptic believes his own sceptical philosophy and therefore in his way takes a side, for scepticism indeed is itself a philosophy. The sceptic judges all philosophies, and to judge philosophies is, as we have said, to philosophize.

The facts which enter into the history of philosophy are all links of a chain which is unbreakable and which in its wholeness is always, in the thought of the philosopher who reconstructs it, a whole thought, which by a self-articulation and self-demonstration, that is, a self-realization, becomes of itself a reality, in and through the concrete process of its own articulations.

The facts of philosophy are in its past; you think them, and they can only be the act, the unique act of your philosophy, which is not in the past, nor in a present which will be past, since it is the life, the very reality of your thought, a centre from which all time irradiates, whether it be past or future. History, then, in the precise meaning in which it is in time, is only concrete in his act who thinks it as eternal.

Is there, then, another history besides the history of philosophy? Were there no other histories, it is clear that our doctrine of the circle of philosophy and its history would not be a special case of the identity of history in time and eternal history, but would be its full and absolute demonstration. Yet we do distinguish from philosophy, (1) Art; (2) Religion; (3) Science; (4) Life (that is, the will and practice as distinct from the intellect and theory). So, then, besides the history of philosophy, we have got, it seems, to find a place for four other kinds of history; with this proviso, however, that each of these forms of mind, in so far as it is distinct from the philosophical, strictly has no history. This leads to an inquiry of no slight interest in regard to the whole theory of mind.

Note

In section 14 of this Chapter I say that the unity of the history of philosophy as forming a thinking which is one whole, belongs as of right to the history of philosophy whose reality is in the thinking of the philosopher who reconstructs it. This important consideration must, I believe, have escaped the notice of my friend, Benedetto Croce, when he disputed the difference here expounded between history of art and history of philosophy, denying that "men have been exercised over one unique philosophical problem, the successive and ever less inadequate solutions of which form one single line of progress." (*Teoria e storia della storiografia,* 2nd ed. Bari, Laterza, 1920, pp. 126-35; *Analogia e anomalie delle scienze speciali.*)

It is true that men have worked at problems which are always different; but man, mind, the spirit which is actually working in the history of philosophy, works at one problem which is its own and unique. System is not to be sought in a history in itself, which has no existence, but in that *real history* of which Croce himself speaks with such insight in the book referred to (p. 5), the history, as he says, "which is really thought in the act which thinks it" (*che realmente si pensa nell' atto che si pensa*): in the historian's mind who writes it. The historian can only determine his object as the development of his own concept, that is, of himself.

And I do not see how that endless multiplicity of philosophical problems, each individually determined and therefore each different from any and every other, which he finds rightly enough in the history of philosophy, destroys the unity of the philosophical problem which every historian finds and must always find in that history. Even for Croce the difference of the distinctions does not exclude but rather requires and implies the unity. So, too, when in his article "Inizio, periodi e caratteri della storia dell Estetica" (in *Nuovi Saggi di Estetica,* Bari, 1920, pp. 108 ff.), he speaks of the different problems into which from time to time the problem of art is transformed, it does not affect the fact that out of all these distinct and various problems, *by their development*, has come the concept of art, or rather, strictly, the concept which the historian of aesthetic has of art when he proposes to write the history of aesthetic, and which is then the "unique" problem of aesthetic, analogous to the unique problem of philosophy.

To deny the unity of the problem would compel us to reject the doctrine of the concept as development; and this is impossible. It would even compel us to deny the unity of each of the single problems among those, however many they be, which constitute the series; because every single problem is also complicated with many particular problems, in knotting and unravelling which the thought of the whole is articulated. Otherwise they would not be a thought but an intuition beyond our grasp. But Croce certainly does not wish to take this path, and to show how firmly he holds to unity we need only refer to the chapter of his book entitled "La distinzione e la divisione," in which he insists on the necessity of not separating the various special histories, which in the concrete are all one history: *general history* (p. 107). This, in its turn, is no other than philosophy in its development, since history coincides with philosophy, that is, just with the history of philosophy.

Analogous considerations are suggested by some of the corollaries Croce deduces from the historical concept of philosophy. As when, for example, he denies the concept of a *fundamental or general* philosophical problem, as almost a *survival of the past*, for the reason that philosophical problems are infinite and all form an organism in which "no single part is the foundation of all the others, but each by turns is foundation and superstructure" (pp. 139-40). He himself cannot but make a distinction in philosophy between a *secondary and episodical* part and a principal and fundamental part (as he does at least for ancient and medieval philosophy. *Nuovi Saggi*, p. 104); and he even speaks of a philosophy *in general or general* philosophy (*in genere o generale*, p. 88), and of a "fundamental philosophical inquiry" (p. 110), which with him, as we know, becomes an inquiry concerning "the forms of the mind, and their distinction and relation, and the precise mode of their relation to one another"; and he cannot conceive philosophy proper otherwise than as "the *foundation* and at the same time the justification of the new historiography" (p. 285). It is true that, having established the unity of philosophy and historiography and admitted even the legitimacy of the partition of this unity into its two elements, he does not think he is attributing other than a literary and pedagogical value to this partition, it being possible "to bring together on the same plane in verbal exposition now one now the other of the two elements" (p. 136). But setting verbal exposition aside, the logical position remains that philosophy, which Croce calls a methodology of historiography, in its role of elucidating the categories constitutive of historical judgments or rather of the directing concepts in historical interpretation, is the basis and presupposition of philosophical historiography. And in a form relative and adapted to the degree of philosophical reflexion possessed by the historian, it is always the basis and presupposition of every definite historiography. This surely means that what is fundamental in thought does not precede it chronologically; therefore it lives and develops in the dialectical unity of thought itself together with the concurrent elements. Thus, to say that the act of the subject is a synthesis of the position of the subject and of the object does not affect the fact that the object may be posited by the subject. What is true of philosophy is true of historiography, not because the one is constituted before the other, but because the unity which stands at the foundation of both when we distinguish them one from another is philosophy and not historiography. It is, that is to say, the active understanding, and not the object understood, in which that activity is made manifest. To say it is the latter is, I am always insisting, to view the matter from the transcendental point of view.

[1] Who wrote with insight: "Sicut rerum omnium, quae in universo sunt, admirabilis est colligatio et nexus et ordo, ita in scientiis contingere necesse fuit, ut colligatae essent, et mutuum sibi auxilium praestarent" ("De Regressu," in Rosmini, *Logica,* p. 274 n.). Rosmini, who founds his concept of the solid circle on the "synthesizing character of nature" (*sintesismo della natura*), formulates it thus: "The mind cannot know any particular thing except by means of a virtual cognition of the whole," the mind therefore has "to pass to the actual cognition of the particular by means of its virtual acquaintance (*notizia*) with the whole; and to return from actual particular cognition to the actual acquaintance, that is with some degree of actuality of the whole itself" (p. 274). But the untenable distinction between the virtual and the actual prevents Rosmini from perceiving the deeper meaning of the circle. He will not let us take it as the identity of the two terms bound together by the circle. It was impossible, indeed, for him to give up the distinction of actual and virtual, because he had not attained to the concept of process in which distinction is generated from within identity itself. Hegel, on this matter more exact than Rosmini, had said: "Philosophy forms a *circle:* it has a First, an immediate, since in general we must begin with something unproved, which is not a conclusion. But what philosophy begins with is a relative immediate, since from another end-point it must appear a conclusion. It is a consequence which does not hang in air, it is not an immediate beginning, but is circulating" (*Grundlegen der Phil, des Rechts,* § 2, Zusatz). On the circularity of thought consult the theory expounded by me in *Sistema di Logica,* vol. i. pt. ii., and the "Superamento del logo astratto," in the *Giornale critico della filosofia italiana,* i. (1920), pp. 201-10.
[2] See on this argument chapter iii. and iv. of my *Riforma delta Dialettica hegeliana,* and also one of my contributions to *La Critica,* 1916, pp. 64 ff. Cf. Croce, *Logica,* pp. 209-21.
[3] By philology is meant the "knowledge of the known," to quote F. A. Boeckh's definition, one which is in complete accord with Vico's (except that in Vico the thought is profounder) "*conoscenza del certo.*"

Chapter Fourteen - Art, Religion and History

In introducing the concept of art in its distinction from the concept of philosophy, I will first direct attention to what appears to me the crucial point in this distinction. A philosophical system excludes nothing thinkable from the field of its speculation. It is philosophy in so far as the real, which the mind aims at understanding, is the absolute real, everything whatever which it is possible to think. On the other hand, a work of art, although it, too, expresses a world, expresses only the artist's world. And the artist, when he returns from art to life, feels that he returns to a reality different from that of his fantasy. The poet courts life, but a life whose value consists precisely in its not being inserted into the life which the practical man sets before him as his goal, nor into that which the philosopher tries to reconstruct logically in his thinking. The impossibility of such insertion lies in the fact that the poet's "life" is a subjective free creation detached from the real, a creation in which the subject himself is realized and, as it were, enchained, and posits himself in his immediate abstract subjectivity. The kind of dream situation described by Leopardi in his poem "Alia sua Donna," and in his "Dialogo di Torquato Tasso e del suo genio familiare," is what every poet and every artist experiences in regard to his own ideal, and, in general, to every creature of his imagination. [1]

This is the deep ground of truth to which Manzoni has given expression in an essay in which he subjects to criticism the historical novel as a form of art (*Del romanzo storico e in genere de componimenti misti di storia e d' invenzione*). He rightly rejects the romance which mingles invention with history as poetry, because the poet's invention or rather his creative subjective freedom is the very essence of poetry, and poetry can allow no limitation in the adjustment of it to the facts of historical reality. Yet he is wrong in so far as he would deduce from this an aesthetic defect in every historical romance. The poet can idealize history with no greater restriction of his freedom than any other abstract material taken as the object of his artistic contemplation imposes on him. Has not Manzoni himself idealized history in *I promessi sposi?* The history, indeed, or whatever the material of art be, is not prized for any value it may possess in itself considered in separation from the art which invests it. The material of art has worth, means, is what it is, by reason of the life it lives in the poet's soul. The matter is not there for its own sake but for the Soul's life, for its feeling. It represents the "I" as it stands in its subjective immediacy.

This is Croce's meaning when he says that art is always and essentially *lyrical*. And it is what De Sanctis meant when he said, with equal truth, that art is form in which the content is fused, absorbed, annulled. But philosophy also is form, as thought, in whose actuality is the object's life. The difference is that art is the form of subjectivity, or, as we also say, of the mind's immediate individuality. Therefore in Leopardi we are not to look for philosophical thought, a world concept, but for Leopardi's feeling, that is, his personality, the very Leopardi who gives concrete life and soul to a world - which is yet a system of ideas. Take Leopardi's soul from his world, go to his poems and prose not for the expression of his feeling but for a philosophy to be discussed and made good by rational arguments and you have destroyed Leopardi's poetry.

This individuality, personality, immediate subjectivity, is not opposed to the *impersonality* which has been rightly held to be an essential character of art. Without this *impersonality* where would be the universality, infinity or eternity by virtue of which the work of art at once soars above the empirical individual, be coming a source of joy to all minds, conquering the force of ages and endowed with immortality? The impersonality of which Gustave Flaubert, [2] an exquisite artist who reflected deeply on the nature of art, who had no doubt his exaggerations and prejudices, speaks, was this universality of mind as a transcendental "I," constituting the present reality of every "I." The personality which must be excluded from art is rather that which characterizes the empirical I, the Self withdrawn from the perfect light of self-consciousness, which in art must prevail in all its effulgent power.

Self-consciousness is consciousness of self; but with a difference. Consciousness of self is one side only, the thesis, in the spiritual dialectic in which consciousness of the object as other than self is the antithesis. Art is consciousness of self, a pure, abstract, self-consciousness, dialecticized it is true (for otherwise it could not be realized), but taken in itself and in abstraction from the antithesis in which it is realized. Thence it is imprisoned in an ideal, which is a dream, within which it lives feeding on itself, or rather creating its own world. Even to common sense, for which the real world is not created by mind, the art world appears a subjective creation. And the art world is in fact a kind of secondary and intermittent creation made possible by the creation which is original and constant, that in which mind posits itself in spatializing itself, in the absolute meaning of that term.

Since, then, the most characteristic feature of art is the raising of self-consciousness in its abstract immediacy to a higher power, it thus detaches itself from general consciousness and withdraws into the dream or fantasy. Hence it is clear that a history of art, in so far as it is art, is inconceivable. Every work of art is a self-enclosed individuality, an abstract subjectivity empirically posited among all other such in an atomistic fashion. Every poet has his own aesthetic problem which he solves on his own account and in such wise that it withdraws him from any intrinsic relation with his contemporaries and successors. Moreover, every poet in each of his works propounds and solves a particular aesthetic problem, so that his works, so far as we regard exclusively their character as art, are the expression of a spiritual reality fragmentary in its nature and from time to time new and incommensurable with itself. There is no genre, there are only particulars. Not only is there not an aesthetic reality such as literature, constituting for the historian of literature a genre, the development of which he supposes himself to trace, but there is not even an aesthetic reality answering to such a phrase as, for example, "the art of Ariosto." Each of Ariosto's comedies, satires, poems or other works, is an art by itself.

It is true we write histories of literature and of the single arts, and, as we said in the last chapter, to understand Ariosto is to understand his language, and to do this we must get away from his poem, and from himself as a definite individual, and go back and immerse ourselves in the history of the culture out of which has germinated his whole spirituality, the spirituality expressed to us in the poet's words. But when we have learnt the language and can read the poem, we have to forget the whole of the long road we have had to travel in order to learn it. Then there is our own mentality acquired by what we have learnt and what we have been, we have to loosen that and forget ourselves in the poet's world and dream with him drawing aside with him out of the high road along which in history spiritual reality travels, just as when we are dreaming the world is forgotten and all the bonds which bind us to the reality of the objects in which dialectically our real life is made concrete are broken. So though it is true that a history of the literature or art of a people is possible, such as we have, for example, in De Sanctis's *Storia delta letteratura italiana,* one of our noblest historical works, one in which we feel as it were the very heart-beat of the dialectical life of mind, yet if such a history would be something more than a gallery or museum in which works of art are collected which have no intrinsic art-relation to one another, - unless it be the light thrown on them by the proximity of kindred works of the same school or of the same period and therefore generally of the same or similar technique, [3] - if it would be more than this then it can only be a history of mind in its concreteness, out of which art bursts forth as the plants spring from the soil. So that a history of art in its aesthetic valuations must always necessarily break the historical thread, and when the ends are reunited the thread ceases to be a pure aesthetic valuation. Aesthetic valuation is fused in the general dialectic of history, the standpoint of which is the unique value of mind as the constructor of history. In short, when we are looking at art we do not see history and when we are looking at history we do not see art. [4]

Much the same, conversely, holds of religion. Religion is not philosophy. We saw this when treating of the immortality of the soul. Religion may be defined as the antithesis of art. Art is the exaltation of the subject released from the chains of the real in which the subject is posited positively; and religion is the exaltation of the object, released from the chains of the mind, in which the identity, knowability and rationality of the object consists. The object in its abstract opposition to knowing is the real. By that opposition knowing is excluded from reality, and the object is therefore *eo ipso* unknowable, only affirmable mystically as the immediate adhesion of the subject to the object. It is the position of Parmenides, and from it Gorgias derived the first motive of his negation of the possibility of knowing. [5] In its absolute unknowability the object not only will not tolerate the presence of the subject but will not even tolerate the presence of other objects. And as there is no atomism which does not necessarily resolve itself into unity, so there is no pure polytheism which does not lead to the idea of a higher divinity which confers the divine power on all the others. The strictly religious moment of religion can only be the moment of mono theism, for in that the object is posited in its opposition to the subject, and the subject cancelled, and there remains no possibility of passing from it and positing other objects, or of differentiating it in any way as first. [6]

If, then, we accept this position of the divine, as the absolute, immobile and mysterious object, is it possible for us, from the religious point of view, to conceive a history, a development? But a development can only be of the subject, and religiously the subject has no value. On the other hand it is impossible that the mind should fix itself at the simple religious standpoint by annulling itself as subject, because the very annulling cannot occur without an affirmation of the activity of mind. Mind is borne, as by its own nature, from time to time aloft above every religious standpoint, shaking itself free in its autonomy by criticizing its concept of the divine and thereby proceeding to ever more spiritual forms of religion. So that in its religiousness mind is immobile, it moves only by continually overcoming its own religious moment and absorbing it in philosophy.

The history of religion accordingly either takes a rationalistic form, and then it depreciates the true and essential religiousness of every particular religion, by annulling the value which each religion in claiming for itself cannot but deny to others. History of religion then becomes the history of the human mind, the mind polarized in the moment of its antithesis, withdrawn from its true dialectic, and dialecticized abstractly as a consciousness in which the moment of free self-consciousness is suppressed. It is then no longer a history of religion but a history of the fundamental dialectic of the mind, which is a synthesis of consciousness and self-consciousness in which religion is deprived of its abstract religiousness and becomes philosophy. Or the history of religion takes a form which maintains the specific value of religion; and then it no longer finds matter for history. History means development, that is a unity of a multiplicity, whereas the religious consciousness admits no multiplicity, it admits neither preparatory theophanies, nor increase and progress such as a dogmatic development which is other than a merely analytical commentary. [7]

As with art, so with religion, in each case history is constructed by bringing it into the universal history of the dialectical development of mind. In this development art and religion are spiritual positions, concepts of reality, and in being such are, essentially, history of philosophy. So that a history of art and a history of religion, in so far as they are really conceivable and therefore possible to carry out, are histories of philosophy, and even so they are histories in time which are resolved into an ideal history just to the extent that they are shown in their own nature to belong to the history of philosophy.

[1] The stanza of the poem is:
    Viva mirarti omai
Nulla spene m avanza;
S' allor non fosse, allor che ignudo e solo

> Per novo calle a peregrina stanza
> Verrà lo spirto mio. Già sul novello
> Aprir di mia giornata incerta e bruna
> Te viatrice in questo arido suolo
> Io mi pensai. Ma non è cosa in terra
> Che ti somigli; e s' anco pari alcuna
> Ti fosse al volto, agli atti, alia favella,
> Saria, cosi conforme, assai men bella.

(Henceforth to behold thee living no hope remains, unless it should be when my spirit, naked and alone, sets forth on new, untravelled ways to seek its abiding-place. When my earthly sojourn newly opened, dark and drear, even then I had my thought of thee, a wanderer on this barren waste. Yet on earth is nothing which resembles thee, and were there anything even to compare to thee in face, in action and in speech, however like it be to thee, it still falls short of thy beauty.)

The following is the passage from the "Dialogue between Torquato Tasso and his familiar Spirit."

Tasso. Were it not that I have no more hope of seeing Leonora again, I could believe I had not yet lost the power of being happy.

Spirit. Which do you consider the sweeter, to see the loved lady, or to think of her?

Tasso. I do not know. When present with me she seemed a woman; far away she appeared and appears to me a goddess.

Spirit. These goddesses are so amiable, that when any of them approaches you, in a twinkling they doff their divinity, detach their halo and put it in their pocket, in order not to dazzle the mortal who stands before them.

Tasso. What you say is only too true. But does it not seem to you a great fault in ladies, that they prove to be so different from what we imagine them?

Spirit. I do not see that it is their fault that they are made of flesh and blood and not of nectar and ambrosia. What in the world possesses the thousandth part or even the shadow of the perfection which you think ladies have? I", surprises me that you are not astonished to find men are men, creatures of little worth and unlovable, since you cannot understand why women are not angels.

Tasso. In spite of this I am dying to see her and speak to her again.

Spirit. Well, this night I will bring her to you in your dream. She shall be beautiful as youth and so courteous in manner that you will take courage and speak to her more freely and readily than you have ever spoken to her. And then you will take her hand and look her full in the face, and you will be surfeited with the sweetness that will fill your soul. And to-morrow whenever you think of this dream you will feel your heart overflowing with tenderness.

Tasso. What consolation! A dream in exchange for truth.

Spirit. What is truth?

Tasso. I know no more than Pilate knew.

Spirit. Well, let me tell you. Between knowing the truth and the dream there is only this difference, that the dream is always and many times sweeter and more beautiful than the truth can ever be.

Tasso. Is a dreamed pleasure then as good as a real pleasure?

Spirit. It is. Indeed I know a case of one who, when his lady has appeared to him in a kindly dream, the whole next day he avoids meeting her and seeing her, because he knows that the real lady cannot compare with the dream image, and that reality dispelling the illusion from his mind, would deprive him of the extraordinary delight the dream gave.

[2] Cf. Antonio Fusco, La filosofia dell arte in Gustavo Flaubert, Messina, 1917.
[3] Technique is an antecedent of art. In art technique is overcome and annulled. This is clearly shown in B. Croce, *Problemi di estetica,* pp. 247-255.
[4] Cf. "Pensiero e poesia nella Divina Comedia," in my *Frammenti di estetica,* Lanciano, 1920.
[5] Cf. *Sistema di Logica,* i. pp. 151-153.
[6] Cf. *I discorsi di religione,* Firenza, Vallecchi, 1920.
[7] See Gentile, *Il modernismo e i rapporti tra religione e filosofia,* Bari, Laterza, 1909, pp. 65-78. For the whole of the discussion in this chapter on the abstractness alike of art and of religion and of their concreteness in philosophy, cf. Gentile, *Sommario di pedagogia come scienza filosofica,* Bari, Laterza (1913-1914), vol. i. part iii. chap. 4, and vol. ii. part ii. chaps. 2 and 4.

Chapter Fifteen - Science, Life and Philosophy

We not only distinguish philosophy from art and religion, we also distinguish it from science. Although science has the cognitive character of philosophy yet *stricto sensu* it is not philosophy. It has not the universality of its object which philosophy has, and therefore it has not the *critical and systematic* character of philosophy. Every science is one among others and is therefore particular. When a particular science transcends the limits of its own special subject-matter it tends to be transformed into philosophy. As particular, that is, concerned with an object which itself is particular and can have its own meaning apart from other objects which coexist with it, science rests on the naturalistic presupposition. For it is only when we think of reality as nature that it presents itself to us as composed of many elements, any one of which can be made the object of a particular investigation. A naturalistic view is the basis, then, of the analytical character of every science. Thence the logically necessary tendency of science in every period towards mechanism and materialism.

Again, every science presupposes its object. The science arises from the presupposition that the object exists before it is thought, and independently altogether of being known. Had science to apprehend the object as a creation of the subject, it would have first to propound the problem of the position of the real in all its universality, and then it would no longer be science, but philosophy. In presupposing the object as a datum to be accepted not proved, a natural datum, a fact, every particular science is necessarily empirical, unable to conceive knowledge otherwise than as a relation of the object to the subject extrinsic to the nature of both. This relation is sensation or a knowing which is a pure fact on which the mind can then work by abstraction and generalization. Science, therefore, is *dogmatic*. It does not prove and it cannot prove its two fundamental presuppositions: (1) that its object exists; (2) that the sensation, the initial and substantial fact of knowledge, which is the immediate relation with the object, is valid. [1]

Philosophy, on the other hand, proposes to prove the value of the object, and of every form of the object, in the system of the real, and its why and how. It gives, or seeks to give, an account not only of the existence of the objects which the particular sciences dogmatically presuppose, but even of the knowing (which itself also is at least a form of reality) whereby every science is constituted. And therefore philosophy, in being systematic, is critical.

In science, in so far as it is particular, with the naturalistic and materialistic tendency and by reason of it, there goes *pari passu* the tendency to empiricism and dogmatism. Through these two tendencies science has continually come to set itself up as a form of philosophy and arrayed itself against the philosophy which has sought by overcoming mechanism, empiricism and dogmatism, to set forth the universal concept of the world in its metaphysical ideality. And so science, in the very spirit which rejects and opposes philosophy, is the partisan of a philosophy: the feeblest and most naive form which philosophy can assume.

In calling science naturalistic we do not mean to identify it with the sciences of nature alone. Besides the natural sciences there are what are called the mental and moral sciences. The moral sciences are equally naturalistic, in so far as they also fail to attain the universality and system of philosophy and have a particular and presupposed object as a fact. All the moral sciences have this character. This is why they are sciences and not philosophy. They build upon an intuition of the reality to which their object belongs, identical with the naturalist's intuition of nature, and therefore, albeit under another name, they conceive reality as nature. Their reality is positive, in the meaning that it is presupposed and not posited by mind, it is therefore outside the order and unity which belongs to mind, pulverized in the inorganic multiplicity of its elements. The value of mind is therefore for these sciences inconceivable.

Even philosophy of mind ceases to be philosophy any longer and becomes simply science when it seeks to explain mind, both in its wholeness and in the elements of which empirically it appears to be constituted, as a *de facto* reality. So, too, what is called *the general theory of law* falls outside the proper ambit of the philosophy of law, because it regards law as simply a diversified phenomenology, a complex of experiential data. The science with this subject-matter must comport itself just as every natural science comports itself towards the class of phenomena to which it refers, determining its general characters and *de facto* rules. [2] We may say then that strictly philosophy has mind and the sciences have nature for their object.

Even the mathematical sciences, which have themselves established the postulates by which the world of pure quantity is constituted, do not treat even their own postulated reality in any way differently from the natural sciences. They have in common the particularity of the object and the dogmatic character of the propositions, a dogmatic character which results from conceiving the object as self-subsisting in its absolute necessity, confronting the subject which can do no more in regard to it than presuppose it and analyse it.

Such being its nature, can there be a history of science in the true meaning of history? It is evident that for science there is no alternative, it must exclude the concept of a unique history of history of science, for the very reason that science breaks up into sciences, each of which, in so far as it is science and not philosophy, is separated from the others and has therefore no essential relations with them. But besides being particular, every science is, as we have said, empirical and dogmatic, because it presupposes the known to the knowing, precisely as Plato presupposed the ideas, which are purely the objects of its knowing, to the mind which knows them. And for the same reason that it is impossible to conceive a dialectic of the Platonic ideas and therefore in the Platonic theory a history of philosophy, it is impossible even to conceive the history of science. There being a definite reality to know, either we know it or we do not know it. If it is partly known and partly not, that can only mean that it has separable parts, and then there is a part which is completely known and a part which is completely unknown. Beyond truth, which is posited in a form which has no degrees, there is nothing but error, and between truth and error the abyss. The history of the sciences in fact for the most part assumed the aspect of an enumeration of errors and prejudices, which ought to be relegated entirely to the pre-history rather than to the history of science. History ought to be the development of science, and science as such can have no development, because it presupposes a perfect truth which we cannot reach by degrees but to which we suddenly leap. Therefore the concept which completely fits the naturalistic sciences is *discovery*, intuition, substantially identical with the Platonic concept of the primitive and transcendent intuition of the ideas.

A history of a science is only possible on one condition: it must not treat the science as a science in its particularity and in its dogmatic character. Just as the history of art and religion is rendered possible by resolving the abstractness of each in the concreteness of philosophy, so in the same way a history of a science is possible. Every rational attempt at a history of the sciences takes each particular science as a development of the philosophical concepts which are immanent in the science itself, by studying every form of these concepts, not for the value the particular form may have at a particular time for the scientific student as an objective determination of reality, but as a degree of mentality in perpetual formation by which the single scientific problems are continually being set and solved. The object it sets before itself is no longer the object which is presupposed by the mind, but the life of the mind. And it then becomes clear that the greater concreteness of this history will not depend on the single histories of the special sciences included in it, but on its being a unique history, representing the dialectical process of the thought which comes to be realized as the thought of nature or as empiricist philosophy.

When we reflect on the necessity which causes the history of science to become identified with the history of philosophy we see that it has its root in the fundamental identity of the epistemological position of scientific knowing with art on the one hand and religion on the other. Science, in so far as it is particular and non-systematic, is, in regard to reality, in the position of art, for art, as we have seen, is not philosophy because its reality is a particular reality and therefore purely subjective. On the other hand, in so far as science does not posit its object but presupposes it as already existing, it makes mind confront a real, whose reality excludes the reality of the mind. Thereby it is in its very nature agnostic, ready to say not only *ignoramus*, but also, and primarily, *ignorabimus*, as religion does before its unknown and fearfully mysterious god. Ignorant of the true being of things, which is inscrutable, science knows only what it calls the pure phenomenon, a subjective appearance, as one-sided and fragmentary as the poet's fantasies which only shine forth in the imagination, in a dream in which the mind is estranged from the real. Science, therefore, oscillating between art and religion, does not unify them, as philosophy does, in a higher synthesis, but combines the defect and one-sidedness of each, the defect of art in regard to objectivity and universality with the defect of religion in regard to subjectivity and rationality. Science claiming to be science in so far as it abstracts from the one side or the other of the concrete unity of mind, finds itself unable to actualize itself unless it can overcome its abstractness. This it can only do in the spiritual act which alone is real as the inseparable unity of subject and object, the unity whose process is philosophy in its history.

We have still to consider one term distinctive of philosophy, - life, practical activity, will. Were this reality something with a history of its own different from that of philosophy, it would seriously impugn our whole position of the identity of philosophy with its history, because it concerns our fundamental concept, and our principle, the concept of mind as unconditioned reality.

But if we set aside the fantastic relations supposed to exist between the will and external reality, relations which empirical psychology tries in vain to rationalize, making volitional activity intervene as a causality of movement in a physical world presumed as transcending psychical reality, - if we set these aside, what criterion of distinction is there between knowledge and will? Every time we contrapose the theoretical to the practical we find we have first of all to presuppose the reality intellectualistically, just as empiricism does and just as Greek philosophy continued to do through out its course, so precluding every way of identifying mind with practical activity. For theory is opposed to practice in this, that theory has reference to a world which presupposes, whereas practice has reference to a world which presupposes it. So that from the theoretical point of view reality is either nature, or idea which is not mind and cannot therefore be valued otherwise than as nature. If, then, morality is the value of a world which has its root in mind, it cannot be conceived outside of the spiritual life. A philosophy which does not intuitively apprehend reality as spiritual - and before Christianity no philosophy did - has no place for morality, nor indeed is it possible for it to conceive practice in general. [3]

Apart from the whole course of our inquiry so far, it is now easy to prove that if we admit this twofold view of mind, theoretical and practical, and maintain that for mind as theoretical activity reality is not mind but simple nature, the result is that we destroy the possibility not only of conceiving the practical activity but even of conceiving the theoretical. The Pauline doctrine presents most vividly the consciousness of the opposition between the *spirit* (object of practical activity) and the *flesh* or *nature* (object of theoretical activity); but Paul makes shipwreck over the concept of *grace,* a concept which has its origin in the impossibility of really conceiving the creativeness of mind as will, once the concept of nature is set up. Indeed, if there is a world which already is all it can be thought to be (and can we conceive anything which, in being thought, is not assigned to the object of the cognitive activity?), and if we declare this world to be a presupposition of mind and hence a reality which must already exist in order that the mind shall be and work, we can then no longer possibly think that it is brought into being by the action of mind. From the naturalistic standpoint (which is necessarily an intellectualistic standpoint, so far, that is, as mind is conceived as the merely theoretical intellect) there is no place for a reality which has its roots in the mind. And yet, on the other hand, if the intellect be merely cognitive and if the whole of reality is posited as its presupposition, how is it itself conceivable? Lying outside the whole it cannot but be nothing.

In all this there is nothing new. We are but looking back and recapitulating an age-long argument, clear to demonstration in the history of philosophy, that a concept of mind as wholly or partially theoretical, in the meaning in which theory is contraposed to life, is absolutely untenable. Life, natural or spiritual, is the reality: theory is merely its contemplation, extraneous to its process, hovering over the world when its long-drawn day is advanced towards evening. The concept is an impossible one. There is no way of conceiving knowledge except as a creation of the reality which is itself knowledge and outside which other reality is inconceivable. Reality is spiritual, in self-creating it creates will, and equally it creates intellect. The one creation is identical with the other. Intellect is will and will has no characteristics which can (speculatively, not empirically) make it a thing distinct from the intellect.

Theory is different from practice, and science is other than life, not because intellect is not will, or will is not intellect, but because of the thought, the real and living act of mind, is taken at one time in the abstract, at another time in the concrete. As the proverb says, it is one thing to speak of death, another to die. So too, the idea of a good action is one thing, the good action another. But the difference between the idea of the good action and the good action itself is not that one is a simple idea, the other an idea actualized, because indeed they are different both as ideas and as actions. The difference consists in this, that in the one case the idea is abstract, in the other concrete. In the first case we have in mind the idea which is a content or abstract result of thought, but not the act by which we think it, and in which its concrete reality truly lies. And in the second we have in mind the idea, not as an object or content of thought, but as the act which actualizes a spiritual reality. An act is never other than what it means. But when we compare two or more acts we ought to notice that we are not in that actuality of the mind in which multiplicity is unity, for in that actuality the comparison is impossible. When an act is an action which is opposed to an idea, the idea is not a spiritual act, but merely the ideal term of the mind which thinks it: an object, not a subject. And equally when an action is completed and we survey it theoretically, the action is no longer an act of the subject but simply an object on which the mind now looks, and which is therefore resolved into the present act of awareness of the action. This awareness is now its real action.

The spiritual life, then, which stands opposed to philosophy is indeed abstractly as its object a different thing from philosophy, but it lives as philosophy. And when it is posited before consciousness as a reality already lived, consciousness resolves it into knowledge in which it reassumes it, and holds it as philosophy.

In such wise, then, philosophy is truly the immanent substance of every form of the spiritual life. And as we cannot conceive a history of philosophy on which philosophy turns its back, it becomes clear that in the concept of the identity of philosophy and its history, and of the eternal reconciliation of one in the other, we have the most perfect and the most open confirmation of the absoluteness of the spiritual reality, inconceivable as limited in any one of its moments by conditions which precede it and somehow determine it. In this concept, if we are not misled, is the strongest proof and the clearest illustration of spiritual freedom. [4]

[1] On the dogmatic and non-systematic character of science cf. *Sistema di Logica*, vol. i. Introduction, chap. i.
[2] Cf. my *Fondamenti della filosqfia del diritto,* Pisa, Spoerri, 1916, chap. i.
[3] I have dealt with this subject in A. Rosmini, *Il principio della morale,* Bari, Laterza, 1914; the *Fondamenti della filosofia del diritto,* chap. ii.; and the *Discorsi di religione,* Firenza, Vallecchi, 1920, chap. iii.
[4] In regard to the identity of knowledge and will, see also Gentile, *Sommario di pedagogia,* i. part i. chap. 14, and part ii. chap. i.

Chapter Sixteen - Reality as Self-Concept and the Problem of Evil

We may sum up our doctrine as the theory that mind, the spiritual reality, is the act which posits its object in a multiplicity of objects, reconciling beginning and their multiplicity and objectivity in its own unity as subject. It is a theory which withdraws from mind every limit of space and time and every external condition. It declares that a real internal multiplication which would make one of its moments a conditionate of anterior moments is inconceivable. Hence history is not the presupposition of present spiritual activity but its reality and concreteness, the basis of its absolute freedom. It starts with, and is summed up in, two concepts, which may be regarded the one as the first principle, the other as the final term, of the doctrine itself.

The first of these concepts is that, strictly speaking, there are not many concepts, because there are not many realities to conceive. When the reality appears multiple it is because we see the many and do not see the root of the multiplicity in its concreteness in which the whole, however many, is one. Hence the true concept of a multiple reality must consist, not in a multiplicity of concepts, but in one unique concept, which is in trinsically determined, mediated, unfolded, in all the multiplicity of its positive moments. Consequently, since the unity is of the subject who conceives the concept, the multiplicity of the concepts of things can be no more than the superficial shell of the nut whose kernel is one concept only, the concept of the subject-centre of all things. So that the true concept, that which alone has a right to be called the concept, is the self-concept (*conceptus sui*). And since we can only speak of reality, in the universal, by means of concepts, so that the sphere of the real osculates with the sphere of the concept, the necessity of conceiving the concept as *conceptus sui* carries with it also the necessity of conceiving reality as *conceptus sui*. That is, the subject who in conceiving the whole conceives himself is the reality itself. It is not, as Schelling, following out in all its consequences the neo-Platonic speculation, supposed, first reality and then concept of self (first Nature, and then Ego), but only self-consciousness or the self-concept, precisely because the concept cannot be understood except as *conceptus sui*. The concept of natural reality, which is not yet I, would not be the concept of self but of other.

This concept of the concept, it is now clear, permeates the whole of metaphysics as science of knowledge, and puts logic in a new light; for physical value, logic has hitherto been understood as a science of the concept in itself, abstracted from the subject who thinks it, as though the concept had for its object the whole of reality, the subject included, reality conceived naturalistically, or idealistically in the manner of Plato. [1]

The other concept, the goal which all our doctrine has in view is the concept of *absolute formalism,* as the conclusion of every science of mind, or rather of every real science. For science must, if it would gain a full understanding of its own object, rise from reality as nature to a complete grasp of the concept of reality as mind. If we mean by *form* and *matter* what Kant meant when he called form the transcendental activity of the mind by which the matter of experience is shaped into a world, the content of consciousness, all that we have explained of the relation between mind and whatever we can consider as opposed to mind authorizes us to conclude that there is no matter outside form, neither as formal matter, that is, elaborated by the activity of the form, nor as raw material on which it might appear that such activity had yet to be exercised. Matter is posited by and resolved into form. So that the only matter there is in the spiritual act is the form itself, as activity. The positive is the form itself, it is positive in so far as it posits, not in so far as it is, as we say, posited.

Even these two concepts, form and matter, apparently so fundamental in their difference, are only one concept. They are the Alpha and Omega of an alphabet which form not a straight line but a circle whose end is its beginning. Form, in fact, can be and must be meant as absolute, it has not matter confronting it, in so far as it is conceived not only as activity [2] but as an activity which produces nothing which it expels from itself and leaves outside, inert and brute, nothing therefore which it posits before thought as radically different from thought itself. So that to conceive thought as absolute form is to conceive reality as *conceptus sui*.

In this concept we have the guiding thread which will lead us out of the labyrinth in which the human mind has been for ever straying, striving after and yet failing to touch anything real outside itself, and always finding itself at grips with something, the identification of itself with which is repugnant to its deepest demands, - evil (pain, error, sin), nature. Let us take care that the thread does not break in our hands.

If reality be conceived as posited, already realized, evil is inconceivable. For evil is what ought not to be, what is opposed to the mind in so far as the mind is what ought to be and sets itself before itself as an end to be reached, and which mind in fact reaches by the manner in which it posits it. What else is pain but the contrary of the pleasure which for each one is, as Vico said, the proclaiming his own nature? The mind's not-being, - that is what is painful. Now if mind (the reality as concept) has being, in the meaning of Parmenides, there is no longer any place for pain. But mind is the negation of Parmenides's *being,* because in so far as it thinks it is *doing,* the non-being of being. So that it is in not being: it fulfils its real nature in so far as this is not already realized and is in process of realization. And hence mind finds itself always confronting itself as its own negation. Hence, too, the providential pain which spurs us on from task to task, and which has been always recognized as the inner spring by which the mind progresses and lives on condition of progressing.

Thus the truth of the concept is assured, because truth is nothing but the attribute which belongs to thought as concept. Were the concept an immediate self-identity with no difference within it as a stone is a stone and two is two, neither more nor less than the determinate sum-total of what is thought, then error would be inconceivable. For error, therefore, we have to repeat the argument in regard to pain. The concept is not already posited but is the positive which posits a process of self-creation which has as its essential moment its own negation, the error opposed to the true. So there is error in the system of the real in so far as the development of its process requires error as its own ideal moment, that is, as a position now passed and therefore discounted. Prove any error to be error and no one will be found to father and support it. Error only is error in so far as it is already overcome, in other words, in so far as it is our own concepts non-being. Like pain, therefore, it is not a reality opposed to that which is mind (*conceptus sui*), it is that reality, but looked back on as one of its ideal moments before its realization.

What we have said of theoretical error applies equally to practical error or moral evil, since intellect itself is will. We may even say that will is the concreteness of intellect. So the true *conceptus sui* is that world self-consciousness which we are not to think of as an abstract philosophy (contraposed to life), but as the highest form of life, the highest peak to which as mind the world can rise. A form which does not rise so high as to cease to be the ground and foundation, the one and single form as it expands from base to apex of the pyramid of life. You conceive the world as other than yourself who conceive it, and the necessity of that concept is a pure logical necessity because it is abstract. But you conceive the world (as you should and at bottom perhaps always do conceive it) as your own reality, there being no other, a self-possessed reality, and then you cannot suppose it outside the necessity of your concept as though the law did not concern you. The rationality of your concept will appear to you as your own law, as duty. What else indeed is duty but the unity of the law of our own doing with the law of the universe? And what else is the immorality of the egoist, with eyes only for his own interest, if it be not the separation he makes between himself and the world, between its law and his law? The history of morality is the history of an ever more spiritualistic understanding of the world. Every new step we take, in ideally tending to the formation of the moral consciousness, is a deepening of the spiritual meaning of life, a greater realizing of reality as self-conceived.

Will it ever be possible, then, to attain perfect goodness (an earthly or a celestial paradise) in a vision of the whole infinite mind if the mind which is the good will as full spiritual reality can only be conceived as development? How can we conceive, either at the beginning or at the end or at any intermediate time, the mind stainless and sinless, if the good will is effort and conquest? If its being is its non-being?

When once the concept of reality as self-concept is understood, we see clearly that our mind's real need is not that error and evil should disappear from the world but that they should be eternally present. Without error there is no truth, without evil there is no good, not because they are two terms bound to one another in the way that Plato, [3] following Heraclitus, said pleasure and pain are bound together, but because error and evil are the non-being of that reality, mind, the being of which is truth and goodness. Mind is truth and goodness but only on condition that it is making them in conquering its own inner enemy, consuming it, and therefore having always the need of conquering and consuming, as the flame needs fuel. A mind which already is mind is nature. A moral character already constituted as a means of governing conduct mechanically and making sin impossible in the same meaning in which, given the law of gravity, it is held impossible for a body lighter than air to fall to earth, is, as any one may easily understand, the negation of all true and real moral feeling. It is the negation of the freedom which Kant rightly held essential for the moral mind.

There are not, then, error and truth, but error in truth as its content which is resolved in its form. Nor are there good and evil, but evil by which good is sustained, in its absolute formalism.

The problem of the Nature which mind finds always confronting it and therefore holds to be a presupposition of its own being, is identical with the problem or pain, or error and or evil. Like Bruno's Amphitrite, from whose womb all forms are generated and to whose womb all return, mind, which in its concrete position contraposes itself to itself, strives thereby to obtain all the nutriment it needs for its life from beginning to end.

The self-concept, in which alone mind and all that is is real, is an acquiring consciousness of self. This Self is inconceivable as something anterior to and separate from the consciousness of which in the self-concept it is the object. It is realized then in realizing its own object, or, in other words, it is realized in the position affirmed when the self is subject and that identical self is object. It is the I. It is the spiritual reality. It is an identity of self with self, but not an identity posited in its immediacy, so much as an identity which is posited in reflexion. It duplicates itself as self and other, and finds itself in the other. The Self which would be self without other would clearly not be even self because it only is in so far as the other is. Nor would the other were it not itself be other, because the other is only conceivable as identical with the subject. That is, in affirming reality, the subject which affirms is the reality which confronts it in the affirmation.

If we accept this doctrine that dialectic is mind in its life, that outside it there is nothing we can grasp but shadows, intelligible only in relation to the bodies which cast them, three concepts emerge as equally necessary: (1) The reality of the subject, as pure subject; (2) the reality of the object, as pure object; (3) the reality of mind, as the unity or process of the subject, and the immanence of the object in the subject.

Were there no subject what would think? Were there no object what would the thinker think? It is impossible to conceive thought without personality, because thought, however dogmatic or sceptical the form of it we would posit, is *conceptus sui*. It is "I." Thence thought is not mere activity but an activity which relies on itself, and therefore posits itself as a person. But none the less it is equally impossible to conceive thought without its term or fulcrum, because the concept of self realizes the Self as object of knowledge. Thought, then, is conceivable on condition that whenever and in so far as the subject is conceived the object also is conceived. Each is real since thought is real, but nothing is real outside thought.

But even thought would itself be inconceivable if the subject in being the opposite of the object were not at the same time the object itself, and *vice versa*. The reason of this is that the opposition is inherent in the concept of thought as *conceptus sui*. The opposition is between self and self. The difference and otherness belongs wholly to the self or I. It is a relation which will never be intelligible so long as we try to understand it by the analogy of other kinds of relation. The "I," to be exact, is not different from itself, but differentiates itself, thereby positing its own identity as the basis of its own difference. So that the thesis and the antithesis, concurrent in the reality of the self-consciousness (being and not being subject), have their fundamental reality in the synthesis. The synthesis is not subject and object, but only subject, the real subject, realized in the process by which it overcomes the ideality of the pure abstract subject and the concomitant ideality of the pure abstract object. This synthesis as the concrete reality of self-consciousness is the process which is not fact but act, living and eternal act. To think anything truly, means to realize it. And who does not know that it is to this realization mind is working, that it may establish the fulness of freedom, the reign of mind, or *regnum hominis* in which all human civilization, all lordship over nature and subjection of it to human, that is, to spiritual ends, consists? What is the progressive spiritualization of the world but the realization of the synthesis, which reconciles opposition even by preserving it, in the unity, which is its own ground and its whole meaning?

But this human perfectibility, this ever more powerful lordship of man over nature, this progress and increase of the life of mind triumphing ever more surely over the adverse forces of nature, conquering them and subduing them, even within the soul itself, making, as Vico said, of the very passions virtues, this march of humanity, as we usually picture it, with its stages, through space and time, - what is it but the empirical and external representation of the immanent eternal victory, the full and absolute victory, of mind over nature, of that immanent resolution of nature in mind, which, like the concept of the necessary reconciliation of temporal history in ideal and eternal history, is the only possible speculative concept of the relation between nature and mind?

Descend into your soul, take by surprise in its essential character, as it is in the living act, in the quivering of your spiritual life, that meaning of our "nature" which grows so formidable in all the vastness of time and of space which you confer on it. What is it? It is that obscure limit of your spiritual being beyond which your living spirit is ever passing out and to which it is ever returning. It is the limit which marks the boundary of the Kantian phenomenon, as in ancient philosophy it used to stand behind the subjective sensation of Democritus and Protagoras, concealing from thought a chaos of impervious and raw materiality. It is the limit which Plato found at the margin of his ideal being, the dark hemisphere encircling the horizon of the luminous heaven of thought. It is the limit which even to Hegel seemed to set bounds to logic and to demand a crossing of it by the Idea which makes nature, by descending into space and time and breaking its own unity in the dispersed multiplicity of the existents which are its particulars. Seen from within your soul, is not this "nature" your own non-being, the non-being of your own inward commotion, of the act by which you are to yourself? It is not your nonbeing as something existing for others to recognize. It is the non-being which belongs to your act itself; what you are not and must become, and which you bring into being by the act which posits it. Consider any definite object of your thought whatsoever, it can be no other than your own definite thought itself. It is what you have thought and what you in your actual consciousness have set apart as object. What else is it but a form of your non-being, or rather of the ideal moment to which you must contrapose it, and which you must contrapose to yourself in order to be yourself a definite real?

Nature, like mind, has two faces, one which looks outward and one which looks inward. Nature seen from without, as we see it before us, a pure abstract object, is a limit of mind and rules it. Whence it is that mind cannot see even itself from within, and conceives itself mechanically, in space, in time, without freedom, without value, mortal. But nature has another face. It is that which it presents to our view when, awaking from that dream which for ordinary common sense is philosophy, and arousing ourselves, and strenuously reasserting our personality, we find nature itself within our own mind as the non-being which is life, the eternal life which is the real opposite of what Lucretius called *mors immortalis*. [4] Nature, then, is the *eternal past of our eternal present,* the iron necessity of the past in the absolute freedom of the present. And beholding this nature, man in his spiritual life recovers the whole power of the mind and recognizes the infinite responsibility which lies in the use he makes of it, rising above all trivial incidents of the universal life, such as resemble in the ordinary view the buzzing of insects on the back of the unfeeling Earth, and attending to the life breath of the Whole whose reality culminates in self-consciousness.

[1] With regard to the concept as *conceptus sui,* cf. Gentile, *Modernismo,* p. 202; *Sommario di Pedagogia,* i. pp. 72-75; and *Sistema di Logica,* vol. ii.
[2] Even before Kant, Spinoza had observed this. "Nec sane aliquis de hac re dubitare potest, nisi putet ideam quid mutum instar picturae in tabula, et non modum cogitandi esse, nempe ipsum intelligere," *Ethics,* ii. prop. 43 sch.
[3] "Socrates, sitting up on the couch, bent and rubbed his leg, saying, as he was rubbing: How singular is a thing called pleasure, and how curiously related to

pain, which might be thought to be the opposite of it; for they are never present to a man at the same instant, and yet he who pursues either is generally compelled to take the other; their bodies are two, but they are joined by a single head. And I cannot help thinking that if Aesop had remembered them, he would have made a fable about God trying to reconcile their strife, and how, when he could not, he fastened their heads together; and this is the reason why when one comes the other follows: as I know by my own experience now, when after the pain in my leg which was caused by the chain pleasure appears to succeed." - *Phaedo,* 60 B.C. (Jowett's translation). This is all very true but not the whole truth. Strictly speaking, Socrates not only has pleasure because he has had pain (which is now a mental image in time), he also had pleasure even while experiencing the pain in so far as he perceived that it was pain. For perceiving, like scratching, is an activity, however small its degree. And this comes to saying that pleasure and pain, like positive and negative, are not outside one another. The negative is contained in the positive in so far as the positive is its own process. Both are one reality. Pessimism with its abstract conception of a limit which it would draw close round the whole life of the mind, does not understand the reality because it is itself a misunderstanding.

[4] Lucretius, *De rerum natura,* iii. 869, "mortalem vitam mors cum immortalis ademit."

Chapter Seventeen - Epilogue and Corollaries

We may now briefly sum up the main features of the doctrine we have sketched.

An absolute idealism cannot conceive the idea except as thought in act, as all but consciousness of the idea itself, if we keep for *idea* the objective meaning, which it originally had in Plato, and which it continues to have in common thought and in the presuppositions of *scientific* knowing, that of being the term of thought or intuition. On the other hand, an idealism which is not absolute can only be a one-sided idealism or half-truth, which is as much as to say an incoherent idealism. It may be transcendent, like Plato's, which leaves matter, and therefore the becoming of nature, outside the idea. It may be immaterial, like Berkeley's, for which all is idea except God, the reality who makes perception be. It may be critical or transcendental, like Kant's, in which the idea is a mere unifying activity of a manifold arising from another source, and the idea therefore supposes its opposite, an unknowable, which is the negation of the idea itself. An idealistic conception aims at conceiving the absolute, the whole, as idea, and is therefore intrinsically absolute idealism. But absolute it cannot be unless the idea coincides with the act of knowing it, because and here we find the very root of the difficulty in which Platonism is entangled were the idea not the act itself through which it is known, it would leave something outside itself, and the idealism would then no longer be absolute.

An idealism conceived strictly in this meaning fulfils the task which Fichte assigned to philosophy and named *Wissenschaftslehre;* a task not fulfilled even by Hegel, for he presupposed to the absolute idea or the idea for itself, the idea in itself and the idea outside itself. That is, to the absolute idea he presupposed logic and nature. In the final solution of the cosmic drama these acquire in the human mind the self-consciousness to which they aspire and of which they have need. Self-consciousness must therefore be said to be their true essence. Hegel's use of the "I" of Fichte, in order to solve the difficulty Fichte's conception gave rise to from the abstractness of his concept of the "I," an "I" incap able of generating the "not-I" from its inward nature as "I," ends in destroying rather than in establishing the absolute reality of the "I." The "I" is not absolute if it has something outside it on which it is based, instead of being the foundation of everything and therefore having the whole within itself. The defect of Hegelianism is precisely that it makes what ever presupposes the "I" precede it. Even without this defect it is unfaithful to the method of immanence which belongs to absolute idealism, and turns again to the old notions of reality in itself which is not the thought by which it is revealed to us. [1]

The idealism which I distinguish as *actual* inverts the Hegelian problem: for it is no longer the question of a deduction of thought from Nature and of Nature from the Logos, but of Nature and the Logos from thought. By thought is meant present thinking in act, not thought defined in the abstract; thought which is *absolutely ours,* in which the "I" is realized. Aid through this inversion the deduction becomes, what in Hegel it was impossible it could become, the real proof of itself which thought provides in the world's history, which is its history. The impossibility of the Hegelian deduction arises from the fact that it starts from the abstract and seeks to attain the concrete, and to pass from the abstract to the concrete is impossible. The concrete for the philosopher is his philosophy, thought which is in the act of realizing itself, and in regard to which the logic of the real, which governs that thought itself, and the Nature on which that logic must be posed as a pedestal of the history of thought, are alike abstract. From the concrete to the abstract, on the other hand, there is but one passage, - the eternal process of self-idealization. What else indeed is the act of thought, the "I," but self-consciousness or reality which is realized in being idealized? And what is the idealization of this reality, realized just when it is idealized, but the dualizing by which the act of thought balances itself between the two selves, of which the one is subject and the other object only in their reciprocal mirroring of one another through the concrete and absolute act of thought? The dualizing implies an inward differentiating of the real which in idealizing itself distinguishes itself from itself (subject from object). The "I" knows, therefore, when it finds itself in its ideality confronting itself in its reality as different from itself. And it is in fact radically different. It is the negation of the real which is idealized. The one is act, the *thinking,* the other is *what is thought,* the opposite of thinking.

The thinking is activity, and what is thought is a product of the activity, flat is, a thing. The activity as such is *causa sui* and therefore it is freedom. The thing is a simple effect which has the principle of its own being outside it, and therefore it is mechanism. The activity *becomes,* the thing *is.* The thing *is* as *other,* a term of the relation to an other. In that is its mechanistic nature. Thereby it is one among many, that is, its concept already implies multiplicity, number. The activity, on the contrary, realizes itself in the other, or rather it is realized in itself as other. It is therefore a relation with itself, an absolute, infinite unity, without multiplicity.

The multiplicity of the thing thought implies the reciprocal exclusion of the elements of the multiplicity and thereby space. The thing thought is nature. It is nature in so far as it is the idea in which the reality has been revealed to itself. So that the Platonic idealism is a pure naturalism rather than a spiritualism. It is the affirmation of a reality which is not mind, and if there be such a reality mind is no longer possible. This is the characteristic alike of a transcendent ideal ism like Plato's, and of the crudest materialistic naturalism.

The difficulty we all experience in understanding this new deduction of nature from the idea as thought is due to the fact that we entirely lose sight of the abstractness of the nature we are proposing to deduce, and restrict ourselves to the false common notion of nature which represents it as concrete and actual reality. In so doing we are ignoring entirely the true character of actual thought as absolute reality. For naturalism has always been the necessary consequence, and as it were another aspect, of intellectualism. We can indeed define intellectualism as the conception of a reality which is intended as the opposite, and nothing but the opposite, of mind. If mind has such independent reality confronting it, it can only know it by presupposing it already realized, and therefore by limiting itself to the part of simple spectator. And the nature it will then know is not what it may see within itself, - that would be spiritualism; but what is other than itself. That alone is nature. But this nature of the intellectualist does not require to be deduced. Were there such an obligation it would be a sign that the intellectualist is right; and then it is no longer a case of deducing nature because, in the intellectualist position, it is itself the first principle. Indeed the problem of the deduction of nature does not arise until we have left the false standpoint of intellectualism and so got rid of the illusion of a natural reality.

In this way we can easily perceive the abstractness of the thing thought as such, or rather of nature in so far as it stands opposed to mind. And then this mysterious nature, impenetrable by the light of the intellect, appears a simple moment of thought: a moment whose spirituality is unveiled in all its purity directly we come to think it in act, in the concrete from which it has been abstracted, in the act of thought in which it is really posited. Since it is impossible - and that it is so should now be abundantly clear to every one - to fix cognitively in the real world, and as it were to surprise, a natural reality without positing it as an idea corresponding to a certain moment of our representative activity and thereby converting the opaque solidity of nature into the translucent inwardness of thought.

There is also in what is thought, taken in itself, a double nature, and its intrinsic contradiction is a form of the restless activity of thought. What is thought cannot be what is now thinkable because it is what is thought, and it is what is thought just because not thinkable. The thing thought is thing, nature, matter, everything which can be considered as a limit of thought, and what limits thought is not itself thinkable. The thing thought is the other of the thinking, or the term, which when it is reached we feel the thinking is stopped. The essence of that other is destined always to be withdrawn from view. We can know the properties or qualities, but behind them there remains the thing, unattainable. And so with everything thought, it is on this condition it is thought, because everything thought is thing, and in so far as it is such, incommensurable with mind.

And yet, because not thinkable, the thing is thought: the thinking is the thing's very unthinkability. It is not in itself unthinkable beyond the sphere of our thinking; but we think it as not thinkable. In its unthinkability it is posited by thought, or better still, it is as unthinkable that it is posited. For it is the nature of thought to affirm, and it is only in affirming that it is. By this I mean that if we regard thought as simply what is affirmed, as the conclusion or result of the affirmation, it is no longer an affirming, nor even a thinking. And as thought cannot not be thought, it affirms itself without being fixed as an affirmation. That is, it posits itself as act which is never *fact,* and thereby it is pure act, eternal act. Nature in the very act in which it is affirmed is denied, that is, spiritualized. And on this condition only can it be affirmed.

Nature, then, is an abstract conception of the real, and cannot be given except as an abstract reality. The thought in which my "I" is actualized can only be mine. When thought is not mine, when in my thinking I do not recognize myself, do not find myself, am not living in it, the reality which comes to be the thought in which my thought meets itself, in which, that is, I meet myself, is for me nature. But to be able to conceive this nature as absolute reality I must be able to think the object in itself, whereas the only object I can think is an aspect of the actual subject.

And also, be it noted, this object is not one which has only a value for knowledge. It is a reality intrinsically metaphysical. The "I," from whose dialectical process the object arises, the object which is then no other than the life of the "I," is the absolute "I." It is the ultimate reality which, try how we will to divest it of the value for knowledge with which we endow all reality, we can only conceive as "I." It is the "I" which is the individual, but the individual as subject with nothing to contrapose to itself and finding all in itself. It is therefore the actual concrete universal. This "I" which is the absolute, *is* in so far as it affirms itself. It is *causa sui.*

Deprived of its internal causality it is annulled. In causing itself it is creator of itself and in itself of the world, of the world which is the most complete that we can think, - the absolute world. This world is the object of which our doctrine speaks, and therefore our doctrine is a doctrine of knowledge in so far as it is a metaphysic.

The world is nature and the world is history. Each term comprehends the other so that we can say the world is nature or history. We distinguish the two domains of reality in the distinction between an other *than* mind and an other *in* mind. The other *than* mind, which is outside mind in general, is nature. It has not the unity, the freedom, the immortality which are the three essential characters of mind. The other in mind is history. It participates in all these essential characters, but at the same time implies an otherness in regard to the spiritual activity for which it is and which affirms it. The earth's movement is a natural fact, but the Copernican theory is a historical fact. What constitutes the difference is not that the historical fact is, and the natural fact is not, an act of the mind identical with that by which I think it, but that it is an act of the mind which is already complete when I think it and present therefore to my thinking with a positive character of autonomy, or objectivity, analogous to that of natural facts. We can even say in regard to it, that from being a spiritual act it has become a fact. The form of otherness from the subject, the fact that Copernicus who wrote the *De revolutionibus orbium celestium* and I who read it are different persons, is not the essential thing which gives the Copernican theory its character as history. It possesses that character because we can speak of historical fact, of fact which has in itself a certain law, which every one who narrates or remembers the history must respect: a law which requires an absolute form of otherness through which the creative spiritual act of the historical fact is different from the historical spiritual act. Caesar, when he wrote his *Commentaries,* must have already completed the facts which he narrated; and were there no difference between the man of action and the writer, there could be no history, or history would be confused with romance. I who am speaking am free to say what I will; but when I have spoken *alea jacta est;* I am no longer master of my words, they are what they are, and as such they confront me limiting my freedom; and they may become the torment of my whole life. They have become history, it may be, in the secret recesses of my own soul.

In this meaning, in spite of the profound difference which it makes between natural facts and historical facts, the difference that historical facts are and natural facts are not, at least are not originally, spiritual acts, nature and history coincide in so far as they imply a form of otherness from the "I" which knows, and apart from which we could not speak either of the one or of the other.

This is not enough. In the ordinary concepts of nature and history, that is, in the concepts which the naturalists have of nature and the historians have of history, otherness is absolute otherness. It is not the otherness we indicated in the proposition that the unthinkable is thought, but the otherness we mean when we find it necessary to say that what is thought is unthinkable. The "nature" of the naturalist is nature without final ends, extraneous to mind; the nature we can only know as phenomenon; the nature of which in resignation or despair we say *ignorabimus*. And the history of the historians is that fathomless sea of the past which loses itself and disappears in the far-offness of the prehistoric, wherein lie also the roots of the tree of civilization. It is the history of men's actions, the actions of men whose soul can only be reconstituted in an imagination devoid of any scientific justification. Naturalists and historians alike are confined to the ὅτι without being able to seek the διότι, because for them otherness is not substantial unity, a moment of the dialectical process. Their object is not that which we only recognize in its opposition to the subject, it is full and radical otherness, or rather multiplicity. And thus it is that nature is displayed in space and time (where spirituality is inconceivable), and history at least in time, which, as we know, is only a kind of space, for time in the before and after of the succession implies a reciprocal exclusion of the elements of the manifold.

Nature and history, then, coincide in their character of spatiality. Spatiality withdraws them both from the mind, if not from the mind as it is generally conceived, at least from the mind as it must be conceived in the concrete; realistic ally, as the actual "I."

For if, with Kant, we make time, or as we should now say the form of spatiality which is time, the form of the internal sense, and so adapt it to the spiritual facts, we are no longer looking at the spirituality of those facts: the spirituality for which they must not be facts but the spiritual act. When we declare that the *Critique of Pure Reason* was published in 1781 but that Kant began to write it towards the end of 1772, we are not thinking of the *Criticism* by which it is one indivisible spiritual act, but we are putting it on the same plane on which we place many other mental and natural facts. Moreover, if we would know what that *Criticism* is, as Kant's thought, we must read his book, reflect on it, and thereby separate it from its time and make Kant's past work our present thought. Thereby time is thought of by the mind as nature and not as mind, thought of as a multiplicity of facts external to one another and therefore conceivable according to the principle of causality, not as that living unity, the historian's immortal mind.

But if from the naturalist's contemplation in which we are lost in the multitude of facts, we rise to the philosopher's contemplation in which we find the centre of all multiplicity in the one, then the Spatiality, the multiplicity,

the otherness of nature and history, which constitute their autonomy in regard to mind, all give place to the mind's absolute reality. The nature and the history of ordinary discourse are abstract nature and abstract history, and, as such, non-existent. The otherness which is the fundamental characteristic of each, were it as absolute as it appears, would imply the absolute unknowability of both, but it would also imply - a fact of much more importance - the impossibility of mind. For if there be something outside the mind in the absolute sense, the mind must be limited by it, and then it is no longer free, and no longer mind since mind is freedom. But the otherness of history and of nature, if we possess the real concept of the absoluteness of the "I," is no other than the objectivity of the "I" to itself which we have already analysed. Nature and history *are,* in so far as they are the creation of the "I" which finds them within itself, and produces them in its eternal process of self-creation.

This does not mean, as those who trust to common sense imagine in dismay, that reality is a subjective illusion. Reality is true reality, in the most literal and unambiguous sense, in being the subject itself, the "I." The "I" is not self-consciousness except as a consciousness of the self, determined as some thing. The reality of the self-consciousness is in the consciousness, and the reality of the consciousness in the self-consciousness. The consciousness of a self-consciousness is indeed its own reality, it is not imprisoned in the self as a result or conclusion, but is a dialectical moment. This means that our intellect grows with what we know. It does not increase by acquiring qualities and preserving them without any further need of activity, but it is realized, with that increase, in a new knowing. Thus it is that our only way of distinguishing between the old knowledge and the new knowing is by analysis and abstraction: for the self-consciousness is one, and consciousness is consciousness of the self-consciousness. Therefore the development of self-consciousness, or, avoiding the pleonasm, *self-consciousness,* is the world process itself, nature and history, in so far as it is a self-consciousness realized in consciousness. If we give the name "history" to this development of mind, then the history which is consciousness is the history of this self-consciousness and what we call the past is only the actual present in its concreteness.

[1] Cf. the last chapter of my *Riforma della dialettica hegeliana.*

Chapter Eighteen - Idealism or Mysticism?

The conception to which I have tried to give expression, a conception which resolves the world into spiritual act or act of thought, in unifying the infinite variety of man and nature in an absolute one, in which the human is divine and the divine is human, may appear, and has been pronounced, a mystical conception. [1] And indeed it concurs with mysticism in affirming that the whole is one, and that to know is to attain this one behind all the distinctions.

Now mysticism has its very great merit but it has none the less its very grave defect. Its merit is the fulness and the truly courageous energy, of its conception when it affirms that reality cannot be conceived except as absolute; or, as it is more usual to express it, there is no true reality but God only. And this living feeling, this intrinsic contact or taste of the divine (as Campanella would have said), is a sublimation of human energy, a purification of the soul, and blessedness. But mysticism has the serious defect that it cancels all distinctions in the "soul's dark night" (*notte oscura dell' anima*) and thereby makes the soul abnegate itself in the infinite, where not only all vision of finite things, but even its own personality, is lost to it. For its personality, as a concrete personality, is defined precisely in the function of all finite things. Through this *tendency* it not only quenches every stimulus towards scientific research and rational knowledge, but weakens and breaks every incentive to action, for action cannot be explained except by means of the concreteness of the finite. Just as we can only do one thing at a time, so we can only solve one problem at a time. To live is to be limited. The mystic ignores the limit.

But while "actual idealism" accords with "mysticism" in what we have called its merit, it does not in its fundamental theses participate in what we have called its defect. *Idealism reconciles all distinctions, but does not, like mysticism, cancel them, and it affirms the finite no less resolutely than it affirms the infinite, difference no less than identity.* This is the substantial point of divergence between the two conceptions. The mystical conception, despite appearances, is to be regarded as essentially an intellectualist doctrine, and therefore ideally anterior to Christianity: the idealistic conception is an essentially anti-intellectualist doctrine, and perhaps even the maturest form of modern Christian philosophy.

Mysticism is usually arrayed against intellectualist theories because, according to the mystics, those theories vainly presume to attain the Absolute by means of knowledge, whereas it can only be attained by means of love, or, as they say, by feeling or will. The difference between the two conceptions is substantially this: For the intellectualists the Absolute is knowable because in itself it is knowledge; for the mystics the Absolute is not knowable because it is not knowledge, but love. And love is distinguished from knowledge in being life, self-transformation, creative process, whereas knowledge supposes (that is, they believe it supposes) a reality already complete, which has only to be intuited. Mysticism, on the other hand, accords inwardly with intellectualism in conceiving its love as an object, and the process of the Absolute as a process which confronts mind, and in which process mind must itself be fused. And *vice versa,* intellectualism coincides with mysticism, in so far as, even in conceiving the object of knowledge as knowable, that is as itself knowledge, it makes that object entirely an external limit to the subject, and the subject having thus posited the object as its external limit is no longer itself conceivable, apart from empty metaphor, except as the subject of an intuitive activity. The truth is that the real characteristic of intellectualism is not that in which it is opposed to mysticism but that in which it agrees with it, that is, in its conception of reality as mere absolute object and therefore its conception of the mind's process as a process which *presupposes* an object already realized before the process itself begins. The intellect in this conception stands opposed to value. Value creates its object (the good or the evil); intellect creates nothing, does nothing, merely contemplates existence, a passive and otiose spectator.

Now, in this respect mysticism is in precisely the same position as intellecttualism, and it does not succeed, in spite of all the efforts it makes to conceive the mind as will (feeling, love), because will is freedom, self-creative; and freedom is impossible where the activity is not absolute. Hence mysticism falls back on the concepts of fate, grace, and the like.

The mystic's absolute reality is not subject but object. It is object, that is to say, from the point of view of actual idealism, because in idealism the subject coincides with the "I" who affirms the object. For even the mystic can speak of the personality, *toto caelo* different from his own, into relation with which his own personality enters or aspires to enter. So that he comes to conceive a personality which is an object of his mind, - that is, of the only mind which for him is effectively mind, - and therefore is not mind.

It is, then, no wonder that in the mystic's reality, so essentially objective and anti-spiritual, there is no place for anything purely depending on the subject, the individual personality, the man tormented by the desire of God who is all, and by the infinite sense of his own nothingness. It is no wonder if all particular things dissolve as illusive shadows. Within the all-embracing reality, particulars are distinguished for the determinating activity of that finite power which in itself is nothing, - the intellect, or rather the personality as cognitive consciousness.

Modern idealism, on the contrary, moves in a direction directly opposite to that towards which mysticism is orientated. Idealism is, as I have said, anti-intellectualistic, and in this sense profoundly Christian, if we take Christianity as meaning the intrinsically moral conception of the world. This moral conception is one which is entirely alien to India and to Greece even in their greatest speculative efforts. The philosophy of India ends in asceticism, in the suppression of the passions, in the extirpation of desire and every root of the human incentive to work, in the nirvana. Its ideal, therefore, is the simple negation of the real in which morality realizes itself, human personality. And in Greek philosophy the highest ethical word it can pronounce is *Justice*. Justice renders to each his own and therefore preserves the natural order (or what is presupposed as such), but it can neither create nor construct a new world. Greek philosophy, therefore, cannot express the essential virtue of mind which is its creative nature, it must produce the good which it cannot find confronting it. How could Greek philosophy understand the moral nature of mind seeing that its world was not mind but nature? The nature need not be material, it might be ideal, but it is what the mind contemplates, not what it makes. Greek morality ends in the Stoical doctrine of suicide, a doctrine consistent with its immanent tendency to an intellectualistic conception of a reality in which the subject has no worth. Christianity, on the other hand, discovers the reality which is not until it creates itself, and is what it *creates*. It cannot be treated like the Greek philosopher's world, already in existence and waiting to be known till the philosopher is ready to contemplate it, when he has drawn aside as it were, when, as Aristotle would say, all the wants of his life are appeased and life is as it were complete. It is a reality which waits for us to construct, a reality which is truly even now love and will, because it is the inward effort of the soul, its living process, not its ideal and external model. It is man himself who rises above humanity and becomes God. And even God is no longer a reality who already is, but the God who is begotten in us and is ourselves in so far as we with our whole being rise to him. Here mind is no longer intellect but will. The world is no longer what is known but what is made: and therefore not only can we begin to conceive the mind as freedom or moral activity, but the world, the whole world of the Christian, is freed and redeemed. The whole world is a world which is what it would be, or a world, as we say, essentially moral.

For an idealistic conception such as this a true mysticism is impossible. The chief presupposition in Brahmanism or Orphism, of which there are many forms even in the modern world, the intellectualistic principle of abstract objectivity, is in idealism definitely destroyed. The whole development of Christian philosophical thought, arrested during the Scholastic period, restarted and reinvigorated in the Humanism and Naturalism of the Renascence, and since then proceeding gaily without serious interruption, may be regarded as a continual and progressive elaboration of anti-intellectualism. To such a point has this development been brought to-day, that even an anti-intellectualism like ours may assume the appearance of intellectualism to any one who fails to appreciate the slow transformation which speculative concepts undergo throughout the history of philosophy. For to-day we say that mind is not will, nor intellect and will, but pure intellect.

There is a point in regard to this anti-intellectualistic conception which deserves particular attention. Descartes did indeed propose to correct the abstractness of the intellectualist conception, and undoubtedly he has the merit that he affirms a certain subjectivity of truth and therefore of reality; but he falls back into the same abstractness since he does not abandon what is the very basis of intellectualism, the presupposition of absolute objectivity. Not only does he not abandon it, he duplicates it. He distinguishes the intellect from the will by its passivity. The intellect with a passive intuition mirrors the ideas, which are in themselves. In this passivity the intellect is defined in a way which will admit no character in it of freedom and spiritual subjectivity. Moreover, it is the will which, with its freedom of assenting or with holding assent from the content of the intellect, is able to endow cognition with its peculiar character of subjective certainty. Now it is clear that in thus driving subjectivity from the intellect to find refuge in the will, we are not only repeating but even duplicating the desperate position in which intellectualism is placed in the opposition between knowing and known. For now we have a double opposition, firstly that between the intellect and the ideas, secondly that between the intellect and the will. The will, in so far as it knows or recognizes what the intellect has received but does not properly know, is itself intellect, and the intellect is itself in regard to the will made an object of knowledge. And whoever reflects carefully will see that the will which has thus been excogitated to supply the defect of the intellect cannot attain its purpose, because if we suppose truth to be objective in regard to the intellect its objectivity must be always out of reach. We should want a second will to judge the first, and a third to judge the second, and still, to quote Dante, "lungi sia dal becco l'erba." [2] In short, intellectualism is here attempting to cure its own defect by an intellectualistic theory of the will. The intellect only draws back, it is neither eliminated nor reconciled. [3]

And the doctrines which, following Kant, make a sharp distinction between the theoretical and the practical reason, conferring on the theoretical a power of knowing and on the practical a power of doing, have no greater success. If the Cartesian anti-intellectualism integrates the intellect with a will, and then discovers that this will itself is intellectual, the Kantian anti-intellectualism juxtaposes a will to the intellect, and the will in this juxtaposition must again discover itself intellectual. Indeed the Kantian will, precisely because it is separated from the intellect and creates a reality which is not the reality, does not attain the full autonomy which implies the absolute immanence of the purpose, and it needs to postulate an extra-mundane *summum bonum* and therefore God and an immortal life of the individual beyond experience. And what is this transcendent world but a real world which it does not create, a world which objectively confronts the will, just as phenomenal nature objectively confronts the intellect? In general, a will, which is not the intellect itself, can only be distinguished from it on condition that, at least for the intellect, there is conceived a reality not produced by mind but a presupposition of it. And when the mind, be it even only as intellect, presupposes its own reality, the reality created by the will can never be the absolute reality, and therefore can never have moral and spiritual value, free from every intellectualistic defect.

There is only one way of overcoming intellectualism and that is not to turn our back on it but to look it squarely in the face. Only so is it possible to conceive and form an adequate idea of knowledge. It is our way and we may sum it up briefly thus: we do not suppose as a logical antecedent of knowledge the reality which is the object of knowledge; we conceive the intellect as itself will, freedom, morality; and we cancel that independent nature of the world, which makes it appear the basis of mind, by recognizing that it is only an abstract moment of mind. True anti-intellectualism indeed is identical with true intellectualism, when once we understand intellect ualism as that which has not voluntarism opposed to it, and is therefore no longer one of two old antagonistic terms but the unity of both. And such is our idealism, which in overcoming every vestige of transcendence in regard to the actuality of mind can, as we have said, comprehend within it the most radical, most logical, and the sincerest, conception of Christianity.

Now such a conception puts us at the very antipodes of mysticism. It is hardly necessary to point out that in it all the rights of individuality find satisfaction, with the exception or those which depend on a fantastic concept of the individual among individuals. In modern philosophy such a concept is absurd, because, as we have shown, the only individual we can know is that which is the positive concreteness of the universal in the "I." That absolute "I" is the "I" which each of us realizes in every pulsation of our spiritual existence. It is the I which thinks and feels, the I which fears and hopes, the I which wills and works and which has responsibility, rights, and duties, and constitutes to each of us the pivot of his world. This pivot, when we reflect on it, we find to be one for all, if we seek and find the all where alone it is, within us, our own reality. I do not think I need defend this idealism from the charge or suspicion of suppressing individual personality.

The suspicion, - I was about to say the fear, - which casts its shadow over the principle that the act of thought is pure act, is lest in it the distinctions of the real, that is of the object of knowledge as distinct from the knowing subject, should be suppressed. Now whoever has followed the argument to this point must see clearly that the unification with which it deals is one than which there can be nothing more fundamental, inasmuch as it affirms that in the act of thinking nature and history are reconciled. We can wish to feel no other. For such unification is at the same time the conservation, or rather the establishing, of an infinite wealth of categories, beyond anything which logic and philosophy have hitherto conceived. Bear in mind that reconciling the whole of natural and historical reality, in the act of thinking (and this is philosophy), does not mean that there is, properly speaking, a single massive absorption of the whole of reality, it means that the eternal reconciliation of reality is displayed in and through all the forms which experience indicates in the world. Experience is, from the metaphysical point of view, the infinite begetter of an infinite offspring, in which it is realized. There is neither nature nor history, but always and only *this* nature, *this* history, in *this* spiritual act.

So then the mind, which is the one in the substantiality of its self-consciousness, is the manifold as an actual reality of consciousness, and the life of self-consciousness in consciousness is the history which is a unity of historical reality and of the knowledge of it. Philosophy, therefore - this consciousness of itself in which mind consists - can only be philosophy in being history. And as history it is not the dark night of mysticism but the full midday light which is shed on the boundless scene of the world. It is not the unique category of self-consciousness; it is the infinite categories of consciousness. And then, in this conception there cease to be privileges between different entities, categories and concepts, and all entities in their absolute determinateness are equal and are different, and all the concepts are categories, in being each the category of itself. [4] The abstractness of philosophy finds its interpretation in the determinateness of history, and, we can also say, of experience, showing how it is one whole *a priori* experience, in so far as every one of its moments is understood as a spontaneous production of the subject.

Determinations are not lacking, then, in our idealism, and indeed there is an overwhelming wealth of them. But whilst in empirical knowledge and in every philosophy which has not yet attained to the concept of the pure thinking, these complete distinctions of the real are skeletonized and reduced to certain abstract types, and these are then forced to do duty for true distinctions, in idealism these distinctions are one and all regarded in their individual eternal value. Mystics are therefore rather the critics than the champions of this idealism since in their philosophy all distinctions are not maintained.

On the other hand, we must not reduce these distinctions to the point at which we merely think them as a number, and thereby conceive them as Spinoza's infinite of the imagination, a series without beginning or end, extensible always and in every direction, and so for ever falling short of completion. In this mode reality would be an ought-to-be, and the reality of the "I" would have its true reality outside itself. The distinctions are an infinite of the imagination, a potential infinite, if we consider them as a pure abstract history of philosophy, as forms of consciousness cut off from self-consciousness. Instead of this, in our idealism the distinctions are always an actual infinite, the immanence of the universal in the particular: all in all.

I am not I, without being the whole of the "I think"; and what "I think" is always one in so far as it is "I." The mere multiplicity always belongs to the content of the consciousness abstractly considered; in reality it is always reconciled in the unity of the "I." The true history is not that which is unfolded in time but that which is gathered up eternally in the act of thinking in which in fact it is realized.

This is why I say that idealism has the merit without the defect of mysticism. It has found God and turns to Him, but it has no need to reject any single finite thing: indeed without finite things it would once more lose God. Only, it translates them from the language of empiricism into that of philosophy, for which the finite thing is always the very reality of God. And thus it exalts the world into an eternal theogony which is fulfilled in the inwardness of our being.

[1] My friend Benedetto Croce has expressed his objection to mysticism in these words: "You cancel all the fallacious distinctions we are commonly accustomed to rely on, and history as the act of thought has then it seems nothing left but the immediate consciousness of the individual-universal in which all distinctions are submerged and lost. And this is mysticism, excellent in making us feel in unity with God, but ill-adapted for thinking the world or for acting in it" (*Teoria e storia della storiografia,* p. 103). This is true, but as a criticism it does not inculpate our idealism, although that might also be defined as a consciousness (not indeed *immediate,* as has been shown) of the individual-universal; because, as Croce points out, mysticism cannot be historical, it cannot admit the consciousness of diversity, of change and of becoming. In fact "either the consciousness of diversity comes from the individual and intuitive element itself, and then it is impossible to understand how such an element can subsist with its own form of

intuition, in thought which always universalizes; or it is affirmed to be a product of the act of thought itself, and then the distinction which it was supposed had been abolished is reaffirmed and the asserted distinctionless simplicity of thought is shaken" (p. 104). Such a simplicity, it must be clear even to the most cursory reader of the preceding pages, is certainly not the kind of simplicity actual idealism affirms. For idealism diversity is precisely a product of the act of thought itself. Only those distinctions are illegitimate which are presupposed and unproved. They are illegitimate because they are not derived from that act of thought which is the unshakeable and only possible foundation of a truly critical and realistic philosophizing and therefore of any efficacious acting in the world.

[2] *Inferno*, xv. 72.

[3] See the special treatment of this point in *Sistema di Logica*, vol. i. part i.

[4] This problem of the categories will be found treated in the second volume of *Sistema di Logica*.

www.ingramcontent.com/pod-product-compliance
Lightning Source LLC
LaVergne TN
LVHW091259080426
835510LV00007B/328